ALSO BY JOSEPH BRAUDE

The New Iraq: Rebuilding the Country for Its People,
the Middle East, and the World

THE HONORED DEAD

THE
HONORED
DEAD

A Story of Friendship, Murder,
and the Search for Truth in the Arab World

JOSEPH BRAUDE

SPIEGEL & GRAU | NEW YORK | 2011

Published in the United States by Spiegel & Grau, an imprint of The Random House Publishing Group, a division of Random House, Inc., New York.

SPIEGEL & GRAU and Design is a registered trademark of Random House, Inc.

LIBRARY OF CONGRESS CATALOGING-IN-PUBLICATION DATA
Braude, Joseph.
The honored dead : a story of friendship, murder, and the search for truth in the Arab world / Joseph Braude.
p. cm.
ISBN 978-0-385-52703-3 (alk. paper)—ISBN 978-0-679-60432-7 (eBook)
1. Braude, Joseph. 2. Murder—Investigation—Morocco—Case studies.
3. Morocco—History—21st century. I. Title.
HV6535.M8B73 2011
364.152'3092—dc22   2010046496

Printed in the United States of America on acid-free paper

www.spiegelandgrau.com

2 4 6 8 9 7 5 3 1

FIRST EDITION

Book design by Casey Hampton

To Ali

The realist in murder writes of a world in which gangsters can rule nations and almost rule cities. . . .

—RAYMOND CHANDLER

PROLOGUE

Muhammad Bari eased out of his bedroom and opened the creaking front door just enough to make his way outside. His wife needed her sleep; she had to get up for work in an hour. Usually Bari's best friend would be waiting for him in the alleyway and they would walk together to a nearby mosque for the dawn prayer. This morning, the alleyway was empty. Bari didn't worry: sometimes his friend slept in until sunrise.

It was December in Casablanca, Morocco's sprawling economic capital on the Atlantic coast of North Africa. An ocean mist chilled the lingering darkness. Bari's teeth chattered as he took off his shoes outside the mosque and placed them in an empty cubbyhole. He performed his ritual ablutions in the washroom and proceeded barefoot into the sanctuary warm with body heat: several hundred people had already lined up on the floor in long rows facing east. The sanctuary's warmth was welcome, but the dawn prayer lasted only ten minutes.

Ordinarily, Bari and his friend would repair from the mosque to a nearby café. If one or both of them had missed the dawn prayer, they would find each other inside. They would sit and talk for hours while people with jobs hurried in and out. This morning Bari arrived alone, and drank his coffee alone, and read the newspapers alone, and watched Al Jazeera alone, and worried about where his friend could be now. *The place where he sleeps does not belong to him,* he thought. *He has to evacuate early so that the men who control the facility do not catch him.*

Could he have overslept? How could he possibly risk sleeping past sunrise?

Bari finally felt driven from his familiar café chair to find out what was going on with his friend, why he had left Bari alone on this morning. He knew where to go. He knew the place well.

The enormous warehouse is enclosed by a spiked metal wall that someone painted red a long time ago. At one end, the wall abuts a field of gravel and dirt bisected by the same train track that slices the city in half; people gather there at night to lie around and get drunk. Nobody ventures over that wall. Nobody is supposed to go inside except the people who work there. Silence ordinarily surrounded the place.

But not this morning. When Bari reached the spiked front gate, it was surrounded by state security. A dozen uniformed police minded a perimeter of yellow ribbon. Auxiliary Forces troops in green fatigues stood guard by the entrance. Plainclothes detectives paced in and out.

"Who are you? What do you want?" one of them barked.

"I'm looking for a, a friend of mine," Bari replied.

The detective locked in on Bari's eyes. He grabbed him by the forearm and pulled him in past the gate to a raucous crowd of cops, who were bending down and peering over and putting down markers and taking pictures and arguing with one another.

There was a rusty smell in the air.

"*That* was a friend of yours?" the detective demanded, pointing.

Bari turned his head toward the stone steps leading up to the guard's quarters, where his friend always slept. What he saw, he did not understand at first. The steps were drenched in red. There was a large *thing* lying on top of them. It had a blood-soaked beard, a couple of teeth, and clothes on. There was a head, but it was mutilated into a different shape. Bari began to feel a rising heat in his head and throat. His temples started pulsating. Now the rest of his body was in on it. He couldn't breathe. He lost his balance.

The detective steadied him by the forearm, which was still clasped tight in his muscular hand.

The lieutenant who questioned Bari over the next three days wore jeans and a charcoal gray blazer. Lieutenant Jabri was genteel, more relaxed than the men at the warehouse, perhaps a little weary of his work. He rarely raised his voice, he never insulted Bari or the other detainee, and he phrased his questions thoughtfully. Rather than refer to the murder victim by name, for example, he always called him "al-Marhum," Arabic for "he who has been granted mercy."

On the third day, he went through the same battery of questions he had asked the day before and the day before that.

"You're sure al-Marhum was never in any trouble?" the lieutenant asked.

"Never," Bari said.

"How would you describe his character?"

Bari combed his scraggly salt-and-pepper beard with his fingernails and shaped it with his knuckles. "I said yesterday he had a good reputation all over the neighborhood and he went to pray in the mosque every morning."

The detainee who sat next to Bari in the lieutenant's office nodded vigorously.

"The last time you saw him?"

"The night before you found him," Bari replied. "It was Sharif the book peddler and me and we had a bowl of *harira* with him."

"Was al-Marhum preoccupied, agitated?"

"No, he was comfortable and maybe almost a little cheerful. He said he was going to do some small deal and he thought it was going to come through."

The lieutenant had been seated at his desk. Now he abruptly stood up and looked down at Bari, who had to crane his neck to meet the lieutenant's eyes.

"How long did al-Marhum sleep in that place? How long did he sleep there!"

Bari twitched.

"The truth."

"Five years."

"Five years," Jabri repeated. "Did you ever visit him inside?"

"Sometimes," Bari replied.

"A lot or a little?"

"Not often. Very rarely." That wasn't true.

"Did he have other visitors there? Was it common for him to bring people in there?"

Bari could feel his own pulse. *The lieutenant must notice the blood rushing to my face,* he thought. "Yes, I do remember that sometimes I would come by and knock and he would say he had people inside and I should come back later."

The lieutenant moved slowly back to the chair behind his desk, fixing his eyes on the other detainee.

The man who sat next to Bari, a man named Attar, was visibly frightened, increasingly so each day. The police had let Bari go around seven o'clock the night before with instructions to come back the following morning—but they had held on to Attar God knows how late. When Bari returned, he found Attar alone in the office waiting for the lieutenant to arrive. He was slumped over in his chair, asleep. Bari tapped him on the shoulder and Attar convulsed. He cried, *There is no power or strength except in God!* and looked frantically in several directions before setting his rose-pink eyes on Bari. "Oh, I'm so sorry," he said. "I'm so sorry."

The stars had come out on the third day of questioning by the time a distant tumult from the ground floor of the precinct drew louder and nearer, banging up the staircase on squeaky wet boots. There was yelling and a nasal, wordless plea. Into the room walked four detectives, all sweaty, and a young man between them in handcuffs. He limped and wore a bandage stained with blood around his left wrist. Eight hands were on his body.

Bari had a son his age.

"What *I* want to know is," one of the detectives began to say.

The lieutenant motioned him to stop talking.

"Brothers," the lieutenant said, "we would like to ask whether either of you has seen this young man before."

He looked at Attar, who shook his head.

"Brother Muhammad Bari?"

"I have never seen him before in my life, and he must not be from our area because I know I would have seen him at least once or twice if he were from here," Bari declared, overdoing it a bit, he realized.

The lieutenant snapped his fingers and an old typist from across the hall showed up with paper. Bari and Attar were made to sign affidavits to the effect that the young man was a stranger to them.

"My brothers," the lieutenant said, "you are free to go."

Attar darted out of the room with barely a *God keep you*.

Bari didn't move at first. He looked at the boy in handcuffs for as long as his eyes would let him. This man's role in Bari's simple life began to dawn on him. Bari stood up and steadied himself, making a tentative approach toward the lieutenant. He took a deep breath.

"This is the man?" Bari asked.

The lieutenant nodded.

"Why did he—"

"The important thing is we have caught him and he will confess."

Another deep breath.

"That's it?" Bari asked.

"Brother Muhammad," the lieutenant said, "try to move on."

Bari went to bed that night weeping and weeping at last.

Because he had been detained, he had missed the funeral. So had Attar. In his tears, Bari could picture it, having lent a hand in the burial of indigent neighbors before. From the great city morgue off the interstate, the body would be thrown into a rickety red and white ambulance and driven 250 yards to the expansive Burial Grounds of Mercy. Down a long flowery lane where amputees and orphans confer blessings in exchange for charity, the dark sack would reach its pit. There are few family plots in Casablanca; lanes fill up with bodies in the order in which they are received. A cleric whom the victim had never met would go through Salat al-Janaza, a special prayer for funerals. The grave would be marked by a long number.

Bari lay awake all night.

When he ran out of tears, he started asking questions of his own.

THE HONORED DEAD

ONE

I t's 9:30 P.M. in Casablanca, and the Al Jazeera sports channel blares off a corner wall to a rapt all-male crowd in the coffee-house near precinct headquarters. A game is on, the score is tied with seconds to go, and the promise of victory for Widad, a local soccer team, looms like a ticking bomb. A thick cloud of cigarette smoke and sweat chokes the room. Most of the viewers are too engrossed to say a word, but four plainclothes police, hunched around one table sipping mint tea, have been trashing the rival Syrian team in Morocco's distinctive dialect of Arabic.

"Donkeys!" they call out, hissing. "Pigs! Go home to your sty!"

My own clear view of the TV screen is obstructed suddenly by an explosion of frenzied men jumping, smacking, kicking, and hugging amid spontaneous cries of "Allahu Akbar! Allahu Akbar!" Every table becomes a war drum, every ashtray a rattling tambourine. One man grabs hold of a table between his arms and crashes it repeatedly against the linoleum floor. A Coke bottle smashes. The acrid cloud over our heads seems to yield a few drops of rain, and in the noise of shouting and cavorting I catch a glimpse of the instant replay: Widad just pulled off an upset victory, thanks to a long-shot goal by native son Muhammad Fallah. The athlete grew up in a shantytown family from the slums a few blocks east.

All four cops join the celebration, banging tables with the row-diest fans—until a shrill finger-whistle from outdoors cuts above the shouting of the crowd. Alerted by the cue, the policemen stand tall, pushing their way clear of the room and out the front door with the universal swagger of their profession.

I march straight out of the coffeehouse with them—as we are formally joined at the hip.

Just outside, a young woman in a brown hooded robe is heaving a wordless plea into the wiry frame of Abd al-Qadir Marzuq, the cops' commanding officer. She squeezes both his wrists. "You have to get him and lock him up tonight or the man will kill me," she says.

Marzuq pries free an arm and points an index finger at each of his pale gray eyes—a North African sign of devotion to a task. "You are my sister," he adds, though she is not.

Three of his four men pile into the back cage of a white van marked NATIONAL SECURITY in blood-red paint. The fourth takes the steering wheel and Marzuq rides shotgun. With two days to go before the joyous Muslim festival of Eid al-Adha and the first big win for Casablanca's home team in five long weeks, police citywide are energized by God and country—and it is a wretched night for any wanted man to wind up captured by the Moroccan security services.

I climb in with the back cage crew and hear a sound like wood chips cracking under my sneakers. The light goes on briefly, and I see what litters the grooved metal floor: thousands of sunflower seed shells, spat out by cops and their prey over months, maybe years, of night raids into the city's teeming slums. The van swerves off the main road and I tumble onto a cold metal bench.

"You almost missed," an officer says, punching me gently in the shoulder. We speed east into the darkening margins of the city.

In the front seat, Marzuq cusses out an ex-wife over his mobile phone, something about their teenage daughter, until a different phone—the one informants dial him on—warbles the Moroccan national anthem out of his vest pocket, ending the chat with his ex.

"Yes!" he shouts into the informant line. "God keep you! Where?"

He nods his head and promises forceful action, with God as his witness.

The van comes to a screeching halt and my benchmates tumble out the back. We emerge by the curb of a circular concrete embankment at an asphalt roundabout near the northeast tip of the city. A rooster crows in the distance; livestock faintly moo and bleat. Nestled among palm trees, a pair of crudely sculpted black lions stand guard. A thousand juicy clementines rolling home for the night on a wagon's back sparkle under the glow of a flickering streetlamp. The man who hauls them averts his gaze at the sight of the white-and-red van.

The police scuttle down a dingy road and into a derelict quarry where goats and sheep are nibbling at the edges of a giant trash heap. At length, they reach the mouth of a dark corridor hewn by parallel rows of corroded aluminum-roofed huts—the beginning of a vast shantytown. A mammoth barbecue somewhere inside lends a palatable after-aroma to the overwhelming stench of human waste.

Marzuq huddles with his men. "Hit them tonight," he says. "Even the small-timers. Hit them hard. We meet at Susu's."

He splits them up in two directions and I follow the boss.

Down a main shantytown artery, electric lighting fades to black. The glow of kerosene lanterns inside shack windows casts a murky green light into alleyways, smoky from the outdoor liver and sausage grills. Almost everything that moves is male and hooded. The artery narrows into a vein. Marzuq snakes through, slowing occasionally to accept holiday greetings from men his age, stopping only to accost clusters of teenage boys. Any three or four hunched inward in silence meet with Marzuq's skeletal fingertips on the neck.

"What have you got?" he demands. Working necks, he shakes loose orange flame-tipped hashish cigarettes—*kufta* in Moroccan slang, meaning "cutlets"—and stamps them out with his boots.

Two bearded men with holy books under their arms stop to cheer Marzuq by name as he spins left into an alleyway. "May every Eid find you well, brother Abd al-Qadir," one says. "God bestow his blessings upon you a thousand times."

Marzuq spies four more kids loitering by a corner hill of rock and debris. He is about to nail them when a distant teenage voice twists his neck like a powerful magnet.

"Hasan!" he calls out to the voice. "Hasan, come over here, you fucking pimp!"

Four boys in the distance run off, leaving one.

"Hasan!"

The teen has a 2Pac baseball cap on backward and a trench coat over his black leather pants. Marzuq charges in his direction and plants two hands on Hasan's shoulders, kneading the flesh.

"What did I tell you?" he says with a rasp. Saliva thickens in his mouth, moistening the vowel-snipped Moroccan slang. "What did I tell you? Open it!"

The boy just shakes his head slowly, eyes open wide.

"Open it, you fucker!"

The cop pulls apart Hasan's trench coat and extracts three little clear plastic bags from an inner pocket. He smacks the kid hard on his neck. Hasan winces with only a clipped *"Tsst"* out of his mouth. Marzuq rips open the bags and spills a brownish powder out, grinding it into the dirt with his boots.

"Fuck off!" the lieutenant cries.

Hasan begins to move—but too slowly. Up the boy's legs from behind comes a full-sole kick from Marzuq's right boot, then a furious kneecap thrust into the small of the young man's back. Hasan walks away fast, holding his back and limping.

All these random hits are just targets of opportunity. Marzuq keeps speed-walking through the sinewy alleys, deeper into the dank shantytown toward his target. Along the way he turns his head toward me. "What do you think of our service?" he asks. "Do you *understand*?"

These sound like rhetorical questions, so I keep quiet.

At this writing, the shantytowns of Casablanca house half a million people, roughly a tenth of the city's population. Some tin-roofed huts date back nearly a century, to the beginning of Morocco's forty-year occupation by France. Most of the youth today are third- and fourth-generation squatters—deprived, like their great-grandparents, of basic human needs. Yet these ramshackle homes have spawned the country's finest athletes, a handful of Arab movie stars, and some of the region's best-loved vocalists—not to mention a few of the world's most deadly al-Qaeda fighters. For cops, these areas are the beating heart of crime and vice. Thievery rings have a way of tracing back here, along with the drug trade's urban foot soldiers, the lion's share of murderers, and, perhaps predictably, the vast majority of their victims. Tonight's expedition is part of an ongoing security effort, dubbed a "purification campaign" by its chief, to hunt wanted men in their hiding places on the strength of informants' tips.

Slowing down behind the lieutenant, I notice a door.

Marzuq and his unit have converged on a two-room cabin of brick with crinkly tin rods dangling off the roof. Shoehorned into the façade's oblong opening is an ornate blue door, from an old house, perhaps, with geometric and floral motifs carved orange and white into a ceramic tile laid over cedar wood in the distinctively Moroccan shape of a giant keyhole. I have seen doors like it on picture postcards, and in the wealthier sections of Casablanca. But they were to be expected there. Here it stands audacious, unnatural in its habitat—a vestige of defiance, perhaps, by whoever installed it; a proclamation of personality.

Marzuq whispers something to his men, and three move off to either end of the portal. Ears against the bricks pick up voices of the family inside. Even I can hear them from a wind-whipped alley's breadth away—arguing, laughing, putting away dishes. The police just stand there like sweaty statues.

From down the lane a girl of about fourteen draws near the home with a knapsack over her shoulders—brown eyes, high cheekbones, jet-black hair. Her approach in the darkness slows, growing tentative as her eyes confirm the shadows of men flanking her entryway. She shrinks back. Marzuq lunges from the shadows and clasps her arm before she can flee. Strands of her flowing hair break ranks in the clammy breeze.

"What do you want?" she demands.

"Tell Mama to open up," he whispers. "Don't tell her we're here. Talk softly!"

"No," she tries to say, pursing her lips. But only the first consonant of her reply meets the air; Marzuq's spade-shaped palm buries her mouth in time to subdue the vowel. He clasps her arm tighter.

"Do it, by the prophet!"

The girl's eyes widen and her chin quivers. "Mama?" she calls out unevenly.

All the sounds inside the home stop. A woman comes to the door, jostling it diagonally off the ground to expose her veiled head.

"Where is Susu!" Marzuq demands, pivoting his head to scan inside. "Where is your Susu!"

"Not here," she says. Her chin quivers, too, and tears slide down her cheek. "Not here, by God."

Marzuq elbows the door wide open.

"Where is he?"

"Please," she says, affecting a gracious smile, "we don't know."

"Bring him out to us or we'll take you all in, by God," he says.

The fourth enforcer signals Marzuq from the shadows. He has noticed something just off the ground by a livestock shack a few feet away: the moonlit glimmer of an undershirt. A man in his early twenties lies there, concealed in part by the hybrid shadow of a worn-out satellite dish on the rooftop and a cow head bobbing out of the window beneath it. From where I stand, I can smell the booze sweating out of his pores.

Marzuq returns the door to its slot and motions his men to surround the boy. The woman opens the door again.

"No!" she cries, grabbing hold of the door for dear life. She is losing her balance in the slick wet blur of her tears.

The police make a human chain around the boy.

"*Yyaaawww!*" the boy wails. They haven't even touched him yet.

Marzuq strikes the first blow—your basic kick in the shins. It is a signal to his boys, just an opening salvo.

Susu flails his arms.

Motioning his men to pitch in, Marzuq lands a bare fist in the boy's stomach, provoking a murmur of dissatisfaction and a half-hearted clench of his left fist.

The other cops join in: Susu's left breast meets the cracked plastic rim of a club; the edge of his neck catches the tip of a rubber boot.

"*Yyaaawww!*" he wails again.

What's he trying to say? I wonder. He lies there motionless, taking the hits like heavy rain. Maybe he is too drunk to feel any pain. Time seems to slow. His smell, his dirt, the brutality of his tormentors are all making my stomach swirl. His helplessness pains me, and I want to throw up.

Other doors begin to open now; neighbors emerge to watch. Three cops continue kicking at Susu's lower body while Marzuq and his subordinate move to pick him up by his arms and legs. They shake him and drag him down the lane as the crowd swells—three dozen, six dozen, a hundred or so. As the numbers grow, the policemen tighten their grip and make haste. Their focus on Susu dissolves and they scan the faces of the crowd with apparent unease. Some onlookers appear to flash anger and solidarity, others satisfaction.

Out of nowhere a little boy in jeans and an ocher sweater points an accusing finger at me. "Who are *you*?" he demands. "What do *you* want with us?"

I feel my heart beating in my neck.

As the detectives approach the edge of the shantytown, a large contingent follows along. It falls to two policemen—the ones with free hands—to push the crowd away. "Go home!" they say over and over. One of them has a crack in his voice. "This is a matter of state security!"

"*What* state security?" someone calls, taunting him.

The cop pulls out his knife and raises it in the air, and nearly everyone draws back.

Our designated driver races ahead to the front seat of the van and starts it up. This is no orderly arrest; it's a getaway. The police hastily unlock the backseat and flop Susu like a fresh-caught fish onto the floor of the cage between the benches. He cringes, evidently pricked from head to toe by shards of sunflower-seed shells. His stench arrests the air we breathe. Everybody is silent—until I open my mouth.

"Who is Susu?" I demand. "What did he do?"

There is no immediate response.

Moroccan law calls for an arrestee with health trouble or signs of injury to undergo a series of medical tests before his arraignment. The van speeds down a minefield of potholes into a residential area of run-down concrete housing, rusty satellite dishes, and laundry lines along the sidewalk. We approach the neighborhood of Dar Laman, home to the King Muhammad V Emergency Ward.

Eventually, through the banged-up Plexiglas window that walls off the front seat from the cage, Marzuq puts his right hand on my shoulder and leans into me, as if to push off into the upper register of his voice. "This is a very dangerous man," he says. "An evil man. He has been stealing for months and evading capture. He stole from homes, he stole from market stalls. Then yesterday in broad daylight, Susu committed a crime of cosmic proportions."

We veer right into a short corridor formed by two white walls, then slow through a blue metal gate. A weary flower grove and a green and red Moroccan flag at half-mast adorn a stubby hexagonal building with a double door directly ahead of us. The guards inside seem to know that a National Security van calls for a stretcher. They wheel one out and bring in Susu strapped down, flanked by police.

"What did he do?" I ask the cop behind the wheel.

"It was in the livestock market," he says. "A man was leading away his sheep for the holiday, just walking it across the street to drive it home. Susu unsheathed his knife, and in full view of a Muslim crowd, he cut a gash across the sheep's stomach, spilling its blood in vain."

The walls of the emergency ward are white, and perhaps eighty people cry out for attention. Pregnant mothers are wailing. Wounded men cry out unintelligibly. Three lonely doctors work the crowd.

"Do you understand what that means to Moroccans and Muslims?" the cop goes on. "It is a crime against the Moroccan people, a crime against Islam. A mass crime, truly—like a serial killer. It is as if we are all his victims. And have no doubt that we are going to deliver him to justice."

I watch Marzuq find the doctor in charge and talk him through what he is about to examine. I can't make out his words from across the hall. The doctor is smiling, nodding his head.

"So what do you think of our service to the nation?" the officer asks me, beaming.

There is no way to evade the question this time. I eyeball Susu on the stretcher—scratched and bruised, breathing fast, drowning in booze—and wonder what *he* thinks. I wonder what possessed him to attack a living paschal lamb before its ritual slaughter on the holiday of Eid al-Adha.

"You brothers are true patriots," I tell the policeman. "God be with you."

His teeth catch a glint of the fluorescent light along the ceiling. He puts his hand gently on the back of my neck. "Thanks, brother."

The cops are no angels. Neither am I. But for now, we're working together.

Out of the 195 or so countries in the world today, a few dozen are liberal democracies that aspire to justice for all, personal freedoms, and individual rights for their citizens—though some deliver on these commitments better than others, and my country, the United States, probably does not top the list. The rest, where most of the world's people live, are dictatorships, autocracies, or failing states. Some of these governments espouse the same ideals mine does but do not begin to deliver on them, while others make no pretext of supporting them at all. Nearly everyone agrees that liberty and justice are good and desirable things, and Martin Luther King Jr. taught us to be optimistic that "the arc of the universe bends toward justice." But what should be done to help make that prophecy come true—and who should be doing it?

Eight years after the American-led toppling of Saddam Hussein, regime change of a different sort happened two thousand miles west of Baghdad, in the North African country of Tunisia. There was no invading army—and in the days of rioting that precipitated the fall of the Tunisian dictator, there were no familiar opposition groups at the helm, Islamist or otherwise. A street vendor, angry at the authorities for confiscating his wares, lit himself on fire. As the tale of the man's victimization by government officials spread across the country, it hit a nerve, and tens of thousands of Tunisians braved police batons and gunfire to end the rule of their oppressor. They confronted, head-on, the dreaded security apparatus that had controlled the country with an iron fist for decades. It was both a fractious movement of social protest and a unified struggle to honor the death of an individual. In a region dominated by foreign powers and transnational movements, the Tunisian revolution demonstrated that the most profound change comes from within, and that the story of a simple man can eviscerate a police state. This sort of justice is no guarantee of justice for all. As the initial aftermath of the revolution has shown, the path toward a free and fair society is not straightforward. Then again, neither is the process of state building that follows military occupation, the aftereffects of which have proved costlier and bloodier.

Tunisia, in turn, inspired waves of mass protest from Algeria to Yemen—notably in Egypt, the most populous Arab country and a center of the region's politics and culture, ruled by a staunch (and notoriously corrupt) ally of the United States. In Cairo, as in Tunis, the groundswell of indignation was not engineered by proponents of an ideology. It stemmed from something messier: millions of personal stories of disaffection, each too humble to have ever been heard alone; an enraged population, conspiring to drown out the official narrative of the state. Every country this trend has reached, in one way or another, now faces the problem of renegotiating the relationship between the authority and its subjects.

For the past few years I have been interested in the intersection of authoritarian states and the masses they patrol. The most poignant site of that intersection is a police precinct, where ordinary people viscerally encounter the power of their government. How cops treat citizens is a reflection of norms set by the upper echelons of their chain of command. How individual citizens respond to their treatment, or mistreatment, speaks to the capacity of the society to press its demands on the state. I decided to observe that interplay in order to see, from the ground, whether there might be a new way of achieving change from within—whether a government and its people, rather than strive to defeat each other, can somehow conspire to become a society. So I went to Morocco, a thousand miles due west of Tunisia, where social disaffection has also long been smoldering. Morocco is governed by a centuries-old monarchy, sturdier than the young military dictatorships that rule some of its neighbors. But of course, no regime is unbreakable.

I arranged a meeting with a senior member of the domestic intelligence service known as the Directorate of Territorial Surveillance. He agreed to permit me embed-style access to a precinct of the Moroccan police for a period of four months in 2008. The arrangement was handled informally, which is not unusual in the Arab world. What is unusual—and remarkable—is that no stipulations were imposed on me, nor did the government ask to see what I wrote before its publication.

Perhaps the Moroccan officials agreed to my request because they felt that in their policing they had something to show off. Or perhaps they felt they were showing off just by inviting a writer in, in the sense that no Arab state had ever before shown the openness to usher a writer into the midst of its security services over a sustained period of time. Either of those possibilities suited me well. I would have been very happy to find in the Moroccan police a model worth emulating by other developing countries and a benign attitude toward the population. At the same time, I was prepared for anything.

TWO

In bed that night after Susu's arrest, I dream a police van is slicing through shantytown alleys too narrow for a donkey cart. Marzuq and his team leap out and smack slum youth with zeal. They finish off all the roughnecks in their precinct and still have enough pep left to drive across town and hunt a new culprit: me. Parking by a row of Lego-brick apartment houses, they shuffle out the back of the van to surround the building where I live. They drag me by the legs into the backseat cage, angry about some unspecified crime, and work me over with their fists. "What you did was unforgivable!" they yell.

After a while the punches stop.

"*Now* you're going to pay."

The clubs are about to come down when I jump up from bed and catch my breath.

Blinding sunlight glares off the mirror I face when I wake up in the morning. The window is open. The sounds of construction and rush-hour traffic mix in the distance, and I can hear Arabic briskly spoken by hard hats along the sidewalk a floor below me. I traipse into the kitchenette and switch on the electric water heater. I wash the peanut butter off one of the spoons in the sink and dump some sugar and instant coffee into a dark brown mug.

It was no great joy to look a policeman in the eye and praise his service while a docile prisoner lay beaten up and writhing on a hospital stretcher. The cop had seemed so eager for my approval, so innocent in his presumption that I would flash a thumbs-up, I felt the need to give him what he wanted. I didn't know what else to do. If instead I'd chastised him for the team's abuse, he and his colleagues might start covering up in my presence—like Adam and Eve after biting from the apple. So I praised the man's service to his kingdom, and he thanked me. But now I worry that my words of flattery will embolden him to behave even worse. I'm spinning in circles. Maybe the mundane brutality of an obscure shantytown arrest does not amount to a hill of beans in the grand scheme of Arab and Islamic affairs—unless of course your name is Susu, or you know enough about him to care about his wounds.

I'm slightly underdressed in the sidewalk café near my apartment in the west Casablanca neighborhood of Ma'arif. My table is surrounded by men in button-down shirts sipping espresso shots in hot milk and puffing cigarettes together over the daily press, which they read with an air of detachment. I peer over my croissant and orange juice at my copy of *Al-Sabah*:

CASABLANCA MAN KILLS STOREKEEPER WHO REFUSED TO LEND HIM A PACK OF CIGARETTES crows one headline in Arabic.

'HOLLYWOOD-STYLE' BANK ROBBERIES ROIL CASABLANCA WITH DISTINCTIVE PROFESSIONALISM AND COORDINATION—A CHALLENGE TO THE SECURITY SERVICES says another.

The front page isn't only about crime. Martin Scorsese just accepted an honorary award at the Marrakesh Film Festival. The price of a paschal lamb is up this holiday season—a boon for rural farmers in the provinces, a crisis for rural migrants to the big city. The enemies of Morocco are reported to be beating the drums of war again on the Saharan front. I continue reading below the crease, however, and there it is again:

POLICE ACCUSE A BARBER IN FEZ OF KIDNAPPING AND RAPE OF FIVE-YEAR-OLD BOY IN HIS OWN HAIR SALON.

DETECTIVES LEARN IDENTITY OF KILLER OF MAN WHOSE BODY WAS DISCOVERED IN A LARGE BAG NEAR NIGHTCLUB ON CASABLANCA HIGHWAY.

The sensational prose under each headline evokes the kind of black-and-white broadsheets that used to spin around and freeze-frame in old American gangster movies and creates the distinct impression that Casablanca, if not the whole of Morocco, is in the midst of a crime wave. I look up from the paper. The incongruous voice of Edith Piaf floats through the steamy smoke-filled air. A waiter in a bow tie winds his way toward me with a silver tray.

"Journalist?" the waiter asks in French, pointing at my recording device.

I nod.

"Where you off to?"

"Ayn Sabaa–Al-Hay al-Muhammadi," I reply, naming the hyphenated precinct to which I have been attached.

"Ah," he says, "the other side of the world."

It is barely fifteen minutes due east, but he's right: last night's shantytown squalor and the humble neighborhoods that surround it feel an ocean away. So do the tortured expressions of the slum dwellers, the roughhousing of the sports fans, and the violence of my "embed" hosts—though to judge from complexion and features alone, any man in this breakfast café could be Susu the sheep slasher's uncle. There is bitter conflict east of here, among the malcontents of a beleaguered population and between them and the agents of the state. The dapper waiter's almond eyes burn golden, and I'm pinned by his knowing glare. What is he trying to tell me? He places a croissant on the table and drifts away. Maybe I need to relax. I've been in Morocco fifteen days.

Casablanca was a tiny, plague-ravaged port town of a few thousand inhabitants, frequented by pirates, when around 1912 French forces designated it the economic capital of a new imperial

Morocco. The army settled tens of thousands of Europeans behind the old stone walls they found here, and once space ran out, they extended the colony westward into new Parisian-style housing. Indigenous Jews, crammed in their historic ghetto in the center, were deemed useful to the empire as civil servants and interpreters. The empire needed manual labor, too: men to crush rocks in recently discovered phosphate mines, work the nascent food and textile factories, and build a railroad to move product to the port. For these responsibilities, they turned to the vast Arab Muslim population in rural areas to the east. They imported them to the city and settled them as close to their new jobs as possible, in tin-roofed shantytowns like the scene of last night's hunt. For security reasons, between the workers' squalid lodgings and the homes of their imperial taskmasters the French devised an invisible line.

A century later, Casablanca is a vast metropolis. The French are all but gone, replaced in the economic hierarchy by new elite classes of Moroccans. But the shantytowns are still here, and so is the line. I've been all over the developing world, and no matter what other unique features distinguish the city I'm in, the line is always clearly marked. For now I'm living on the right side of it, to the west, but my work with the police will naturally bring me to its other side.

In Morocco, you know you are driving west of the line when you see homes flatten out and spread in four directions and imperial palm trees shoot up pencil-thin, in perfect parallel rows, toward the cloud-flecked sky. Girls in miniskirts and sharp-dressed boys hold hands by eucalyptus groves at the fringes of enchanting public parks and make out in the shadow of nightclub lights that color the Atlantic shore. There is a neighborhood of majestic villas called "California" a short walk from the place I'm staying, named for its climate by the American troops who landed with General Patton in 1942. The Muhammad V Sports Complex where last night's soccer match was played lies manicured and brightly lit each night, just down the street from my breakfast café. Art galleries and a five-screen surround-sound "Megarama" greet the crashing waves along the coast. Moving east toward the city center through the ritzy neighborhood of Anfa, five-star hotels and eateries spill into a broad commercial hub. White buildings thicken and grow a dozen stories tall, the logos of foreign companies strewn against the emerging skyline. Across the street from a line of rambling office buildings and sidewalk cafés, a coffee-colored stone clock tower built by the former occupiers looms over the medieval city's heavy stone wall. Historic keyhole-shaped Marrakesh Gate, which used to lock in the Jewish ghetto, leaks beggars and hustlers now, prostitutes and pushers, in green, orange, and brown robes. You have come to the border.

The line is a thick physical and psychological buffer zone of forbidding structures: a bleak civil prison, three cemeteries, a municipal butchery and livestock market, and a sprawling, razor-wire-tipped military base named Jankeer, Moroccan slang for a demon, on either side of the railroad tracks that slice the city roughly down the middle. A long industrial strip of factories and warehouses shields west from east behind a maze of iron gates and noisy machinery, shrouded at times in thick black smoke.

Just beyond the smoke lies the other side of the world.

Here, the air is literally harder to breathe. It is policed, like the rest of urban Morocco, by myriad security and intelligence services—their names, uniforms, and division of labor a further bequest of the state's European forebears. The General Police, who wear blue and white, are supposed to manage vehicular and animal traffic, break up street fights, and deter muggers and carjackers during their daily neighborhood patrols. The Auxiliary Forces wear green fatigues and share responsibility for the security of some government installations as well as the teeming open-air markets, where a rigged scale or a turf war among butchers has been known to send meat cleavers flying. Neither of these police divisions has much to do with violent crime of a political or religious nature, unless it happens to erupt in plain sight. Neither division, for that matter, has any investigative capacity whatever. On the other side of the security spectrum, by contrast, the plainclothes Public Intelligence Police have a free hand to infiltrate mosques, political parties, student groups, and gangs—and to build files on the citizenry, one ideologue at a time. The PIP, in turn, is but a poor man's cousin to the more powerful Directorate of Territorial Surveillance, a full-on domestic intelligence agency, reputedly with spies inside slums and government offices, beyond the borders of the kingdom, and within the security services themselves.

Beneath the lofty realm of intelligence agents and above the small-time patrols of the uniformed police lies the large, plain-clothes detective cadre to which I have been affixed: the Judiciary Police. Like the American FBI, they gather evidence, interrogate witnesses, apprehend suspects, and arraign the alleged perpetrators of "grand crimes." That is a loose designation, roughly equivalent to a felony, which theoretically crams terrorism, drug offenses, and illegal immigration into a file cabinet with robbery, rape, and murder. Their jurisdiction spans the kingdom, though in practice all but the elite units are linked to the terrain of one precinct each. I use the word "precinct," though in the case of Casablanca it denotes a larger territory than, say, an American urban precinct, and the very concept of a precinct bears refining before it can be neatly grafted onto an Arab city. My precinct, the fifth of seven citywide, has a reputation for packing the entire range of Moroccan criminality into a few square miles.

Before I left for Morocco, I got the lay of the land from a friend who studies global trends in violence for a living. While the government here is a moderate, constructive player in the politics of North Africa and the Middle East, the country is also an international hub for terrorists and drug cartels.

The criminals who garner the most attention, Moroccan jihadists, have proved themselves to pose a lethal threat both within the country and beyond its borders. The Moroccan Islamic Combatant Group, an al-Qaeda affiliate established by Moroccan veterans of the jihad in Afghanistan, took credit for serial suicide bombings in Casablanca in 2003 that claimed forty-five lives. A year later, the organization struck in the Spanish capital of Madrid, in subway bombings that left two hundred people dead and a thousand wounded. It is an elusive and murky organization, composed of autonomous cells in Morocco, Europe, and various Muslim countries, each with a local leadership that has been difficult to identify and thwart. The group aims to topple the government in Morocco by undermining domestic security and damaging its Western allies—with the ultimate goal of supplanting the kingdom with an Islamist regime. It has drawn foot soldiers not only from the ranks of the urban poor but also from among the gainfully employed. It is responsible for dispatching dozens of suicide bombers to Iraq, Afghanistan, and other places where the fight is on against American or Western troops. And it is only one of several jihadist groups operating inside the kingdom today.

Meanwhile, the northern tip of the country between the Rif mountains and the Mediterranean Sea is the home base of a massive industry for the cultivation and export of cannabis resin, commonly known as hashish. At this writing, 760,000 Moroccans in the region's villages live off cannabis cultivation—yielding $13 billion in revenues annually and making Morocco the largest producer and exporter of cannabis resin on earth. Using Spain as a key transfer point for illegal shipments of drugs, the product is moved via speedboats, fishing boats, yachts, and trucks into Belgium, France, Italy, the Netherlands, and numerous other destinations across the European continent. These well-established trafficking routes have caught the attention of Latin American drug cartels, which have begun to smuggle cocaine and heroin into Europe via Morocco as well. Romanian and Russian crime organizations have also been traced to Moroccan soil, making the kingdom both a point of origin and a significant transit point for the global drug trade.

When organized crime and terrorism come together, the potential to destabilize a country is enormous. Witness Ansar al-Mahdi, a local jihadist organization independent of al-Qaeda. The group's charismatic leader met with drug barons in the country's north and made plans to open an explosives factory and a training camp for firearms with their support. Drug barons apparently found it appealing to use Islam as a cover for their crime operations; the chaos of an insurgency would create the perfect environment for them to run their business. For the leader of Ansar al-Mahdi, the alliance with drug lords fit into his broader scheme of combining his ideological ambitions with criminal activity. He had previously hatched a plot to rob banks and armored transport vehicles to help fund his movement, and when he was busted, he made use of his two-year stint in prison to recruit hardened criminals to assist him after their release.

He was not alone among Moroccan jihadists in devising such strategies. An even more ambitious group of criminal Islamists was the Belliraj organization, a broad-based conspiracy broken up in 2008. Belliraj funded its operations using professional thieves all over the world. Its supporters robbed an armored truck in Luxembourg, making off with 17.5 million euros; they stole gold jewelry in Belgium and melted it in Morocco for resale. Most disturbingly, the Belliraj network arranged a quid pro quo with Latin American cocaine traffickers to provide security for its drug operations in Morocco in exchange for money.

In other words, terrorism has gotten complicated. The anger and frustration of urban poverty still spawns jihadist operations, but so do a host of other factors—some ideological, some purely criminal. According to Morocco's interior ministry, the Belliraj organization drew its recruits from all levels of Moroccan society. The secretaries general of two political parties were implicated in the conspiracy, as well as successful businessmen, a university professor, pharmacists, travel agents—and, of greatest concern, a police captain. The Ansar al-Mahdi group managed to lure into its network several women who lived in the upscale Casablanca neighborhood of Anfa. Two were married to pilots in the national airline—an alarming potential threat for obvious reasons. At least five members of the armed forces had joined the organization. For Morocco's kingdom, which survived two bloody coup attempts by military officers in 1971 and 1972, the infiltration of the armed forces by jihadists is a big deal. Nor are terrorists the only criminal element to have penetrated the security establishment in Morocco. In 2006, authorities arrested the head of security at Morocco's royal palaces. He was tried and convicted of colluding with a drug lord during his seven-year stint as head of the Judiciary Police in Tangier. Several high-ranking military officials have also been imprisoned for their collaboration with the cannabis underworld.

Moroccan security is a vexing undertaking—more complex for the commingling of terrorism and drugs, and more dangerous for the fact that the security services themselves have been compromised. The problems are emblematic of new battles being fought in developing countries around the world—from Latin America and the Caribbean, where drug cartels flourish, to jihadi battlegrounds to the east, where the gravest threats no longer come from enemy states, but from nonstate actors that thrive on weakness and chaos. The security services are battling not invaders, but factions of their own populations whose allegiance lies elsewhere, people who would love nothing more than for the state to fail and anarchy to be unleashed. Common homicide, to judge from the screaming headlines I read this morning, may also be on the rise—but the Directorate of National Security has other, more pressing concerns.

Late December rain is pouring outside the glass windows of the sidewalk café, and palm tree shadows sail gray over diesel traffic. I hail a fire-engine red Peugeot *"petit taxi"* and, once inside, watch the city hide its skyline behind block after block of white concrete apartment buildings. Satellite dishes lie prostrate in clusters on every rooftop, now hosed down by the cold rain.

"My Iraqi brother!" cries the man behind the wheel, smiling broadly into the rearview mirror. "Brother in God, brother in blood!"

He has noticed that I speak Arabic with an Iraqi accent and figures he knows the rest. I wasn't exactly born with this accent, but it's strong enough that he wouldn't be able to guess that.

"O Iraq, land of Saddam, land of manhood! Your martyred leader Saddam is our hero, brother, God have mercy on his soul! God destroy the enemies of Iraq, enemies of the Arab and Islamic nation: the Americans, the Jews, the effeminate among the Arabs! God make Iraq a graveyard for their children!"

He rockets northeast off a shopping strip on Gandhi Boulevard, windshield wipers squeaking, then slows into the mire of traffic that swells the neighborhood of Anfa.

"They said they came to bring democracy to Iraq," the driver goes on. "See the rivers of blood they brought with their false democracy, brother. And they killed Saddam, the only man fit to rule Iraq since the days of al-Hajjaj!" He proceeds to quote a poem attributed to the latter, a bloodthirsty eighth-century governor in Baghdad. It rhymes in Arabic: "O people of Iraq, people of treachery and hypocrisy . . . I can see ambitious eyes, long necks, and ripened heads, so it is time to harvest them. Indeed, it is I who will cut them off!"

The Arabic language, as spoken today by rich and poor alike, brims with poetic references and poignant tropes from a bygone age. Most of them are beautiful and wise, but more than a few speak to a vision of the world that is torturous and stark.

"Am I right about this world, brother?" he asks. "A strong people need a strong ruler, do they not?"

There is only one acceptable answer—the one I always give, from North Africa clear across to the balmy waters of the Persian Gulf: "Of course, my brother. I know that you are right."

"Don't worry, my dear one," the driver assures me. He goes on to quote the prophet Muhammad: "On the hour of judgment the Muslims will fight the Jews and kill them, until the Jews will hide behind the stone and the tree, and even the stone and the tree will say, 'O Muslim! O servant of God! There is a Jew behind me, come and kill him!'"

I am numb, by now, to this golden oldie. I ask the man to turn on his radio.

At length, beyond a gas station and a row of oil-stained body shops on Émile Zola Street, we reach an angular gray and white three-story building with long, narrow slits for windows. A bilingual sign hangs over the second floor, French script in green, Arabic in red: GREATER CASABLANCA SECURITY SECTOR—JUDICIARY POLICE DIVISION.

I count out the man's fare and make off out the door and up nine concrete steps into a pasty-white first-floor landing. An Auxiliary Forces private in green fatigues salutes, guarding the entryway from behind a white linoleum bar. He asks for an ID card. On a long linoleum bench built into the side wall, an elderly woman sits weeping softly.

I am just about to hand the guard my passport when a handsome man in his early forties pops his head out the leather-cushion-padded door of the frontmost office. He is clean shaven, hair slicked back, and wears a snazzy yellow leather jacket over a half-unbuttoned dress shirt. The woman half-rises to approach him, only to sit down again when he fails to meet her eye.

"Welcome home!" he tells me, putting his arm around the uniformed private's shoulders. "So he asked you for ID, eh? Come on in."

Lieutenant Mustafa Sharqawi, the chief of the Judiciary Police Precinct 5, motions me to follow behind him.

An oversized desk at the far end of his office sits beneath two regulation portraits hanging overhead: King Muhammad VI sipping mint tea, and his late father, Hasan II, peering inscrutably off-camera. There is a refrigerator with sodas in one corner, a telex machine with screaming instructions from central command in the other. I take my seat next to a small adjoining table where a box of Romeo and Juliet Havanas sits next to a yellow porcelain ashtray with three grooved cigar rests, shining spotless.

Three hundred middle-aged pounds with a bald head extends his hand from across the table, beaming at me already.

"Lieutenant Abd al-Jabbar," Sharqawi says, "my esteemed deputy."

A mobile phone on the desk rings. The chief nixes it with his thumb. "So how many pages of material you think you have so far?" he asks, and grins into his phone, scanning text messages.

My mouth malfunctions and nothing much comes out.

"You know," Abd al-Jabbar volunteers, "all of us here at Precinct Five, all of us work for a hero."

"God have mercy on your parents, brother Abd al-Jabbar!" the chief cuts in, raising his voice. "God have mercy on your parents!"

"Don't let him stop me from telling you," the deputy insists. "Don't let him stop me! He's the hero of Hay Farah!"

Sharqawi dribbles the air beneath his right hand to tone the lieu-tenant down, and it seems to work. Somebody knocks at the door. It's the elderly woman from out front. The chief waves the peti-tioner off with the back of his left hand. Granted a moment of peace, he gives me a long hard stare. "So what do you think of Casablanca?" he asks. "Is it safe from crime or what?"

"Well," I begin to say, "I do love Casablanca, but you know—"

"Stick around here and months from now, I guarantee you will not have found the sort of crime you see in Western cities, or most Arab countries. For one thing, we have gun control, so already you know that the murder rate is going to be lower. Second of all, we have very simple people here, with very simple needs. Simple, poor, uncomplicated people."

"Some of them are Islamist militants, no?" I ask him.

"Very rare!" he nearly shouts. "Very rare!"

"That whole issue is exaggerated," the deputy adds.

"When a man kills somebody around here," the chief says, "usu-ally either he is drunk or on drugs or he has worked very, very hard to make that man dead because he had to do it with a rock or a stick or something. A knife. Last week down the road, for example."

"It was a stick," Abd al-Jabbar interjects.

Sharqawi clenches the space between his eyebrows and aims it straight at the deputy's big mouth. My mind's eye, meanwhile, con-jures a bloody stick, the primal weapon.

"Not only do we work to deny the criminal the essential weapons of his craft," he goes on, "but the knights of law enforcement are *very* strong, *very* patriotic, and we have informants everywhere. Also"—he pats his hand on a small pile of thick paperback books—"now we have the rule of law. You know what is the rule of law, I think."

I can make out the Arabic titles along each spine. They are in fact books of law: a new edition of the Moroccan penal code, a slimmer volume about the laws governing media and reporting, and a book on the security services and their prescribed powers.

"We have the rule of law, and we have human rights. Human rights is something that we in the Judiciary Police cherish very highly."

"You were saying a murder happened down the road last week?" I ask.

He waves the back of his hand in the air like a flag and goes on with his lecture: "I think you will find that we honor the human rights of our citizens and do not tolerate *any* infractions." Then he leans in my direction only slightly. "Have you seen anything that would lead you to say otherwise?"

I stumble again for a suitable response, fearing for my status.

"Because if you have," adds the deputy, "we would launch a full investigation, and if necessary, we would fire the man who did it. We are very proud of our record here. You know, now there is a Complaints Division and anyone can file a complaint about a policeman to the king. Praise God, no one has ever complained about our precinct."

"But tell me, have you seen anything," Sharqawi persists, "anything at all, that would tarnish the good reputation of our precinct? Last night, for example, during your expedition with Officer Marzuq?"

"I only just got here, Lieutenant," I reply. "I'm here for the big picture."

This appears to placate the chief. His eyes close briefly and he nods. He opens them again and smiles broadly.

Something tells me the beating of Susu in the shantytown is the last police beating I'm ever going to witness in Casablanca.

"I often wonder, you know, why the Jews love our kingdom so much," Sharqawi says. "You are a Jew. Can you tell me? Because I really want to know."

The answer, not short, is a mystery to many Moroccans. I break off a little piece of it: "The late king, Muhammad V, God have mercy on his soul. He saved Morocco's Jews from the Nazis."

"God have mercy on his soul!" Abd al-Jabbar chimes in.

"And God have mercy on your parents," the chief tells me. "You are welcome here—welcome, welcome."

I ask him again about the murder.

"It was last week," he says. "We all worked very hard last week. A man was found—in a warehouse, beaten to death with a stick.

There was a lot of blood. Not all of it was his. I got there and I was afraid, deep inside, that we would not find the man who did it. But by the grace of God Almighty, and by the grace of the forensics police, and by the grace of the detectives here at our precinct, we were able to catch the perpetrator within three days and persuade him to confess. Praise God."

"Three days, by God!" Abd al-Jabbar says. "That is a very long time in Casablanca."

"You know," the chief cuts in, "if you want to see an example of how we operate, you can read our file on that killing." He hands me a staple-bound thirteen-page document in Arabic with a red stamp on the top of page 1 beside the heading,

JUDICIARY POLICE IN AYN SABAA–AL-HAY AL-MUHAMMADI, CASABLANCA
TO: THE HONORABLE PROSECUTOR FOR THE KING
SUBJECT: DELIBERATE MURDER AND THEFT

"This is a secret document," he adds. "For your eyes only."

I fold it up and put it in my briefcase.

"Let's have lunch," the chief suggests. "I bet you never ate Berber food."

The chief ushers his deputy and me out the office door and locks it behind him. I follow them into the car parked out front and wonder, having read so many raucous headlines about murder, rape, and grand theft all over the kingdom, why a thirteen-page police file about a common homicide should be designated "secret."

THREE

There is a cultural imperative among Arab police to conceal certain things from the public. It dates as far back as the ancient world, but for the moment I will rewind to 2003. On May 16 of that year, two months into the American-led invasion of Iraq, a dozen young men strapped on homemade explosives and blew themselves up in Casablanca. Forty-five bystanders died and a hundred suffered injuries in the deadliest terror attack in the history of the kingdom.

Like September 11 in America or July 7 in England or March 11 in Spain, the tragedy shattered a veneer of naïveté. Elites in the country used to describe their society as "the Moroccan exception"—free somehow of the terror and civil strife that afflicted other Arab and Muslim lands, thanks to social accord between rich and poor, a policy of cultural accommodation with the West, and a tradition of tolerance toward minorities. The six sites targeted by suicide bombers that day, each in a ritzy imperial-palm-lined section of the city's west, seemed calculated to demonstrate otherwise: a Spanish restaurant, the Belgian consulate, an Italian restaurant owned by a Jewish family, a Jewish cemetery, a Jewish community center, and the fabulous five-star Hotel Farah, popular at the time among Western tourists. The identity of the twelve suicide attackers pointed clearly to the presence of a tortured underclass. Each bomber, the police eventually learned, was a local boy in his twenties from the slums. Like other incidents of mass carnage from New York City to Bali, the tragedy of May 16 was like a bloodstained mirror held up to the state and its society—a mirror that, in this case, was as quickly smashed.

On the eve of the attack, liberal activists in Morocco had hoped that the new king would move swiftly to introduce transparency in government and rein in the historical excesses of the Moroccan security apparatus. He had promised as much in his inaugural address, and he had begun to make good with a few swift decisions of immense significance. He fired his late father's notorious top cop, announced a general amnesty for political prisoners, offered to compensate some victims of prior police brutality, and invited the leftist opposition—his late father's lifelong political adversaries—to join the ruling parliamentary coalition. He had even established a government project to redress the abuse of civilians by his father's regime—a more modest version of South Africa's Truth and Reconciliation Commission. But as of May 16, there were new priorities. The rattled population overwhelmingly craved a restoration of security, and the monarch's key allies in Washington and Paris backed a massive crackdown on Islamist militancy in the kingdom. The king's enforcers arrested three thousand people in connection with the attacks, most on vague or unknown charges. An overhaul of the country's mosque leadership followed, spearheaded by the intelligence services. New security detachments were deployed to several Moroccan cities, along with new forms of counterterrorist training. Meanwhile, covert cooperation with Morocco's Western allies reached new heights. As has widely been reported, the kingdom has played a prominent role, throughout the Bush years and allegedly ever since, in the United States government's "extraordinary rendition" program, which enabled terrorist suspects to be flown in secretly for interrogation and torture by Arab governments on behalf of the CIA. Details of these actions were concealed from the Moroccan public.

Farah, which means "joy," also happens to be the name of the squalid district where several of the May 2003 suicide bombers had lived. Remnants of their jihadist cell were flushed out from the same area four years later in a celebrated epilogue to the 2003 tragedy. On the morning of April 10, 2007, a hundred police and snipers followed an informant's lead to a dilapidated four-story building in the east Casablanca neighborhood known as Hay Farah. A young man inside fled to the roof and promptly blew himself up. Another, apparently on the verge of following suit, began to fumble with his clothes when a sniper shot him down; nine pounds of explosives were later removed with great care from his body. A third member of the cell managed to escape the building and blow himself up along the road, wounding a cop and nine civilians. The last of the four detonated his bomb close enough to the police commander's retinue to injure three officers and claim the life of one. A few days later, friends of the militant cell blew themselves up near the United States consulate, wounding a Moroccan bystander. But by then the public's attention had come to focus on the death of the police officer.

My "embed" host in Casablanca, Precinct 5 chief Mustafa Sharqawi, commanded the massive police operation on April 10. He has become a legend among police for his exploits that day. His beefy deputy is just one of many colleagues in the security services who have taken to calling him the "hero of Hay Farah." Few civilians, however, are aware of Sharqawi's role in the famous operation—or the names of his comrades in arms—because that information has been designated "secret."

The widely reported "martyrdom" of the policeman during the April shootout sparked an outpouring of solidarity, patriotism, and bereavement kingdomwide. The monarch ordered family reparations and a royal funeral procession to be led by senior officials and hundreds more police. They were joined by thousands of civilians. Children brought flowers; old women wailed. Yet the name of the man they were burying was largely unknown, absent from various media reports. The name had been designated a secret, though it was soon released to the public because of the extraordinary circumstances of his death.

Newspaper coverage of more ordinary violence in Morocco resembles Western crime reporting in most respects. Journalists probe the human impact of murder, rape, and theft on family and society, culling a cautionary tale, where the facts permit, out of the spectacle of a man gone wrong. Upon closer inspection, however, there's a hole at the center of these stories, crucial facts glaringly omitted: the names of the victim, the perpetrator, witnesses and suspects, police, the judge—any proper noun, really, that would ground the incident in its real-life context. Full-color photographs of a crime scene or a bust are generally published with faces or eyes obscured. Bystanders quoted in the body of the story are identified by initials or a first name at most. All such details are commonly designated "secret" in Morocco, along with many other Arab countries, and perhaps with good reason.

The rationale, police tell me, stems from the perils of *thar,* an ancient Arabic name for the sort of clan-based blood vengeance that used to fill in for justice in the premodern world and still does from time to time. It is the same custom that drove the Hatfield and McCoy families to kill each other for thirteen years in the West Virginia and Kentucky backcountry and led an Italian immigrant to New York, in the opening scene of *The Godfather,* to ask Don Vito Corleone to kill the boys who raped his daughter. Since the twentieth century, Arab states have aspired to supplant *thar* with some form of law enforcement and a court system—but far too often, according to my guides among the security services, the traditional morality of vengeance still kicks in. When it does, it can spiral out of control. *Thar* most commonly rears its head in rural areas and among rural migrants to the big city—aided and abetted, cops say, by the release of too much information about a given police action. Name a killer or a suspect in a newspaper article, and the victim's family is liable to pursue a campaign of retribution against his relatives. Name a cop or a witness, and either the criminal he put away or the criminal's loved ones at large will seek payback—maybe not today, maybe not tomorrow, but soon and for the rest of his life. Even the divulgence of a murder victim's name may pose a danger to her loved ones if, as is likely, the family of the man who killed her regard his imprisonment as a crime in itself, worthy of retribution.

So it is judged best to keep all these names secret. Secrecy itself, in the eyes of the state, remains a prerequisite for national security. This imperative has survived the 2003 attack and thrived in its aftermath—newly grafted, with some high-profile exceptions, onto the novelty of al-Qaeda-style violence.

But in the age of megaterrorism, with a global audience paying unprecedented attention to the annals of justice in Muslim societies, it is an open question whether future blackouts will be sustainable. Holes in the state's monopoly on basic facts are emerging and growing, poked at every day by Arabic Tweeters and Facebook users, a newly feisty local press corps, and nosy outsiders like me. A few small-time weekly tabloids in Morocco, reporting exclusively on crime, dared to print the parties' full names and photographs in their coverage—but several editors were prosecuted or sued for the offense, and their policy of naming names was effectively squelched.

Only through greater openness, Moroccan liberals contend, can the country ultimately escape the ancient cycles that have inhibited social progress and stoked the extremist worldview that enabled the tragedy of May 2003. And if there are relationships worth severing among terrorism, other forms of crime, and broader social trends, they suggest, such insights cannot be uncovered in the darkness.

These are the arguments elites make, anyway. But there is another case for openness that you have to see to understand. I noticed that on Thursday mornings off Grand Army Avenue near the heart of Casablanca, a crowd used to form in front of a newspaper kiosk. Men, women, and teenagers elbowed each other and occasionally swore at each other. They wanted the same thing and there wasn't enough of it to go around. No sooner had someone bought a copy of one of the gutsy new crime tabloids than she walked a few feet away and stood there to go through it slowly, page by page. Some of the crowd followed her, angling for a view of the newspaper over her shoulder.

So these are the victims. So these are the killers. So these are their names. So this is where it happened.

A few people began talking softly. "I *live* there," a man said. "I know that *family*," said another.

I saw a boy start crying. He pointed to a picture of someone his age who had been stabbed to death. "Can I take this page?" he asked. "He was my friend, and we never had a camera." The woman nodded and handed him the whole issue.

I went to see the embattled editor of one of these tabloids once, a few weeks before the government intimidated him into suppressing names and images like the rest of the Moroccan press. He told me it was too bad the authorities were hassling him. "Printing these things is like minting money," he said. "We can't supply enough copies." I asked him why he thought the genre was so popular. "Everybody loves to read about crime, right?" he said. "All over the world it's the same."

I'm sure that's true. But in the crowd that gathered Thursday mornings where bare truths were briefly on display, I felt I could discern an altogether different kind of popular demand. It was the pent-up desire to know and to remember an individual human life— the kind of life that in most authoritarian countries sometimes ends in darkness, bundled up and buried in the locked cabinets of state security. The crowd craved an end to this form of inhumanity. They wanted to be part of the cycle of acknowledgment and grief that naturally follows an untimely loss. They wanted to experience that cycle together. They were trying to be a community.

Critics of the Arab world sometimes indict Arab society as a whole for being complicit in the scourge of terrorism. There are no civic bonds in these places, they argue, so Arabs can't come together to cut away the violent strand in their midst. These critics are at a loss, however, to imagine what it would take to build that sense of community that they say is absent.

I flip through the thirteen-page case file on the recent murder of a man at a warehouse in Casablanca and imagine the crowd that would form off Grand Army Avenue if I got a loudspeaker and announced what it was that I held in my hand. These thirteen pages name a victim, a killer, a dozen witnesses, suspects, bystanders, and detectives. In graphic detail they describe the end of a life. They cite the testimony of ordinary people who have been enlisted to help solve the riddle of his death.

The document ends with an answer.

I look up from the case file and ask Chief Sharqawi why it's a state secret.

"Because we're not just police," he says, as if it's obvious. "We're guardians of the social fabric."

Behind the wheel of his unmarked Peugeot 206, the chief's head swivels evenly left and right, surveying the sidewalks as he navigates. It's merely drizzling now. Perched on the bumper ahead of us, three boys in their preteens hold tight to thin steel pipes lining the back of a delivery truck—a free ride. By the honeycomb-patterned wall that shields a large warehouse from the street, a grimy-looking man in his fifties works one of the hexagonal bricks with a stick. At this the chief slows the car and stalls a moment, only to pick up the pace again.

"He's just a poor brother," the deputy Abd al-Jabbar declares. "Probably he stows his valuables in the wall."

The boss's muscular hands turn the steering wheel gently.

What was left of the rain tapers off, and the muddy sky of Precinct 5 blushes a firebrick mist over the horizon. Stubby palm trees give way to junior shrubs along the sidewalks. Royal Army Avenue loses some of its girth and coarsens as the three of us reach an older section of town. Ramshackle storefronts crop up on either side displaying cow hides and cauldrons of stew. The crowd outdoors dresses more traditionally now: every woman wears a cloak of brown or black, her head tightly wrapped in a bright-colored headscarf. Men bundle up in loose-fitting hooded djellabas. Only the sheep wear white. A day before the Eid festival, they nearly outnumber pedestrians as we approach the Casablanca municipal butchery and livestock market, the New York Stock Exchange of paschal lamb. Each customer comes out clasping the hind legs of his purchase and marches it on ahead of him by its front legs, wheelbarrow style, into the backseat of a car. This must be where Susu the sheep slasher perpetrated his "crime of cosmic proportions."

"Tomorrow is the holiday," Sharqawi explains. "Every good

family in Casablanca should acquire a lamb for slaughter. Like your turkeys."

His posture is relaxed and his talk up-tempo as we ride through the deteriorating streets. He scans the many faces along the sidewalk, slowing the car from time to time as if to home in on something. His deputy keeps silent and stares straight ahead. Only Sharqawi's window is wide open. I open mine a crack. The pedestrians aren't smiling much. Most of them are raising their voices at each other; they want to be heard over the sputtering traffic. I try to pick out an Islamist militant—so many supposedly hail from this neighborhood—but all I see is poor people and sheep. I wonder what Sharqawi sees. I wonder if he would ever really tell me. I wonder how I can draw him out.

"Can you share some more about what you did that day at Hay Farah?" I ask him.

"It's a war to the death with those dogs," he says. "They hate the police. They call us tyrants. And we hate them, too. We call them apostates."

"Why do you suppose they call you tyrants?" I ask.

He shrugs, parks his Peugeot by the curb, and gets out. "Come and have a look," he says, diving into the crowd. "Come see a *real* Islamic society."

A space seems to open up as Sharqawi and his deputy move through it.

"A blessed Eid and every year may you be well, dear Lieutenant!" a man cries.

"And *you* be well!" the chief replies.

A buxom woman in her forties runs toward the chief and hugs him tight, planting twin kisses on his cheeks—an aggressive move for a woman in a headscarf, I'm thinking. He returns the kiss and whispers something in her ear before motioning me closer.

"Tell him what you do for me," he says to her in Arabic.

"*Je suis informatrice!*" she whispers giddily in French.

I try to talk to the self-proclaimed informant, but Sharqawi drags me off toward the market square where people are haggling over livestock.

"You wouldn't guess from her veil, but she's a prostitute," he says. "She's been at it for twenty years and she knows everybody. A great asset."

The veiled "informatrice" sports the happiest smile in the meat market, which otherwise brims with angst this holiday season. As the newspapers have reported, a 10 percent spike in the cost of feed across North Africa is causing livestock farmers to raise the price of their lambs, while unemployment in Casablanca stands at a twenty-year high. What's more, the edges of the market square are reportedly teeming with "sheep scalpers," whom many have blamed for jacking up prices further. Scalpers allegedly use their cell phones to track the price per kilo from one market to the next with the ruthless efficiency of international currency traders—and coordinate with shady regional sheep distribution networks to hoard and squeeze supply. Perhaps they are more a scapegoat than a true culprit, overblown by the establishment for popular consumption—but buyers are wary, and government-licensed brokers of livestock in the market square take pains to flaunt their crinkly laminated ID cards. It's a reassuring way to get negotiations started—though when they name their price, they meet shock and distress.

"Give a Muslim brother a break," a customer says.

"Usury is forbidden!" another exclaims.

The broker just shrugs. Usury has nothing to do with it. Meanwhile, he faces troubles of his own. A further strain on the pricing of an animal, according to local media, stems from the cash that brokers have been paying in protection money to Auxiliary Forces personnel, the uniformed guardians of order in the markets. I notice one Auxiliary private, dressed in green, twirl his black baton in the air, only to stop the antic immediately upon sighting Chief Sharqawi and his deputy, whom he promptly salutes.

The impact of the price hike, in any case, has been devastating for lower-income families, because the slaughter of a sheep during the Eid festival is a religious obligation for believing Muslims—a commemoration of the patriarch Abraham's willingness to sacrifice his son before God. Some households have been selling off treasured clothing and household wares in the old city markets to come up with the needed cash. A mile down the road from the slaughter-house, several dozen civil servants have staged a protest for the past few days in front of the local district governorate where they work—dressed up in wool with sheep's head masks to cover their faces—because the advance pay they were promised for the holiday did not come through. "I'm thinking of moving out of my neighborhood," one protester is quoted as telling the local daily *Al-Sabah*. "What will people say about me because I can't buy a sacrifice for Eid? I prefer to die than hear that sort of talk." His name, as well, is left out of the story.

I think that the secret of Susu the sheep slasher's crime might be hiding somewhere in this collective emotional morass. The police were not mistaken when they dubbed it "a crime of cosmic proportions"; to kill a paschal lamb in Morocco before one of the holiest days in Islam is to make a harrowing symbolic statement. One might even think of it as an act of terrorism—a form of protestation through violence—albeit for an obscure, purely local cause. These are the ideas that run through my head as I watch young men grow despondent in a spiked and unjust sheep market. But I'm only theorizing—clutching at straws with no access to the source of the cosmic crime. Susu was stone drunk when Marzuq and his men took him away. Maybe when he's sober, he has a story to tell. Maybe his story would inspire others. His life and his imagination are what matter to me. They matter to me as much as Susu's crime and the bloody mess he made matter to the cops.

"I want to buy *two* today," Chief Sharqawi says to one of the sheep brokers, then turns to me. "They're for Lieutenant Jabri, our chief investigator," he explains, "and Officer Marzuq, whom you met last night. I already got one for me and my family. I'm going to pay for two more and tell the guys to just swing by and pick them up. They've earned it."

I listen in on the negotiations. The broker asks for 3,000 dirhams, about $400. Sharqawi agrees to the asking price, but the broker taps him on the shoulder and winks. "For *you*, we lower it," he says, which is not usually the way haggling works.

"Because we do good things," Sharqawi tells me, "we get a discount."

Two more buyers standing close by shake their heads. One of them keeps shaking his head, with mounting fervor, until a word leaps out of his throat: "Tyrants!"

Sharqawi turns to face him silently, with an icy grin.

The fellow's friend puts an arm around him and jostles him away as if he were drunk. Sharqawi's shoulders relax, his deputy pats him on the back, and the three of us make off.

We lunch on boiled cows' feet and a blood-red stew of beans with hearty bread and sweet mint tea, on the second floor of an open-air restaurant by the slaughterhouse. The chief and his deputy eat like soldiers, hearty and fast.

Delicately, I describe last night's incident in the shantytown and inquire about Susu: "It's a strange sort of crime, to slash a sheep in broad daylight. Why do you think he did it?"

"Why?" Sharqawi says, pouring tea out of the pot into cups, back out of the cups into the pot, and so on—a prevalent technique for cooling and mixing. "The kid was crazy and drunk. He's a criminal. Criminals like him don't have a why. The important thing is he was a menace to the market and to the Moroccan people and my men stopped him."

"Can I meet the kid?" I ask.

The chief puts down the cow's foot he has been working on and looks me over carefully. "Now *I* want to ask *you* why," he says out of his throat. "Why would you want to talk to *him*?"

I lower my eyes toward the meal and dunk a clump of bread in the red bean stew.

"You should be asking us *how*," Sharqawi says. "How we find him. How we stop him. How we keep the streets safe from animals like him."

He pays the bill and hands me a toothpick on the way out. We get into the car and drive back the way we came. I've just been given a piece of advice, though from his tone of voice it sounded almost like an order. The question is whether to follow it.

FOUR

On the first night of Eid, the city is a soup of flashing lights, stirred by the winds of an Atlantic storm. Half a million grills, under white tarp and concrete shelters, scent the soggy air with the smell of meat. Nobody starves, somehow. Strangers come together. Children emerge from apartment houses with bags full of raw animal parts for the people huddled outside. On street corners, over wood and bits of coal, the pent-up unease of the week before the holiday gently dissipates; every Muslim man, woman, and child finds their chunk of lamb. Police are on holiday, too, gone from the slum alleys, and for the moment, so is crime. So are most of the drugged-out teens. A quarter of the population has left Casablanca for the towns and villages that reared them, and of the celebrants who remain in the city, not a single believing Muslim— to borrow a data point fervently insisted upon by Chief Sharqawi— would dare commit a crime on Eid. Heavy rain is no grievance, he says, even under the porous tin roofs where it makes mud out of the floor and mucks up everything. The families inside have loved ones out in the vast, parched farmlands beyond the city. For them, and for the whole of Morocco's economy, rain is a gift from God. Prayers from the shantytowns are wafting up against the downpour: a year of health, success, and safety for the king and all his people; mercy and eternal rest for the ones who did not live to see this feast.

As for me, though I'm not Muslim, I pray for unbridled access to the innards of my adopted precinct, and I win invitations from five police to follow them home and join in the celebration. There is enough room in my stomach to take several of them up on it. Over their holiday tables, I learn who specializes in which investigative field—the drug war, illegal immigration, racketeering, car theft, armed robbery, crimes of honor, homicide—and manage to secure roaming privileges on each floor of their stark linoleum-tiled head-quarters. From their wives I learn that if you haven't marinated your lamb kebabs for a good six hours, you can alternatively steam the meat in a tain—a clay dish with a conical lid—for half the time with saffron, cumin, cilantro, pepper, and salt, and your husband will be equally pleased. Marzuq's wife, a hairdresser, tops her glistening bed of couscous—fluffy, flour-coated semolina wheat granules—with a traditional tangy good-luck stew of seven vegetables originating in the northern inland city of Fez. Her teenaged son wants to be a cop like Dad. Chief Sharqawi's wife, in her kitchen a mile away, has judged savory spiced lamb to be better off alongside raisins, onions, and chickpeas over couscous in a sweet brown mess.

"And you can tell the other wives I said so," she adds.

All the police I visit live in lower-middle-class parts of town and dole out giblets and meat scraps for the poor, like the rest of their neighbors.

It's a family holiday. I know I'm only here to work and am an outsider in this culture, but I can't deny it: I'm lonely. As I wander from home to home I pass boarded-up markets and cafés. My embed hosts in the police force are preoccupied with their loved ones. The holiday brings state and society together under the aegis of Islam. Cops, through their hospitality and charity, are consecrat-ing the ties of blood and religion that bind them to their jurisdiction and separate them, in a sense, from me. In my isolation I am re-minded that the agents of this regime and the cultures and traditions that surround them are part of the same continuum. But there remains a divide: Chief Sharqawi was able to brush away my speculation about Susu's crime the other day, but the broader environment is full of divergent voices, reduced to whispering about the same offenses, the same fearsome "purification campaigns"—but far beyond the earshot of headquarters.

Violent crime resurges immediately after the holiday, and back up goes the wall between the security services and their enemies among the population. Masked men who have managed to acquire rifles and tear gas cannons pull off two more bank robberies in Casablanca and the neighboring township of Muhammadiya. A notorious drug baron flees the kingdom's central prison and six guards are investigated on suspicion of helping him escape. A "purification campaign" in another precinct goes horribly awry when a lieutenant and his team of three, driving their Peugeot sedan along an alley in a shantytown, find themselves surrounded by thirty young men wielding daggers and jagged rocks. "Get out of here or we'll kill you!" they cry. Though badly outnumbered, the cops refuse to stand down. In the bloody confrontation that ensues, a dozen boys and all three police are wounded, and one youth mutilates a lieutenant's left eye. Cops claim the assailants were druggies and alcoholics, though a press report suggests they had joined an Islamist faction and were essentially trying to conquer the shantytown, to make that small, squalid piece of land their own sovereign territory.

"In our precinct we *never* let things get out of hand that way," Sharqawi assures me.

It appears to be true that the slums in his care are free, for the moment, of overtly organized unrest, and most of the crimes his agents handle are "simple and uncomplicated," as the chief has declared more than once. Officer Marzuq, like an alley cat with a bird between his teeth, drags a teenage boy in one night who beat his mother for drug money. A twelve-year-old girl and her father arrive the next day to complain about digital photographs of her and a schoolmate French-kissing that turned up recently on the Internet. Three boys caught pulling up a section of the railroad track for cash face a long string of questions that lead police to their garage full of poached scrap metal and stolen household appliances. Murder, as well, rears its head in Precinct 5—a steadier trickle of cases than at any time in recent memory, cops say. But these crimes, too, prove as run-of-the-mill as the cheap booze that fueled them.

"Most of the time when there is a killing, the culprit, ultimately, is freedom."

That is the wisdom of Lieutenant Rashid Jabri, fifty-one, director of criminal investigations for Precinct 5, who cracks homicides in an office spanning half the second floor. Detectives follow him around and savor his sparing words like sweet mint tea. He wears blue jeans, like most of his subordinates, but flashes distinction above the belt: black button-down shirt, smooth pressed charcoal gray blazer, gold watch, salt-and-pepper mustache. Jabri does not seem to lay a hand on anybody except in amity. But there is fire smoldering in the gaze behind his reading glasses, and any suspect he probes can feel it.

"What I mean," he explains, "is that my countrymen, in a few short years, have seen the relaxation of so many restrictions on their behavior that there is a new kind of chaos, if you will. It is like the chaos of a child who leaves the home of his father for the first time. Homicide is on the rise, and it is a consequence of their newfound freedom."

In front of a cluttered desk, a grizzled man with one arm in a cast has been unburdening himself of his sins to Jabri's chief subordinate, a wiry twentysomething in a black leather coat. Behind the desk, Jabri peels a mini-muffin from its paper foil and hands it across to the man's good arm. The man brings it to his mouth and chomps down grimly, raining crumbs and brown sugar bits onto the floor.

"Bring him tea," Jabri instructs a cop on the far side of the room. "The important thing is that he has agreed to confess."

I listen to the murderer talk, on and on, about his ginned-up quarrel with a friend named Yusuf over a prostitute. "And I'm drinking and drinking and drinking," he says, as if that were his crime. The call girl was standing right beside him while the fight happened, he recalls—amused, at first, "even after the first few punches." The friend picked up a stick, so Yusuf pulled out his knife. They wrestled each other to the ground, and Yusuf managed to dislocate and fracture the man's arm on the way down. Enraged, the man plunged his blade into Yusuf's throat, three times from behind, and finished him off for good. The prostitute ran away, gushing tears and screaming for the police. Twenty-five minutes later, Marzuq came for him and the dead body with four men, a stretcher, and a van.

The young detective nods, jotting down notes. Tea arrives. Jabri winds around the desk to serve it. He pours a long, steaming stream into the glass from on high while resting his free hand gently on the detainee's shoulder. A stenographer lugs a bulky manual typewriter into the office from a room across the hall. Now the dress rehearsal is over. It's time to tell the story all over again, for the record.

"What made you decide to confess?" I ask the killer.

He shifts the determined focus of his bloodshot eyes to me, projecting the same mix of remorse, humility, and awkward sweetness he has been conveying to the young detective.

"Nobody ever treated me so nicely before," he explains, and he waves his good hand, with a trace of pride, over the little teacup and saucer.

Under Moroccan law, Lieutenant Jabri does not owe his detainees the right to remain silent, make a phone call, or consult a lawyer while in custody. The country's criminal code, like its French antecedent, grants the Judiciary Police the power of *garde à vue*—prearraignment detention. He may hold and question someone for a maximum of 72 hours without any interference. This authority comes with stipulations, to be sure. Jabri is supposed to respect the human rights of his suspects, and to give them a holding cell to sleep in if questioning drags on. Should 48 hours of interrogation prove insufficient, he can obtain a one-time 24-hour extension, pending a judge's approval. Once he completes his inquiry, Jabri is obliged to submit all his findings, in a confidential written report, to the court's examining magistrate. Before a murder case can be brought to trial, the magistrate must reinvestigate the crime on his own, using the police report solely as an advisory memorandum. The magistrate then presents his new, independently gathered evidence to a panel of judges in a contested hearing, with a defense attorney present to argue over procedure and facts. This new, unhurried investigation by the court aims, at least in theory, to supersede the more hasty findings of police.

Alas, theory is one thing and practice is another. Moroccan courts—police precincts, too, for that matter—are underfunded, inadequately staffed, and generally overwhelmed by their caseloads. As a result, the magistrate's reinvestigation of a crime usually suffers delays, often lacks thoroughness, and sometimes, unbeknownst to the accused, amounts to little more than a rubber stamp on the homicide detective's original secret report. Thus defendants may in effect be tried and convicted without due process, largely on the strength of a rushed, unchaperoned police investigation, the written outcome of which they do not even have the right to see. This does not necessarily mean that an innocent person will end up convicted, or even charged, nor that the drunk killer whose confession I just witnessed deserves anything less than to be found guilty. It only means that justice, in all its complexity and nuance, occasionally hinges on Lieutenant Jabri.

I watch the grizzled man's story yield a two-page report for the examining magistrate after half an hour or so of typing and editing. A brief formal confession is read back to the killer, who signs off on it by marking an X in place of a signature. The stenographer makes a photocopy of the confession and the two-page report and hands all the material to Jabri, who reviews it and promptly signs his name. The young detective in the leather coat tucks one copy in a worn red folder and makes off, arm in arm with the prisoner, to the latter's arraignment, while Jabri files away the original and lingers in the office. By the edge of his cluttered desk he takes a pile of national identification cards, confiscated in a recent forgery bust, out from under a bronze statuette of Jerusalem's Al-Aqsa mosque, and broods over them, one after the next.

"May I get a copy of that homicide report?" I ask him. In my briefcase, after all, I have already stowed another of his recent works, the thirteen-page case file on a warehouse murder, which was handed to me for reasons unclear—probably on a whim—by the precinct chief before the holiday. I am thinking it would be nice to build up a collection.

"No," he replies.

I can hear the long, tubular bulbs that light the room emit their faint mechanical hum.

"I'm sorry. If Chief Sharqawi says you may read it, of course I would be happy to share it. But as for me, legally I do not have that authority."

A cop walks in with two espressos in hot milk on a round tin tray and lays them down on the desk beside the lieutenant's domed paperweight. He slips out and closes the door behind him gently, as if a baby were asleep in the office.

"You know," I tell Jabri, "last week the chief was kind enough to give me your report on the warehouse murder. Since I have already been authorized to study that information, I'd love to talk it over with you."

He stirs in a sugar cube, fixing his eyes on the coffee in the glass. "The warehouse murder," he says. "You have read that file?"

The truth is, barely. I bluff my way through a compliment: "I see it was quite an involved case, difficult to solve. The chief says your team did masterful work, and it's hard to disagree with him."

He whisks the espresso shot and milk again, then raises his head and smiles with all his teeth. "I should probably talk you through it, show you the crime scene if you are interested. It is not often, you understand, that a member of the security services is found to have killed a man in cold blood."

At this my stirring spoon misses the cup.

"We are all human and prone to error, tragic error," he goes on. "An agent of the state is also a son of the people he serves, for better and worse."

Jabri's mobile phone rings and he takes the call—something about an arrest beyond the city limits. I lunge for my briefcase and begin to read the report in earnest:

Case file D35/2944.

At approximately 9:40 A.M., this precinct and security patrol number 35 received notification from the Hall of Communications that a man had been found murdered at warehouse number 18 at the passageway of villas in the Ayn Sabaa section of this city. Movement was immediately made to the crime scene together with a team of scientific and technical police.

The Arabic prose is formal, eloquent, and clean—a far cry from the cuss-filled slang of the men who ride in the National Security van.

Upon reaching the entryway we found the grounds to be spattered with blood, in the midst of which were traces of the bare footprint of an unknown person. A wooden stick was coated with blood, and beside it lay the body of the deceased—thrown on its back, its hands stretched out—wearing black trousers, a green shirt, and a green coat, bearing a deep wound on its right temple. The blood had totally covered its face. In life the victim's name was Ibrahim Dey, a Moroccan national, born October 8, 1961, in the region of Butabi, from the parents Ali the son of Abdullah and Khadija the daughter of Ibrahim. He was a bachelor and a real estate broker. He was deliberately murdered in a bestial manner, the skull of his head and face smashed in.

I scan the next few pages and find discussion of an autopsy, a dozen interrogations, the scrutiny of phone records, and a search of area hospitals for a wounded man.

"That was a hectic week," Jabri cuts in, eyeing the report in my hands, his phone call finished. "The kind of week that reminds me why I don't like being a police lieutenant."

He speaks to me in formal, nearly classical Arabic, the language of his report, temporarily eschewing the Moroccan dialect that I hear him naturally using the rest of the time.

"Always we are compelled to work late into the night," he says, "to sacrifice our time with family. And the work is just not letting up these days. On the contrary. It is not a life I would recommend to anyone. My sons, God willing, will not be policemen. I will not allow it. My oldest son is learning English and he will have a more fulfilling professional life. I expose him to broad horizons, always I try to broaden his understanding of the world. I have been to Disneyland, you know. Universal Studios also."

"Ah," I tell him.

"How are you, Mister?" he says in thickly accented English.

Better play along, I figure. *"Very well, sir!"*

"Let us now speak English then. You will help me rehearse for my son."

"Your English is not bad!"

Jabri recalls, haltingly, that twenty-five years ago his parents died in a road accident and he had to assume financial responsibility for his younger brothers. In joining the police academy, he gave up on his original dream of going to medical school. The security field, he explains, offered the most time-efficient path to a paying job that could also satisfy his desire to serve the public somehow. Between a ten-year stint with the uniformed police and his present, more senior position as the area's ranking plainclothes detective, he has worked the streets of Precinct 5 for the past twenty-three years.

I indulge his effort at a language lesson, correcting a mistake in gender here and there, and nod solemnly at the life story that comes out. In my head, I want to slash through all this talk and make him tell me what drove a member of the security services to beat a man to death in a warehouse.

"This is from my son's teacher," he says, and hands me the boy's membership card for an American cultural institute in Casablanca. *"Best student in the class."*

"I would love to meet this young man!" I exclaim in Arabic, hoping he will code-switch back to his mother tongue along with me.

Jabri's mobile phone rings. He raises his eyebrows moments into the terse conversation.

"Sorry, I gotta go," he says in Moroccan dialect—no longer classical Arabic, let alone English.

As he hustles out the door, I take it as a good sign that a senior detective is leaving me alone in his office, which is packed with case files from wall to wall. I'm tempted to peek into a cabinet or two, but instead, I focus on the one file that now belongs to me.

Much of the thirteen-page document chronicles three long days spent interrogating witnesses about the personal history of the victim, forty-seven-year-old Ibrahim Dey. In life he called himself a real estate broker, but he was not the sort of real estate broker who had an office or a home address. He was a homeless real estate broker. For the past five years he had been sleeping in the night guard's quarters of the warehouse where he was to die. The salaried watchman, a friend of Dey's, would meet him every evening by the iron front gates and leave the facility in his hands rather than mind it round the clock as he was paid to do. This informal arrangement turned out to be news to the man who owned the property, a businessman named Marcel Toledano, who fired the guard and forswore all knowledge of Ibrahim Dey upon learning of his murder on the premises. The warehouse is described as a storage depot for used freight canisters. The document does not make clear whether the canisters are for sale, or in use, or serve some other purpose.

Dey is remembered by friends as a kindly, pious man without an enemy or sin to his name. A book peddler named Sharif is quoted telling police, "He was a good, stable man who performed his religious obligations punctually and did not smoke or take any intoxicant or narcotic." A ten-year friend of Dey's, Muhammad Bari, reportedly added, "He enjoyed a good reputation. He faithfully carried out his prayers in the mosque of Ayn Sabaa." Both men recalled that they had seen the dead man only the night before and treated him to a hot bowl of *harira*—a bright orange peasant's soup of boiled lentils, carrots, and squash. He had been in a cheerful mood, they said, anxious about a property sale he believed was about to go through. He thought he would make a lot of money, Sharif recalled. Of course, he always thought things like that.

An affidavit stapled to the back of the case file contains a short confession to murder by a man named al-Raddad Murtaziq. The police report that they found him convalescing from glass cuts to his wrist in the Muhammad V Emergency Ward, toward the end of their investigation. He had been brought in by ambulance on the night of the murder, after a uniformed policeman heard him crying out for help in a side street of Ayn Sabaa. He told the doctor he had been attacked, and he signed the hospital registry as "X the son of X." When detectives arrived to question him, he made up a home address in the neighborhood that police immediately recognized as bogus, and he falsely claimed to be a construction worker. In fact, he lived in the Jankeer military barracks, at the western edge of eastern Casablanca—and he was no construction worker.

DNA testing matched his blood with splotches on the warehouse wall, and his footprint proved identical to the one near the dead body that had been made in a puddle of the victim's blood. Murtaziq eventually confessed to the murder and admitted to stealing two coats from the victim, one white and one black, which he wore while making his escape in the cold of night, as well as 20 dirhams—about $2.66. For this he was charged with murder and theft.

"He killed him over pocket change?" I ask Chief Sharqawi. An hour and a half has passed and I'm no longer alone. Lieutenant Jabri and I have agreed to sit down with the boss and his deputy in the main office downstairs, to request formal permission for my visit to the warehouse grounds where Ibrahim Dey was killed.

"Happens all the time," he replies. "We have seen murder over a cassette tape, murder over a pack of cigarettes. Poverty, you know."

"Seems like a lot of work, beating a man to death with a stick for twenty dirhams and a couple of coats."

Jabri nods and shows me his teeth again. "He had no prior acquaintance with Ibrahim Dey," he says. "He had never even been to the warehouse where the killing happened, actually. He was absent without leave from the barracks that night, wandering along the railroad track, and he says some drunk boys started chasing him. He told us he climbed a wall to escape them. That is how he wound up in the warehouse, just looking for a place to hide. And Dey, who was supposed to be guarding the place, came up to him in the dark and started poking at him with a stick. Poor brother didn't know much about self-defense, I suppose. Murtaziq took the stick away from him and beat him until he was dead."

"These sorts of things will happen in a third-world society," adds Sharqawi's deputy, Abd al-Jabbar. "A poor young man, serving his country, wanders off alone and gets lost somehow. These are the silent tragedies."

"What was the nature of his service?" I ask. "He lived on an army base, but Lieutenant Jabri said he was involved in domestic security? I don't understand."

"You *will* understand," Sharqawi says. "You absolutely will. And you know, there is much for you to learn, and we want to help. Did you know that the best-loved music group in North Africa is based right here in our precinct? I'm talking about Nas al-Ghiwan, of course. We want to introduce you to them."

The chief's diversionary chatter drawls on awhile, and I begin to feel my own pulse.

"But what do you think of our investigation?" he goes on. "Did we catch the man or what?"

"Well," I reply, fumbling a little, "from the way it reads, I feel that it's a model police investigation. But to really understand it—"

"You hear that?" Sharqawi tells his deputy. "Model police work."

"Yes, but I feel that to really understand it, to appreciate it properly, I should have a chance to see the crime scene, meet some of the people who are named in the report, and really learn about the circumstances. That warehouse, you know."

"Of course," Sharqawi says. "Jabri? Crime scene tomorrow—and let him meet, what's his name, the night guard?"

Jabri shakes his head. "Attar. Attar is the night guard. But I don't think he will be particularly amenable. He's a Berber, you know. Very stern, a man of few words. Let me think about the right man for you to meet. Possibly Sharif, the book peddler."

"How about the owner of the warehouse?" I ask.

"Toledano?"

I nod.

Jabri eyes his boss and both men's eyebrows do a quick flip. "The whole thing is a little sensitive—a little political, you understand—because the owner of the warehouse is a Jew."

FIVE

t is rarely boring to learn what police consider "sensitive" or "political"—especially for me. The lieutenants of Precinct 5 already know that, like the owner of the warehouse where Ibrahim Dey was killed, I'm Jewish. But they don't know exactly what kind of a Jew I am. Nor are they aware of the extent to which I'm familiar with the field of law enforcement. Back home in the United States, beginning when I was a college student, I worked with the FBI for five years on Islamist terror cases. Later on in life, a few years after grad school, I was arrested by federal agents on charges of international smuggling. Politics snaked through all these experiences, and by the time the Feds were through with me, you might say I had gained some sensitivities of my own.

Before September 11, terror groups not dissimilar to the ones that now plague Morocco were operating on American soil. The public was largely unaware of their presence, and the FBI lacked the tools, personnel, or legal license to pursue them half as aggressively as many of its agents wanted to. Most of the field offices did not have an Arabic translator on hand to listen in on a suspicious conversation. Red tape blocked agents from attending a sermon in a mosque, or opening a file on someone based on his ideological views. A firewall prevented the Bureau from pooling certain types of information with the CIA and other intelligence agencies. The Bureau is an arm of law enforcement, after all, not a spying unit, and a lot of people felt it should stay that way.

Yet the domestic terror threat was real.

My first little project on behalf of the FBI was steered by the Washington field office. It involved a dumpster in northern Virginia. It didn't smell very good in there, but there were some documents in Arabic among the refuse, generated by a guerrilla group that has since been designated a terrorist organization and banned from the country. My FBI handler was under the impression that he couldn't legally go rummaging around in the receptacle himself, because no ongoing criminal investigation justified the search. So he found a way to inspire an Arabic-speaking Near Eastern studies major in college to do it for him—that would be me—and it sounded something like this:

"Now, Joe, you know we can't go into that dumpster. We can't even ask *you* to go into that dumpster. But we all know you're kind of a cowboy, and there's nothing to stop you from going into that dumpster because you want to. Once you're in there, there's nothing to stop you from hauling away as much of their typewritten shit as you like. And once you've hauled it away, there's nothing to stop you from reading it. And once you've read it, there's nothing to stop you from telling us anything it says that we might wanna know about. Hell, you could type up a translation and hand it over to us along with the originals. You could write a memo tying it all together. It's a free country, Joe."

I was nineteen at the time, and the prospect of helping to bust the group in question warmed my heart. It was an organization that counted the United States, Israel, and Arab states that had signed peace treaties with Israel among its enemies. When I jumped into that dumpster, it smelled like roses. And after I found mostly shredded documents among the rotten food, I bought some glue and started a new career in macramé.

Between 1994 and 1999 I had dealings with FBI field offices in seven American states and sustained involvement with three of them. Thousands of Persian- and Arabic-language documents, recordings, and videos now in U.S. government custody are the outcome of these efforts—and most of them did not come out of dumpsters. We found creative ways of working within the confines of laws we didn't like. I relied on my handlers for guidance in this regard. Their own instincts, in turn, were informed by the institutional culture of their organization. One agent I had worked with later reflected on this dynamic in a letter he wrote after he retired:

> When I went to the FBI Academy, we were lectured on "letters of censure." They were internal administrative punishments administered for violations of rules, regulations and policies and were usually signed by the FBI Director and placed in your personnel file. But we were also told agents who never got a censure were likely not aggressively conducting their investigative work. If your efforts supported the mission and the censure was simply due to poor judgment, you took it as a needed lesson and moved on with your career and life.

Being a non-FBI employee, there was never any risk of personal censure to me. "One day we won't need you at all and I'm sure we'll all be happy about it," a different field agent told me. "It's only a matter of circumstances and politics."

Years later, September 11 and the PATRIOT Act proved her right.

While the Bureau had its reasons for making use of me, I had my own motivations for being used. One was the feeling that I was doing something good for the country. Another was the rush that came along with it. But there were also motivations of a different sort that I understand better in retrospect.

One night during my senior year at Yale—I was twenty-one by then—a van sped past my residential college and paused a block and a half away, engine purring. The driver had his usual instructions from the New Haven field office to avoid the appearance of waiting for me in front of my dorm.

"Just get in quick."

We raced to a nearby town and made contact with a dozen or so armed field agents who had been passing time in unmarked sedans, covertly circling a small-time mosque. The driver turned up the volume of what sounded like an AM radio, but instead of a baseball game, a tense conversation in Arabic, fuzzy with static, came through the speakers. The van's receiver was tuned to a wired microphone that a Muslim worshipper inside had agreed to wear under his clothes. "This guy is Iraqi," my handler piped up from the backseat. "He hasn't slept in two weeks, ever since the cleric in there supposedly started threatening to break his arms and legs. If you hear the imam breathe so much as a word that sounds like a personal threat to the guy, just say so and we're going to bust down the friggin' door."

Fair enough.

The agent went on to explain that the preacher, an Egyptian national, had issued the threat because the Iraqi worshipper was planning to join an "infidel" organization—in this instance, a local Masonic lodge. Would the preacher make the mistake of issuing a new violent threat into a hidden microphone? My handler hoped so, because there were more serious activities to which the preacher had been linked but that would be harder to prove. The four of us sat there tense and sweating. The van's stuffy air seemed to aggravate a palpable urge on the part of the agents to move out and storm the place.

"Come on, Joe, what's he saying?"

I concentrated on the layers of a nuanced Arabic-language power play between the cleric and his disaffected follower. I heard the Egyptian dialect, paper-light but confident and laced with Qur'anic phrasing, as well as the worshipper's Iraqi accent—heavy, somber, and, tonight, uneven.

"I mean to steer you toward the straight path, my son," the preacher said. "My advice is only for your benefit."

"But you have terrified my wife and me," the congregant replied.

There was a pause, broken by the cleric's warm chuckle. "Our only reckoning is with God, my son."

"Come on, Joe, where's it going!" my handler cried.

I felt distracted.

Homing in on the vulnerable voice of the Iraqi man, I kept thinking about my mother. Her accent in Arabic is similar to that of the man I heard through the live wire feed. Like the owner of the Casablanca warehouse where Ibrahim Dey was murdered, my mother is a Jewish native of an Arab country. She was born in Baghdad in the 1940s, back when "Iraqi Jew" didn't sound like a contradiction in terms. Those days are over now, of course. In 1951, as a little girl, my mother fled Baghdad to the State of Israel along with her family and approximately 125,000 other Jews. They left behind 2,600 years of history dating back to the exile of the Israelites to Babylon after the destruction of the Temple of Solomon in Jerusalem. What survived in her head were the faintest memories, a handful of songs, the fusion of Arabic and Hebrew that she grew up speaking with her family in Jerusalem, the splendor of Iraqi Jewish cooking—and a most unusual way of thinking about the Middle East. While many strangers to the region see Arabs in black-and-white terms—villains, victims, seething masses—the Arab world to my mom is a landscape of a thousand colors, a place of history and music and glory and love, albeit with some scorpions crawling around. Her accent in Arabic is a reminder to me that I'm connected to that world myself, and when I hear it spoken, no matter by whom, I feel a primordial bond.

Sitting and sweating in the FBI van that night, I looked at my handler, the driver, and the other armed agent and reflected on the reputation I had earned as a "cowboy." I didn't feel like much of a cowboy at the moment. I listened in again on the live wire feed. The Egyptian cleric wasn't threatening anybody. Perhaps he never had. Or maybe he had and would again, but tonight he could smell the wire under the Iraqi's shirt. Maybe he could smell us sweating outside. I hadn't heard him threaten anybody, in any case, and I told my handler as much. We drove away with an empty set of handcuffs, and I went to bed thinking about the Iraqi man who hadn't slept in two weeks, wondering if he was in danger.

My mom worked long hours during much of my childhood. She often came home tired, too tired to tell stories. Meanwhile, what I learned about the Middle East was taught to me in Jewish day school in Providence, Rhode Island, where I grew up. We learned about the Jewish people's historic connection to the Land of Israel, millennia of bloody persecution that followed the exile from our ancient homeland, and the wars of existence Jews fought after the establishment of the State of Israel. Arab lands were places of great danger to the Jewish people, and I learned to visualize them much the way my Eastern European classmates perceived their grandparents' snuffed-out ghettos.

It wasn't until after my parents' divorce that Mom earned something of a reprieve from her long hours of work and enjoyed the time and peace of mind to sit alongside my brother and me and begin to talk about her more complicated heritage. She is a proud Israeli who knows that life in Iraq had grown untenable for its Jews when she and her family were forced to flee as refugees, and who remembers the celestial thrill of touching down safely in Israel. But she also remembers being sprayed with DDT upon arrival, and facing poverty and discrimination for years in a nascent state dominated by Eastern European Jews. Her success as a Hebrew news broadcaster on the Voice of Israel radio and television speaks to the acceptance she and many other Iraqi immigrants eventually won in Israeli society. But the stigmatization of the Arabic music and language they knew at home—indeed, the overall marginalization of Middle Eastern Jewish culture in Israel—speaks to the forced repression of memory that she and her coethnics endured there.

Of Iraq, she remembers idyllic moments from her early childhood. Behind high, vine-shrouded stone walls, she used to listen to her nanny tell animal fables under a palm tree's fragrant shade. Roses, gardenias, lemons, strawberries, and okra grew in a garden flanked by water fountains. There were family outings in a bustling town, pastoral scenes at home that changed with the seasons. There were Muslim friends who came to visit at the home of her great-grandfather, the chief rabbi of Baghdad, and Jewish neighbors who advised a Muslim king on how to build up the Iraqi state. When winter's cold crept into her house, the Persian carpets were spread across the chilly tiles on the ground floor, only to be rolled up and transported to the rooftop for the summertime, "when the family went up and slept in the open air to keep cool," she recalls.

Through her parents, she has also learned in chilling detail what the end of Jewish life in Iraq was like. In 1941, Iraqi nationalists from the military and security services, along with German-backed fascist groups and hoods from Baghdad's slums, stormed Jewish neighborhoods and killed several hundred Jewish men, women, and children in what became known as the *Farhud*—Iraqi Arabic for a pogrom. Jews were the killers' targets, but some lived in mixed neighborhoods, and Mom would hasten to point out that numerous Muslims risked their lives to protect their Jewish neighbors.

The stories people share can be mixed up sometimes—like reams of shredded paper in a dumpster. But young people, being narrative builders, tend to want to glue the shreds together. In high school after my parents' divorce, I grew closer to Mom. Following years of exposure, via my dad, to the stirring songs of early Israel, Mom and I started listening to Arabic music together. I tried to sing the words, which she helped me learn as best she could. She adored those words—they were mostly love songs—and I came to understand that despite her formative years in Jerusalem and the trauma that ended her family's long history in Iraq, she saw herself as more than a proud Israeli. She is a proud Iraqi, too. It's the sort of pride that courses through the blood—the kind a son can easily inherit from his mother.

In college and grad school I studied the history of Arabs and Islam and devoted days and nights to refining my knowledge of the Arabic language. It was a labor of passion, marked by conflicting emotions. Part of me thought of Arabic as the language of my ene-mies, but Mom had shown me that it was also the language of fam-ily and long-lost friends. Maybe there were new friends to be made,

I kept thinking. I read voraciously about Iraq and its people—history, memoirs, Iraqi government paraphernalia, old maps, new maps, whatever I found in the library. I tried to stitch the country together in my head. I dreamed of visiting. I even dreamed irrationally of living there. Would that ever be possible? No, of course not—maybe half a century ago, but never again. For two generations now, the population has been systematically brainwashed to hate people like me. *Maybe I could change their minds. Don't be ridiculous.* What to do with these mixed feelings was an ongoing, burning question.

One outlet for my passion was the FBI. But plainly, I had another interest that law enforcement couldn't satisfy: I craved to overcome a fifty-year detachment from my roots and reconnect organically with what I came to think of as the motherland.

Eventually these conflicting aspirations, playing out beyond the realm of youthful fantasy, met each other head-on and crashed.

But all that happened years ago, and now I'm a grown-up, level-headed Middle East specialist enjoying time as a fly on the wall at Precinct 5 in Casablanca.

Really.

SIX

Next morning I have an appointment with Lieutenant Jabri to visit the grounds of the warehouse where Ibrahim Dey was killed. He is late, and the door to his office is locked, so I go back down to the first floor and sit quietly on the long linoleum bench built into the side wall of the foyer. I look down into the cold white tiles and think about the murder.

So the killer was connected to the security apparatus with which I have a relationship, and the crime scene, by freak chance, was a warehouse belonging to a member of my tribe—one of the few remaining Jews in Morocco. These two uncommon elements feel stranger yet for the trivial motive of the crime and the commonness of its victim, a pauper in the real estate business who, according to his friends, never bothered a living soul. Ibrahim Dey comes across as a man who would neither cross an Arab cop nor make trouble for a wealthy Jew.

Newcomers to the seedy side of Casablanca might also find it unusual that a homeless man, squatting in a storage depot for five years, would try to make a living selling houses to other people. For locals, however, the fact that he was a homeless real estate agent would be the least remarkable detail in the thirteen-page case file on

the gruesome murder of Ibrahim Dey. In the northeast neighborhood of Ayn Sabaa where he died, street peddlers of chewing gum
and cigarettes dabble in real estate, too. Aging prostitutes with any
sort of a client base dream of transitioning into the field. Real estate
is to Ayn Sabaa what the movie industry is to Hollywood: that mystical, king-making specialty of the realm that once turned a handful
of immigrants into tycoons and has been drawing in starving hope-
fuls ever since. The other day I watched a bearded vagabond by a
sidewalk café pour coffee dregs out of the left-behind cups on each
table into a plastic mug. He sat down and struck up a conversation
with one of the customers, sipping his drink like a pampered prince.
In the course of their talk he found occasion to produce, from the
breast pocket of his moth-eaten coat, a business card proclaiming
that he, too, was in real estate.

This obsession stems from the peculiar history of Ayn Sabaa, a
section of town that stretches up along the Atlantic shoreline to the
bitter end of Casablanca's drab smokestack- and slum-filled east.
The neighborhood contains the typical concentration of ramshackle
dwellings near its factory hub, much like an area immediately to its
west, the teeming capital of the shantytowns known as Al-Hay al-
Muhammadi. But the dense population of the slums has never
spilled into certain patches of Ayn Sabaa—patches like the area
around the warehouse where Dey was killed, sparsely inhabited and
eerily subdued. Old, prohibitively priced European-style villas lie
there, the only villas east of the railroad tracks. They were built by
German colonists in the early twentieth century, who, like the French
across town, forcibly prevented Moroccans from living nearby.

With the country's independence in 1956, the Germans began to
leave, selling their homes at whatever price they would fetch to the
few local inhabitants whom they had gotten to know personally.
There were barely any Moroccan elites in the east to fill the fancy
spaces the foreigners were leaving behind. So a handful of green-
grocers and dairy farmers, most of them migrants to the area from
the rural south, managed to acquire valuable property at going-out-
of-business prices. They parlayed their acquisitions in land swaps
and investments and came of age, over a couple of booming

decades, as the new bigwigs of the neighborhood. It took the German community a generation or so to clear out—long enough to turn the sport of angling for a piece of land into an enduring pastime for the people of Ayn Sabaa. The late Ibrahim Dey would have grown up in the shadow of this quirky history. He inhabited an environment in which to say you were in real estate did not necessarily mean you had actually sold a house or even gotten around to living in one. You might just manage to pull off both feats at any moment, though. To be in real estate was partly a license to dream, in your waking hours, of a better life than the one you had.

Aside from his vocation, the victim's name and distant birthplace—the mountain hamlet of Butabi, according to the police file—suggest he also shared a common lineage with most of his neighbors in Ayn Sabaa, from the penniless to the upper crust. They are Moroccans, all right, but their mother tongue is not Arabic. They call themselves Amazigh, and they hail from the southern Moroccan Atlas mountains where Dey reportedly was born. Westerners and Arabs generally refer to them as Berber. At least 40 percent of Morocco's population shares this identity, along with tens of millions in neighboring Algeria and Tunisia and smaller populations in Egypt, Mauritania, Mali, and Niger. The presence of Berbers on all these lands predates the Arab invasion of North Africa by centuries—and in periodic insurrections over the past 1,200 years, Berbers have shown that they do not enjoy being ruled by others. I know enough about Arabic nomenclature to observe that while Ibrahim Dey had Berber roots, the confessed killer al-Raddad Murtaziq appears to be of Arab stock. Add to this charged ethnic mix the overlay of religion—a Muslim guard for a Jewish businessman in a Muslim country—and the case becomes what Chief Sharqawi has termed "political" and "sensitive."

For the moment, I will assume Lieutenant Jabri to be correct in concluding that Murtaziq killed the man in the dark without even knowing his name and simply made off with some pocket change and a couple of coats. Even a crime so impersonal might risk stoking divisive tensions, should too much be learned by the public about its diverse cast of characters. That is what I have been encouraged to believe, anyhow, based on the received wisdom of Precinct 5. For all I know, the cultural background of the police themselves could add to the sensitivity of the situation. The lieutenants I have met all identify as Arab, except for the 300-pound deputy chief Abd al-Jabbar, who owes 150 of those pounds to a Berber mother.

In this homicide investigation, then, a predominantly Arab-run detective unit, policing a massive Berber population, learned that one of its fellow Arab enforcers had taken a Berber life—a rural migrant, the salt of the earth to his neighbors. The crime happened, at that, on the property of a businessman whose Jewish faith rounds out a perfect micropicture of Morocco's heterodox history. It feels to me as if the victim, Ibrahim Dey, was at the center of something—something vague and elusive that I might find hard to put into words even if I knew what it was. What does it mean when an obscure, marginal, individual life brings together so many disparate elements of his society to mark his death? Maybe if I really understood who Ibrahim Dey was, he would turn out not to have been quite so marginal.

Jabri apologizes for the delay and opens the side door of his unmarked car for me. We drive east into the dusty midday glare of Mulay Ismail Street, a smooth six-lane thoroughfare of flatbed trucks and sputtering red cabs. The steel-blue sky, clear of rain at last, is thinly veiled by a few ribbed clouds.

"This week I want you to come to my home," he says. "We would be honored to have you eat with us, meet my three cubs."

His olive cheeks flush a trace of pink.

"It would be a greater honor for me, Lieutenant."

We reach the twin lion sculptures I have seen before, at the concrete roundabout in the heart of Ayn Sabaa from which Marzuq and his men launched their night raid into the nearby shantytown. We turn up a hushed side street, the Passageway of the Villas mentioned in the case file. There they are: crumbling two-story imitations of the kind of swank, gated European-style housing that crowds the west side of town—one villa with peeling pink paint, another with a panicky dog strutting around and around on its stucco balcony. Across the street, a tall, uneven wall spans the block, its concrete worn to the bone. An audience of little boys watch a teenager draw a bearded man in chalk on it. Over their heads in the distance beyond the wall, a wide electrical grid slings into the horizon. We pass by the youths and park in front of a rusty red steel gate tipped with sharp spades pointing skyward. Number 18, the metal door says.

"This is it."

The lieutenant gets out and knocks.

The last time I walked into a Jewish-owned property in a Muslim country, it was the synagogue in Baghdad where my great-great-grandfather used to preach. This place doesn't feel so sacred.

A watchman, short and pale with curly tufts of brown hair sticking out the back of his baseball cap, seems to recognize Jabri. He opens the door wide without putting out his cigarette or saying a word.

"Is that the guard Attar?"

"New guard," Jabri says. "They fired Attar immediately, remember."

We step into a vast dirt field of giant tubular freight canisters mounted off the ground on steel legs. The newer ones stand in a row directly ahead of us; mangier carcasses lie farther off, with mushrooms and weeds growing out of gashes in their metal casing. To the right, sunlight scatters on the dirt beneath an overhanging patchwork of ruffled sheet metal positioned to shield a tractor and a pair of freight trucks from the elements. The vehicles are parked in front of a clearing of crabgrass and some plants, where four wide steps lead up to the front door of an old three-story building made of stone. The stone building looks as if it had been built back when there were no freight canisters—just poor men with strong backs.

"I see the rain has washed away most of the blood," Jabri observes, waving his hand over the stairwell. "This was *all* blood. Look."

He grins over a faint darkening of the stone, like a shadow in the shape of a grape cluster.

"What is this place?" I ask.

"It's just a warehouse," he replies. "One of hundreds in Casablanca."

He leads the way into an unlit corridor. The door shuts itself behind us and I follow the sound of Jabri's footsteps, groping the handrail of a three-level spiral staircase. At length we reach a dank, echoey pair of rooms. Jabri opens another steel door to the blinding sunshine of a walled-in rooftop. The electrical grid lies overhead within spitting range. I gather that the railroad tracks, the great dividing line of Casablanca along which the killer allegedly walked to the crime scene, stretch directly underneath.

"This is where he climbed over?" I ask.

"No, come on, look at where we are. Obviously it would be too high for him to climb."

He grips me gently by the waist and rotates my body ninety degrees. From my new position it is possible to look over to an adjoining warehouse in which the wall blocking off the train tracks stands only about ten feet tall. The low wall doubles as the backside of another stone building, joined to the one we stand on in a broader maze of rooftops, ledges, and outer walls stretching ahead of me and behind me, on and on from one warehouse to the next.

"Look carefully at that section of the wall down there."

I squint in the sunshine and notice thousands of shards of broken glass lining the top of the concrete—glued-on salvaged bits of bottles and windows, perhaps—their sharp ends standing in a long, prickly row.

"That's razor wire, Moroccan style," he says. "In Casablanca, we recycle."

He probes my face for a smile and finds one.

"The perpetrator al-Raddad Murtaziq told us, as you know, that he climbed up there to run away from drunk boys by the tracks down below. It was pitch dark. As soon as he reached the top of the wall he cut his wrist on the glass shards. He couldn't see, but he knew he was bleeding and he started to panic. He felt his way over to that roof over there. All he could do was keep climbing, keep looking frantically for a way down. He climbed in this direction. Look here—blood."

Dark spurts mar the inner edge of the wall beside us.

"See there—blood. We took DNA samples from here, and from the victim's body, and we also took samples from the official guard who should have been here that night, Attar."

"You suspected Attar?"

"Of course. We didn't let him go until DNA testing proved this blood on the wall was not his. That was the point when we broadened our search, and I sent my men to all the city's hospitals to look for a cut-up man who had been bleeding heavily."

"What made you suspect Attar in the first place?"

"We caught him in a lie." The lieutenant's jaws tighten around the words.

I feel a chill down my spine, but I don't show it. The words hit closer to home for me than Jabri knows.

"He told us that Ibrahim Dey only filled in for him on guard duty once in a while at night," he goes on, "like when Attar would get sick or something. In fact we learned from Dey's other friends that the victim slept here every night, had been for years. So of course I wondered what else Attar might be lying to us about."

"How do you make a man tell the truth in a situation like that?"

Jabri's gaze drops to my chin and he begins to form an answer with his lips. He appears to reconsider, and chuckles to himself. Then he starts again: "Speaking only for myself, you understand."

His eyes ask for a nod of indulgence, which I grant.

"I find that there is no better way to extract the truth from those we interrogate than to show them respect for their human rights. Any other tactic, say a more brutal tactic, only imposes artificial calculations on the suspect that would send us further away from the truth. That is how I question a suspect, and the same goes for the two detectives who report to me."

Jabri turns his back to me. He moves to the edge of the roof and motions me to follow.

I watch him retrace the rest of the tragedy as he and his boys have pieced it together. The story line he builds is tangled and weird. Maybe it's so weird that it actually happened. Or maybe the story line is wrong. Al-Raddad Murtaziq, frantic, climbed down from the top roof of the building to a second-floor portico, then jumped another story to the ground, bleeding all over the place. The sound he made when he landed woke Ibrahim Dey from his sleep. Dey came out with a stick. Murtaziq heard his footsteps and ran off to hide under one of the nearby trucks. Dey found him there and poked at him. Murtaziq angrily got up to resist, and Dey backed up in fear—walking backward, in Jabri's reenactment, all the way back to the stone stairwell in front of his lodging. Which is where Murtaziq grabbed the stick and clobbered him repeatedly, bashing his skull in.

"The perpetrator was overcome by remorse and dread after realizing what he had done," Jabri explains. "He started running around the grounds, unsure what to do. He had lost control of his senses. He found the outhouse on the far end and went to the bathroom. He found a jug of water on the ground and tried to wash his hands off. We found blood on the handles of the jug as well. Eventually he came back to the body and watched Ibrahim Dey breathe his last breaths. Then he got out and dragged the corpse inside the building by its bare feet. He dragged it all the way into the victim's room. Inside that room he found the victim's mobile phone and a couple of coats. He tried to use Dey's phone to call his father for help, but the phone was not charged. So he took a cigarette from the counter, the coats from the wall, and twenty dirhams, and made off—back up the way he came."

Jabri points to a rusty iron ladder, an obvious way to reach the second-floor portico from which Murtaziq allegedly had jumped.

"Why do you believe he climbed the ladder, for example, when he could have climbed the staircase inside as we did?" I ask him.

"I'm telling you what he confessed to exactly, nothing more and nothing less. We brought him back here after he confessed, to make him show us precisely what he did, and this is simply what he showed us."

"Why would he climb back down to the railroad tracks if he was running away from the boys down there in the first place? Why not walk out the front gate?"

"Presumably by this point," Jabri replies, "he was less worried about an open fight than of being caught for murder."

"I still would like to see the room where the victim slept."

The lieutenant nods. We reenter the dark hallway. He opens a door beside the spiral stairs and finds a light switch.

A heavy fragrance gushes out of the room in a thick cloud. The rusty odor of blood is faintly mixed into it, but mostly, I recognize the distinctive, hearty aroma of *za'atar,* wild oregano. In my high school days when my mother was cooking, the latter smell wafted out of her kitchen all the time.

Beyond the open door lies a room full of color and light.

The bottom half of the chipped white walls has been painted with sunshine orange stripes in one area, a solid coat of yellow in another. A large disheveled blanket on the corner cot where the victim slept is a tapestry of symmetrical flowers and celestial orbs in honeydew, crimson, and ocean blue. The countertops are busy with boxes of tea and herbs—dried sprigs of wormwood, *za'atar,* and mint—and a polished round tin serving pan, known in Arabic as a *siniya,* the signature disk of Moroccan hospitality. There are pots and glass cups, wires and bits of scribbled-on Styrofoam and paper—hours of doodling, apparently, with stray words, names, and phone numbers. A TV in a corner alcove tops a worn carpet, embroidered with the image of Jerusalem's Al-Aqsa mosque. To me this island of brightness, improbably tucked into a gnarly field of machinery and scrap, has the aroma of childhood and the cerebral chaos of a college dorm room. I feel somehow uncannily at home.

"Where is the bread and olive oil to go with all that *za'atar*?" I ask Jabri.

He laughs. "These are Berbers, brother. They boil *za'atar* in hot water and call it tea."

So a man died here.

Carpets of red and blue cover the floor. I imagine the victim's bare feet landing on the cloth at night, every night, his fibrous safeguard from the cold concrete. I look more carefully at the carpets. Drops of blood are woven into the fabric now. I notice a constellation of brown smudges and feel ice striking me all at once from the neck straight down. I try to make myself look somewhere else.

On a coffee table with a paisley plastic covering out of the 1960s, a yellowing booklet in Arabic lies open.

I move toward it, curious what Ibrahim Dey might have been reading before he died. I am about to bend down for a peek.

"Look here," the lieutenant cuts in. He points to a coat hook on the wall. "This is where Murtaziq found the two coats and took them. Look here." He points next to a different counter with another teapot and some dried leaves. "This is where he found the cell phone and tried to call his father. If only he had managed to reach his father on this phone"—he chortles again—"our job would have been a lot easier."

I am peering at the Arabic booklet out of the corner of one eye. "Some of the personal effects in here might belong to the new guard, of course," Jabri adds. "I'm not sure. Anyway, you wanted to meet some of Ibrahim Dey's friends, yes?"

I nod.

"Well, I have arranged to introduce you to one of them. He will be waiting for us back at the precinct by the time we get there."

He puts his hand around my forearm and motions me cordially out the door.

"Anything we can do for you, brother, you know it is our duty to oblige."

SEVEN

Sharif the book peddler, one of the witnesses named in the thirteen-page case file, is busy counting his fingers when Jabri and I walk back into precinct headquarters. A clean black coat covers his short frame and all but the shabby white collar of his sweater, which is stained the color of his teeth. His eyelids slope toward his shoulders, and whisker-shaped wrinkles under each socket appear to scurry off his face. At the sight of the lieutenant he springs up from the linoleum bench. Jabri motions him back down.

"Take good care of this young man, all right? You understand what to do."

"Understand what to do?" Sharif replies. "Oh, Lieutenant." His Arabic is boxy and pedantic. "We are Berber."

I wonder what Sharif means by that.

Jabri leaves me in his hands.

Sharif scuttles out to the curb and flails his arms at red taxis whizzing by. He is very busy today, he tells me several times, very busy every day. It is so hard to make a living in Casablanca.

"What do you do exactly?"

"I sell law books to judges, attorneys, anybody who needs to read them, or have them around. Yes, that's what I do, you know. I am also involved in real estate."

"How did you know the victim, Ibrahim Dey?"

A cab pulls up. Sharif opens the front passenger door and puts a finger ominously to his lips on the way in. I sit behind him in the backseat. All he deigns to say during our ten-minute ride from precinct headquarters back to the black lion sculptures of Ayn Sabaa is that I ought to pay the fare.

The seven palm trees lining the concrete embankment at Ayn Sabaa are surrounded by a noisy circle of storefronts, kiosks, a bakery, and two large cafés. By one shop, a heavyset woman in a pink hooded coat haggles over the price of a secondhand mobile phone, waving her SIM card in the air to press her case. Teens next door are browsing pirated DVDs of American blockbusters, on display by the hundreds and selling for the equivalent of $1.25 each. In a greasy glass case by an outdoor cash register, whole spiced chickens on metal spears slowly orbit an electric heat lamp, shedding fat onto a pile of French fries.

Sharif jumps out of the cab and sizes up the scene while I reach for my wallet.

"This is where he spent his days," he calls out over the traffic.

My eyes pan the scene. I sniff the exhaust fumes and touch the nearest palm tree.

"Every shopkeeper on the block knew him. Poor, unlucky man. We were so full of sorrow when he died, I could never tell you. We cried a lot. Such a harmless, peaceful man. There isn't much to be said about him. You know, he was vague."

"Vague?"

"Reserved. But we will talk to the neighborhood and you will find out everything you want to know. Do not worry. We are an open society."

He grips my hand and we fly across the roundabout to a glass display case of cookies, jam, chips, and chocolate spread, presided over by a man in white who is even shorter than Sharif.

My escort talks to him in Shilha, a Berber mother tongue, which I do not understand. The chatter drones softly, punctuated by the gutturals of a few Arabic words Sharif sticks in, which I can easily make out: "Judiciary Police" and "American investigator."

Not the words I would use to try to break the ice if it were up to me, I'm thinking.

"I don't know anything," the shopkeeper tells me suddenly in Arabic. "I barely knew him. I have no idea. I don't know."

"It's okay, it's okay," Sharif tells him. "You can talk to him. It's just a sociological study."

The shopkeeper draws a long breath. Cautiously, he takes in the whole radioactive sight of me. Then I see his eyes veer off into a middle space.

"Ibrahim Dey was like the moon," he recalls. "Known to everyone and no one."

The flesh around his eyes loosens up and he relaxes enough to blink.

"Tell me more."

"He had relations with the whole neighborhood. You would find him in that café there, all day long, with his Qur'an and his prayer beads, talking to anybody who could spare the time, the big and the small. People said he was *majdub.*"

I am not familiar with the word.

"*Majdub!*" he says again. "A poor man who could bring you good luck."

"Like a beggar who blessed you when you threw a coin into his can."

"More than that. People could turn to him for counsel. They knew they could trust him. It was said that he opened accounts and never closed them. Trust was something especially strong with him. You could tell him your private stories and get his opinion, and be sure that nobody else would tell them back to you. And yet his own stories, his secrets, were never on the table."

I picture the teapots in his bedroom and smell the *za'atar* in my nose.

"What kind of secrets could a poor man have?" I ask.

The man in white grants me a patient, parental look, as if I had just asked him how babies are made—but not an answer.

"What did he live on?"

"He was a middleman, you know. A broker of all that is necessary in life. If your chicken rotisserie had a missing spoke, he knew a man who could find one. If you ran out of eggs, he knew a wild hen that would lay one. Now and then he brokered the sale of a toaster, maybe a refrigerator. I bought a bathroom plunger through him once. His coat was full of business cards—like the Internet. He was also in real estate, of course."

Sharif claws at my shoulder and intimates that people are busy, especially Sharif. I am being dragged away, though the shopkeeper is just warming up.

"I will tell you something," the man says, beginning at last to smile. "All of us who got lost in the stresses of our business would feel some happiness when Ibrahim Dey came by. There was a sweetness about him. You felt that he had not lost sight of what was important in life. You wanted to share in a little bit of his freedom. He was a very free man, not tied down by anything, really. And he knew his Qur'an, by God. Always he was ready to quote from the holy book and the traditions of the prophet. Why they killed him I do not understand."

They.

I pry Sharif's paw off my shoulder.

"Was he involved in politics?" I ask.

"God forbid."

"Really," Sharif interjects, "time is precious."

He moves me along to a snack shop nearby. Six bearded men at one table are glued to Al Jazeera off a corner wall. Egyptian Muslim Brotherhood cleric Yusuf al-Qaradawi is holding court on-screen, sticking up for suicide bombings against Israeli civilian targets. "There is no such thing as a civilian in Israel," he explains. Meanwhile, the mustached proprietor juggles fresh-squeezed juice and scrambled egg sandwiches on a tin platter.

Our mention of the name Ibrahim Dey slows him down, almost disorients him. He serves the last order and puts away the tray. I watch his eyes moisten.

"Come sit down," he says.

We sit off in a corner, at the table farthest from the din of the television.

"I gave him something to eat almost every day, God have mercy on him. Except the days when he was away."

"Where would he go?"

"He was a wonderful man. The most pious, humble man I ever met. Where did he go?"

The question, repeated, seems to mean something different to him. He, too, suddenly fixes his eyes into a thousand-yard stare.

"Sometimes he just went to the center of town, on work I assume. People sent him there on errands. We all need somebody to grease the wheels of the bureaucracy for us. It was said that he was especially good at it. Sometimes I would have business in the administrative section of town myself, and I would see him there, hopping off a bus with a manila folder under his arm, probably trying to shepherd a driver's license or a typewritten form out of one big building and into the next. Other times, I think he went farther away—outside Casablanca. I wouldn't know where."

"He died a bachelor, right?"

"Certainly a bachelor," the proprietor says. "With what money would he marry? Marriage needs baksheesh. No, this was a simple man, God have mercy on him."

A flatbed truck makes a wet, grating racket on its way around the curved road.

"His best friend that I know of was a man named Muhammad Bari," he adds. "He is the one you should talk to. Another fixture here. They had some things in common."

"Like what?"

"Both of them would sit around all day in that café over there. Poor Bari. For him it must have been like losing a stomach."

Sharif's mouth is twisted by now in awkward contemplation. "I don't know if we have time to look for Bari."

"Oh, come on," I tell him. "I saw the name Bari all over that police file and I want to meet him. Quit screwing around with me, Sharif."

My guide trains his eyes on my mouth and points. "Screwing around with you. I wonder whether you would talk to the police like that."

He has a point. I'm a little gun-shy with police these days.

The proprietor swivels his face between the two of us and peers curiously at Sharif. "I am here every day," he tells me. "You can come back and we can talk some more if you like, anytime."

"Thank you. Maybe *you* can introduce me to Bari."

"All right, all right," Sharif says. "Let's go."

A little angrily he darts ahead, a speed-walk around the curve, and ducks under a yellow-and-orange tarp that frames the sprawling patio of the Tizi Ousli Café. By the time I catch up with him, he has made it well inside the building proper, which is packed with chain-smoking newspaper readers from various walks of life. Like Ibrahim Dey's bedroom, the coffeehouse appears specially contrived to drink in and savor the sunlight. Windows are wide, tall, and polished, and a dozen mirrors have been mounted on all four sides of the inner Ionian columns that fortify and ornament the building. If you sit in the right spot, you could surreptitiously eyeball any table in the hall, thanks to the reflections of the room's four corners in the glare of each mirror. A mist of boiled *za'atar* wafts across the room, mixed in with boiled wormwood, lemon balm, fresh mint, and coffee—a greenhouse in steam, stained with the bitterness of tar.

Sharif is standing over a middle-aged man in a natty trench coat with a war-torn, shaggy brown lining—a relic from the days of disco, perhaps the only coat the man owns. He sports a salt-and-pepper mustache and a beard of mostly salt. He has three deep gashes on each temple, inflicted decades ago perhaps, by a very sharp knife or the talons of a bird.

"Muhammad Bari."

He nods solemnly and puts his hand on the table near a seat he appears to have in mind for me.

I take it.

"I understand you were quite close to the gentleman," I tell him.

"Where you are sitting now," he says, "he would always sit there with me." His eyes squeeze out a tear and his voice climbs weakly into an upper register. "Since that terrible day I have barely slept. So much is lost."

Bari speaks Arabic, like Sharif and the rest of his Berber acquaintances, with the sort of insistent classical precision one learns in a village mosque—though hardly a long vowel makes it through his graying beard unmuffled. The parallel cuts in his temples echo the wavy grooves in his forehead. His left eyebrow leaps asymmetrically upward in a diagonal hook shape, flashing a permanent expression of intrigue.

"You saw the body?" I ask.

"I saw the crowd and the police around the warehouse. I saw the blood on the stairs. Don't ask me about the body."

"I'm sorry."

"I often would stop by to visit my friend inside," he goes on, "always in the evening. But this time I came in the morning because Ibrahim Dey was missing at the mosque and didn't show up at the café. I went to the gate and asked to see my friend. They took hold of me and pulled me inside and showed me." His head droops toward the table as if he were nodding off. "I spent three days with the police answering questions. They held me in their headquarters and I even missed the funeral, God have mercy on him. So many of his friends missed it, too."

He stirs up the black bottom of his espresso shot, darkening the hot milk, and drinks.

"So you are with the Judiciary Police?" he asks.

"I am studying them."

A mischievous smile forms under his beard. "Usually it is they who study us."

Sharif opens his mouth, but an acquaintance from the next table over taps him on the shoulder, and for a moment Bari has me all to himself.

"Sharif was sent by the Judiciary Police to guide you here?" he whispers.

"That's right."

Bari smiles more broadly now. *"When the crow is your guide,"* he says, reciting a proverb, *"he will lead you to the corpses of dogs."*

"I don't follow."

"His purpose is not to guide you but to mislead you."

EIGHT

t does not surprise me that a predominantly poor population like Morocco's would devise a rich vocabulary to distinguish among its vagabonds and beggars. Something about the late Ibrahim Dey caused his friends to regard him as *majdub*—capable of conferring good fortune on anyone who spoke to him kindly or threw him a buck. I wonder what that something was. I wonder who would kill it. I wonder why his friend Muhammad Bari would think the police would keep me from finding out. Bari may hold the key to a deeper understanding of Ibrahim Dey and what his life meant to the people around him. I would like to learn more. Perhaps he would be willing to help.

At twilight, an hour or so after parting ways with Sharif the book peddler, I say good night to the cops at Precinct 5 and ride a taxi back to Ayn Sabaa on my own. An apricot glow behind the darkening clouds has made a gazebo of silhouettes out of the palm-tree-lined embankment. At the Café Tizi Ousli, ashtrays are full and tables are empty—though Muhammad Bari, as I'd hoped, is still at his post, puffing an acrid Cleopatra, rummaging through a pile of leftovers from the daily press, and wiping down his swollen eyes.

"May I join you?"

Again, he offers me the hallowed chair of his lost friend.

"Earlier today you said you felt I was being misled."

The chapped fingers of his right hand smooth his beard and form a triangle, until he lets loose the white tuft at the bottom. He lays down his cigarette gingerly on the ashtray and narrows his eyes into slits.

"I am sure of it," he replies.

A waiter appears in front of us and says something chummy to Bari in their native tongue of Shilha. Both faces turn keenly toward me.

I order coffee for the two of us.

"What did the police tell you about the reason my friend was killed?" Bari asks.

"That this man from the army base happened into the warehouse and got in a fight with Ibrahim Dey. He stole some money and a couple of coats."

Bari grins. *"If at noon the king declares that it is night,"* he recites, *"behold the stars."* Then he picks up his cigarette and flicks off the absurdity of my explanation.

"You don't believe them," I observe.

"This is Morocco. Police always give mundane reasons like that when they don't want us to know what actually happened. There is a major conspiracy at the heart of this murder; I just know it."

He peers at the cindery stub between his fingers as if he has never seen fire before. He decides against restoring it to the ashtray.

"But there are lots of mundane murders in Morocco, too," I suggest, and point to the Arabic newspapers on his table. "Every day."

Bari takes a fierce drag and lets the smoke out through his nostrils. "This wasn't one of them."

The waiter sets down our hot drinks and sugar cubes and falls back toward the coffee bar in nosy slow motion. I look him in the eye and he speeds off.

"That warehouse is not a place people wander into randomly," Bari says. "He must have known where he was going, this young man. He must have studied the place to figure out how to get into the warehouse from the back wall. He was *hunting* Ibrahim Dey, God have mercy on him."

At his own mention of his friend's name, Bari loses command of his voice, as he did this afternoon. "I am sure of it," he says again. The cadence drifts like a leaf into the same blustery upper register. I can see nights without sleep in his reddened eyes.

"You know the killer was a soldier," I tell him.

Bari's eyes moisten. "I didn't know that for days. It was only a rumor at first, and then a friendly policeman finally told one of my friends. They don't tell us anything around here, usually. I'm telling you, he was *hunting* Ibrahim Dey."

"You were such a close friend of his. Can you think of a reason why someone would hunt him down?"

Bari fumbles for his drink and sips it. "He knew a great deal about so many people. I'm convinced he *knew* something."

"Like what?"

"Something to do with terrorism, the drug cartels, maybe both. Something about that godforsaken warehouse. Somebody powerful felt threatened by him and sent this man to kill him. That is the only reasonable explanation."

"And you feel police are aware of this but concealing what they know from you, from me?"

"They are involved somehow. They must be. Whatever it is they know, I know they are concealing it. They would lie to you for sure, like nothing."

They would lie to you for sure. I reach for the napkin by my coffee cup and wipe a few sweat beads off my forehead.

"How can you be sure?"

He appears to take umbrage at the question. "Because I have lived in Morocco all my life."

I look the old man over in his muddied trench coat, stinking of tar. He is plainly unemployed. He has probably not been through grade school. But it doesn't take schooling to know that cops are not obliged to tell the truth. That said, I have read the detailed case file on this murder and enjoyed a tour of the crime scene led by the man who cracked it. Wouldn't it be easier to cover up a lie by denying me all that access, showing me a different case? Or perhaps Chief Sharqawi wasn't thinking carefully in handing me the document—the kind of sloppiness I have to thank for witnessing a brutal police beating in the shantytown. I freely admit that Jabri's rendering of the events surrounding the murder sounded patchy, but sometimes a little patchiness reflects a story's authenticity. Cops lie, sure, but usually not for the hell of it. Sometimes they tell the truth because it's more complicated to lie, especially when there is an obvious culprit. The crime of the century was an open-and-shut case—yet civilians, especially in this part of the world, still believe there was a conspiracy and a cover-up. I wonder where Bari stands on the matter.

"Question," I tell him. "Who attacked New York on September eleventh?"

Bari grins with his eyes closed.

"The answer to this question is also a mystery," he declares. "We are all aware that the United States government concealed a great deal about the hidden hand in that operation. Certain people are known to have been warned in advance not to go into the building that morning. A certain *group* of people. Thousands of them, you know, who did not show up to work that day."

That would be Jewish people he's talking about. I lost a Jewish friend in the Twin Towers myself. I'm outraged that this canard continues to this day. Bari's "truths" deserve some skepticism.

"Question for *you*," he demands. "You know what your so-called guide Sharif told me when he ran up ahead of you today?"

His voice has drifted back to where he can pilot it smoothly.

"He said, 'Do not go anywhere with the man you are about to meet. Give him a few simple answers to his questions and let me move him along.' "

Something about the quote rings true. I can picture that sniveling book peddler, just beyond the range of my ears, contriving to keep something from me. I wonder what he thought I shouldn't know, and at whose behest.

"Maybe he was simply uncomfortable showing me around," I suggest. "What makes you think the police told him to say that?"

"He does business with the police. They buy law books from him. Everybody around here knows that."

"Muhammad," I ask as if I have known the man awhile, "police have a terrible history in Morocco. I get that. But do you not see signs that they are changing a little?"

"How?" he replies.

"You were held for questioning three days, you said. Did Lieutenant Jabri or his men beat you during that time?"

"Well, no."

"Did they threaten you in any way? It's okay, you can tell me. I do not answer to them."

"No. They were very polite. Jabri especially."

"So is it possible that once they had finished their investigation, they told you the truth about what they learned, more or less?"

"It would be easier for me to believe them if they *had* beat me," he explains. "You just know there is something rotten going on when police in Casablanca are acting like saints."

A soccer game is on tonight and it starts in a few minutes. The evening crowd has begun to drift in. Across the hall, the waiter switches the house TV to the Al Jazeera sports channel and puts the volume up.

Bari hunches diagonally toward the center of our table.

"Whatever it is about the murder of Ibrahim Dey that police are hiding, you know, might just have saved my family from years of suffering. Even in death this man brings luck."

"How do you figure that?" I whisper back.

"Fifteen years ago my nephew was arrested and held in Precinct Five," he explains. "Same headquarters, maybe some of the same police. There had been a murder. The boy was innocent. So were all his friends. But they were all dragged in, and police beat them, on and on. They told each of the boys to pay seven thousand dirhams cash to the homicide detective if he wanted to go free. They said, 'If you don't pay, we will blame you for the killing and it will be years before you can prove your innocence from behind bars.' Then they beat them some more."

"Was Jabri in charge?" I ask. "Chief Sharqawi? Were they around at that time?"

"I don't know who was involved."

"Well, how do you know what was said?"

"I helped the boy pay his bribe!" he cries.

I remind him with a queasy index finger to my lips that he had just been whispering.

"I had my own bakery back then and some cash to chip in. My brother is a farmer and there was a little rain at the time, praise God. We managed to come up with the money together. But that was a different era for us, for the weather and the rain, for everybody. Now our money situation has changed. I haven't worked since I got cancer three years ago. Look at me now."

He puts out the stub and yanks his coat straight with both hands.

"Imagine if you were me," he goes on. "You sit in that precinct for three days answering the same questions over and over again, waiting for them to shake you down for cash, wondering how much the price of bribing a detective has gone up after fifteen years of inflation. You are so afraid of what your family, your children would be forced to do to come up with the money that all your other normal human feelings are frozen solid. It was three days before I could allow myself to mourn for Ibrahim Dey."

I flip through my own past in search of three full days in which I managed to put a heated emotion on ice, and come up short.

"When they told me I could go I was so relieved," he says, "first on the way home I cried tears of joy. Then I pictured the funeral. I felt the sweat in my neck and a terrible chill, and at last I started crying for my friend. I cried for him because he will never get to enjoy the things in life that all men enjoy—a family, a loving wife, a home—though he gave so much comfort to others. I cried for myself: it hit me that I'll never be able to go see him at the warehouse again. I am going to be all alone during the day. Then, in the dead of night, I began to think about *why* he died. I realized that whatever the secret was, its concealment must have been priceless for somebody in power. Such a big secret that Lieutenant Jabri had to let me go without shaking me down! Why else would he have treated me so well, tell me?"

"Look, the only reason I'm giving you a hard time about this is that I have seen the internal police file myself. I have a copy of it. What's in it isn't any different than what you heard from Jabri."

Bari puts down his drink. "You have the case file?"

Whoops.

I nod uneasily.

"Would you show it to me?"

"I'm sorry. They asked me not to."

In an instant Bari's face grows sullen again, and meek. He resigns himself to the coffee I bought him.

The soccer game has started now. Casablanca's Widad is squared off against another Moroccan team, Hasaniyat Agadir, from the Berber stronghold of Agadir in the kingdom's south. For the café's Berber clientele seated all around us, there isn't even a question of dual loyalty: resounding boos for Widad betray a unanimous desire to throw their putative Casablanca home team under the bus.

From one end of the coffeehouse to the other, only Bari and I are agnostic about the game.

He is settling back, soggy-eyed, into the brooding state I found him in. The noise all around us lends a new intimacy to our meeting.

"Every day I would find him here, like the tables themselves," he says over our second round. "Like the newspapers. The most trustworthy, pious, God-fearing man you will ever meet. Ten years I knew him. Four years we sat together every day. As the saying goes, *Only God lives forever*."

I nod solemnly. "You were best friends."

"He was *my* best friend," he says. "For him there were others. Sometimes I would go to visit him at night at the warehouse. I would knock on the gate and he would come out and say, 'I have people here.' "

"Who were they?"

Bari shakes his head. "They must have been people he was try-

ing to make business deals with. He was always trying to make a little money. They probably visited him there. But I don't know.
Maybe a man came in who wasn't who he said he was. Another
friend of his was Attar. He was the official guard at the Jew's warehouse. They were very close. Attar is even more deeply hurt. Police
suspected him, and then the Jew fired him from his job. You know
it was a Jew."

"I heard."

"You would know it was a Jew who owned that warehouse the
day Ibrahim Dey was killed because there was practically an army
of state security everywhere, inside and out, looking at every detail
to make sure they took care of everything. The government will go
to hell and back to protect the Jews here. I don't understand why.
You are Muslim?"

The acid question. As usual when I'm asked, the roots of my hair
prick into my scalp.

Bari is a stranger to me, I remember—a stranger in a dicey section of a Muslim capital, distrustful and detached from the Jew-
friendly regime that rules the place. I do not owe him the truth. But
it just tumbles out.

"I am Jewish."

I search his eyes with sudden fear. Whom will he tell?

He stops to look me over, too.

Words bubble up through his beard in a more supple tone: "So
you are asking about this case on behalf of Toledano, the warehouse
owner?"

"I do not know Toledano. I don't know any Jews in Morocco at
this point."

He nods and puts a couple of fingers on my left hand. I feel the
calluses up and down them and spy the nicotine stains in between.
His cut-up temples squeeze in tightly.

It hits me that he is smiling—warmly, even.

"You should meet Attar," he says. "Maybe you can help him get
his job back."

My breathing eases.

"How about right now," I suggest.

He snatches a glance at the scoreboard on TV and gets up, pointing to the way out.

I pay the waiter.

At the curb just outside the café, I swallow a breath of the chilled night air and open the back door of a red Peugeot taxi for Bari. He tumbles in, sidles over to the far side like a little boy, and pats the nearer backseat space for me to take right beside him. He instructs the cabbie to head down Ali Yaata Avenue, an east Casablanca artery cleared of traffic by the soccer match, to the factory and shantytown hub of Al-Hay al-Muhammadi.

Attar's apartment building, he explains, happens to border a well-known landmark there: the barbed-wire fence of the Jankeer military barracks.

NINE

Like Bari, I'm wary of law enforcement, too. That might sound strange coming from somebody who moonlighted with the FBI for five years. But long after learning what it feels like to go after people, I learned what it feels like when people go after me. Along the way, I lost a friend. He was my best friend in the world, the big brother I never had. He isn't dead, but all contact between us has been severed, and I think that in his eyes, *I'm* dead. It's my fault that this happened. I broke the law in the United States and faced a federal prosecution that became a burden for everyone who cared about me. My own bad judgment was in turn compounded by actions of the U.S. government that appear to have served purposes other than justice, and my friend, who had done no wrong, was assailed for no good reason.

I'll call him Ali.

We met when I was a senior in college, majoring in Near Eastern Languages and Civilizations, and Ali was a graduate student in the same department. He showed up late on the first day of a seminar in Arabic and Islamic paleography, the study of medieval manuscripts. He had fair skin and light brown eyes and wore a thick black beard.

At the end of class the professor paired off students to take on the first assignment together, and my designated partner was Ali. We were assigned to edit an excerpt from a treatise attributed to an eighth-century Muslim scholar from Basra, now a part of southern Iraq. Ali and I walked across a field of grass to a basement hangout in the center of campus known as Machine City, where tables and chairs surrounded an island of vending machines. He bought us coffee.

"So, where are you from?" he asked.

"I'm from here, but my mother is originally from Baghdad."

His eyes lit up and blood rushed to his face. "I'm from Baghdad, too."

"My mom is Jewish," I added. It probably came off sounding like a threat.

Ali opened his eyes a little wider and inhaled softly through his mouth. "I'm Muslim," he said.

We code-switched into Arabic, and beloved Baghdad held our conversation in a vise grip for the next hour. We covered neighborhoods, street food, holy sites, shared history. I was talking about a romantic ideal I had learned to conjure in dreams, while he was talking about a real place, but somehow we were both on the same page. He couldn't think of a single thing he didn't like about the city of his childhood—aside from the butcher who had been ruling it for decades.

"You know you talk like an Egyptian," he observed.

I felt ashamed and shrugged. "That's because I studied colloquial Arabic in Cairo."

"Well, that's shit," he said. "I'm going to teach you to talk like an Iraqi."

An invitation followed to the modest apartment where Ali made his home with a wife who wore a headscarf and their son, then a toddler. For the three and a half of us, she put dinner for twelve on the table, then mainly sat there and watched Ali and me talk, eat, eat more, and talk more. Eventually she said, "*Yalla,* boys, go out and eat ice cream somewhere so I can clean up this mess."

So began a friendship that lasted nearly ten years.

Both of us turned out to be hypersensitive klutzes with a pen-

chant for daydreaming through any class in which the topic wasn't
Iraq. We kept each other out of trouble as best we could. Ali's wife,
one tough lady, used an Iraqi expression to describe our friendship:
"two asses in one pair of pants" (*tizayn bi-fad ilbas*). My mother
observed that there was no daylight between our respective versions
of any story—like "a dog bearing witness on its tail" (*kalb yish'had
'ala 'as'osu*).

The people closest to us. came to view us as brothers fairly
quickly, but at the core of our relationship lay turbulence and unrest, born of generations' baggage. He was the first Muslim I came
to love, and I was the first Jew he came to love, and what each of us
had grown up feeling in our hearts about the other needed to be re-
considered. We used to take long drives after dark up and down the
Northeast corridor, and while Ali's CD of Muddy Waters gave
groove to the cold night air, we tried to work through our differences in the safely enclosed space of the sedan. This was no inter-
faith kids' camp; each of us had baseline convictions about the other
that had hardened as we grew up. There was yelling in the car sometimes, offset by long spaces of silence. But in time, these altercations
proved to be merely a phase in our deepening friendship. We came
to see the divisive politics of the Middle East as so much ambient
noise. I learned to view the Arab world through Ali's eyes. Over the
years he inspired me to spend time working, studying, and living in
a dozen Arab and Muslim countries, from Saudi Arabia and the
Gulf states to Lebanon and Jordan to Tunisia and Morocco, and
even the Islamic Republic of Iran. Once I did a fellowship at an Arabic and Islamic manuscript archive in the Gulf. The requisite skills
came from our paleography class, but my comfort level with the
Arabian setting came from Ali. It was sometimes challenging to live
in many of these countries as a Jew, but I have happy associations
and friends in each place now, and in my mind I trace them all back
to him.

Five years after we had met, Ali invited my mother and me to fly
to London to celebrate the wedding of his older sister. Over
cardamom-infused tea on the second day of the celebration, Ali introduced my mother to his grandfather. At ninety-one, the man had

all his wits about him and a pair of piercing brown eyes. He looked into my mother's.

"You are of the blood of Na'im Aslan," the old man declared.

Blood, as it had with Ali five years back, rushed to my mother's face.

"He was my uncle," she said.

"He was my brother," the old man replied. "He is the heart that beats inside me."

In a city the size of Baghdad, the odds that Ali's grandfather and my great-uncle would turn out to have been best friends were thousands to one. Yet back in the 1920s, he recalled, the two of them had gotten to know each other as classmates in school. They became inseparable. One year they traveled from Baghdad to the mystical city of Safed, in what is now Israel, and studied together there. It was a different time in Iraq and in Palestine, a time of porous borders and easy love among peoples who would later grow to hate each other. Na'im Aslan had died years ago. Ali's grandfather was in the sunset of his life. Yet two generations later, our families had found a way back into each other's hearts through Ali and me.

The old man and my mom put their arms around the two of us. "Be good to each other, boys," he said. "God brought you together."

In America in 2003 the drums of war were beating, and the butcher's days in Baghdad were numbered. The prospect of a new government in Iraq stoked our fondest dreams. The country could reconstitute itself and lead the region as a force for peace, a model of tolerance, an arsenal of bright ideas, an economic powerhouse, a regional superpower. Why not? Iraq had played that role before. Both of us wanted to be part of this historic change, which we believed to be inevitable. I wrote a book called *The New Iraq* in which I laid out a vision for the Iraq of the future in light of its resplendent past. More than anything in the world, I wanted to go there and play some role in the reconstruction.

With his prestigious academic background and family in the

Iraqi capital, Ali felt that he was well positioned to go into politics there, or work with the Pentagon's governing authority, or forge some pragmatic combination of the two. He made plans for a homecoming and meanwhile worked what contacts he had in Washington to try to win the interest, if not the trust, of the Bush administration. For me as a Jew, the prospect of organically entering the political fray in Iraq was unrealistic. The possibility of working with the U.S. government in Iraq appealed to me. I also imagined starting an Arabic newspaper in Baghdad. It would be quirky, feisty, truth-seeking, unrelenting. Nobody would like it, but everybody would read it. Some eccentric American investors had my back.

And so Ali and I went off, each on our own, to live out our respective fantasies.

I'm going to recount what happened to me along the way, and at first it may seem a little off-topic. But don't worry; it's not.

I crossed the Kuwaiti border on foot into southern Iraq in May 2003. A car was waiting for me on the other side. A Baghdadi businessman whose brother in the States had read my book had reached out to me by email a few weeks earlier. "I know that you're Jewish and that your dream is to be here. My family worked with Jews in the good old days, and it would be an honor to host you." I checked him out with an aging friend who knew family names all over Iraq, and I decided to take the man up on his invitation—rather than enter the country "on the back of a tank," as they say in Baghdad.

He gave me a bedroom with a radio in it, fed me as much as I could eat, and provided two armed Iraqi guards to be with me at all times. Flanked by these beefy, mustached sentries, I wandered the city like a nine-year-old in Disneyland. I walked through the old neighborhoods and markets and spent time with the legendary booksellers of Mutanabbi Street. I got to know people my own age as well as old-timers who remembered the good old days. I visited Muslim holy places, the tomb of an Iraqi monarch who had reigned while my family still lived there, and the synagogue where my great-great-grandfather had preached and a handful of frail Jews still lived. During the day, I mainly gathered price points for my newspaper venture. At the Suq al-Ghazal, an open-air market where local journalists hung out, I inquired about their salary expectations. Elsewhere in town, I inspected a couple of clunky printing machines that only recently had been used to crank out government propaganda. Toward the end of my trip, in front of a bookstore near the U.S. government's "Green Zone," I met a Pentagon official I had known in Washington—a man who didn't like me very much. "What are you doing here, Tsemah?" he said, using my mother's maiden name. "You're twenty-eight now. That's too old to be looking for adventures. Get out of here before the whole place blows up."

The U.S. government had already begun to botch the reconstruction effort through a series of mistakes that enraged the region and the world. Perhaps the first colossal misstep, a crime against the Geneva Convention, was the American army's failure to protect the Iraqi Museum—the most important repository of ancient artifacts in the Middle East. Looters stormed the unguarded facility and made away with thousands of antiquities. Now children on the streets were peddling these items for whatever cash they would fetch, and private collectors in the West were keen to get their hands on them.

My host in Iraq said he was outraged over the disaster, which is exactly how I felt. He suggested I might be able to help do something about it by helping to recover artifacts and taking them to the proper authorities. I liked the idea—both for an altruistic reason and for a self-serving reason. It seemed right to help make up for the damage my own government had done, even in some small way. I also thought that by helping the United States in its restoration efforts, I could earn brownie points with American officials who now held power in Iraq.

"What do you have in mind?" I asked him.

A young boy walked into his office with a little blanket the following day. "This is Muhammad," my host said, patting the boy on the back, "the king of the black market."

Muhammad chuckled. Then he unrolled his blanket on the desk and waved his hand over a dozen or so cylinder seals—the sort that were rolled in clay in lieu of a signature, two thousand years before the birth of Jesus.

"Pick three," my host said.

I hesitated at first. If I bought them, regardless of my motives, I risked encouraging kids like Muhammad to acquire and sell more of them. On the other hand, if I didn't, a collector could eventually acquire them and they would vanish from public view for years. I didn't want that to happen. But were these relics even authentic? I had studied medieval manuscripts, not ancient artifacts, but felt these items were probably real because so many pieces like them were floating around the streets of Baghdad, and where they came from was not generally in dispute.

"Okay," I said.

Two hundred dollars later, I was the temporary custodian of three little pieces of ancient Babylon, each possibly older than the Torah.

The question was where to take them. The museum, to my knowledge, had not yet been reestablished as a secure installation. Despite subsequent claims by American military personnel that a campaign was being waged to reclaim artifacts, I saw no evidence of this effort in the chaos of Baghdad at the time. I listened to U.S. Army radio in Arabic before I went to bed at night, and most of what I heard was a looped message calling on Iraqis to turn in their weapons at various depots that had been established all over the city.

So I decided to take the seals back to the United States.

Before my trip, Ali and I had tried to make contact with some of the Pentagon officials who were now in charge of Iraq policy. I had managed to have a phone conversation with Abe Shulsky, then a prime mover at the Pentagon's Office of Special Plans. We talked about the possibility of my visiting his office to explore job prospects in Iraq. I liked the idea of bringing the relics directly to him, or one of his colleagues, to make a dramatic demonstration of how easy it is to acquire these items and urge them to recover thousands more. At the very least, they would know to whom to deliver the relics—and I would get a pat on the back for having handed them over.

Upon my arrival at John F. Kennedy Airport in New York, a federal agent was waiting at the mouth of the plane. She checked each passenger's passport as they departed, and when she saw mine, she let the rest of the passengers go. She took away my customs form, then asked me to come with her.

Being no stranger to the "Axis of Evil," I had been hassled by Customs a number of times before, though no one had ever pulled me aside at the gate. Sometimes agents would detain and question me for two or three hours, then take away files, business cards, books, and disks, only to return them by mail a week or two later. My mom provoked their suspicions as well, probably because she looks Middle Eastern and her passport says she was born in Baghdad. When we returned together from Ali's sister's wedding in London, for example, an agent escorted her into one of their white-walled rooms and kept her there for an hour.

But enough about Customs.

I had made several boneheaded decisions, while filling out my customs form on the plane, that reflected a combination of petulance, hubris, and naïveté. Because I wanted to avoid being grilled for three hours at the airport, I had omitted Iraq from the short list of countries I had just visited. Because I wanted to deliver the cylinder seals directly to the Pentagon rather than let a customs agent confiscate them, I had not declared the items on my form. I made no effort to conceal the antiquities; they were the first thing you'd find when you opened my briefcase. What these actions added up to was a halfhearted attempt to waltz through Customs without giving the seals up. As I would soon know well, that's a federal crime. Having worked with the FBI and believing that another federal officer would understand my motivations, I figured that if they questioned me, I could simply explain what I was doing and have no worry that Customs would doubt me.

I would have to learn how arrogant I was the hard way.

The agents opened my briefcase and removed the items, then asked me what they were. I told them what I thought they were, how I had acquired them, and why. After holding me for a little while, they confiscated the items and sent me home. "Maybe we'll call you later about how you can help us retrieve more of them," one of them said.

A few days later, the same agents flew in to visit me in Cambridge, Massachusetts, where I now lived. I welcomed them into my apartment. They behaved much like my FBI handlers. They indicated that they needed help in recovering more artifacts and alluded to the possibility of enlisting me in the recovery effort. I felt at ease, thinking I was assisting law enforcement just as in old times. It was of course sublimely naïve of me to accept the agents' claims at face value. They asked for a more detailed description of how I had acquired the items, where, and in whose company, taking assiduous notes as I walked them through every recollection I had. I was so used to thinking of myself as an asset to the Feds that I couldn't imagine the agents were actually trying to build a case against me. They left, and for several weeks I thought little of the meeting we had had.

One reason I put the matter aside was that a few days later, Shulsky's office at the Pentagon got back in touch with me and flew me to Washington for a series of meetings about employment in Iraq. Among other sessions, I spent forty-five minutes with then Deputy Secretary of Defense Paul Wolfowitz. He had read my book and was curious to know what I thought of the country on my recent trip. He asked what my plans were for the next year or so. I told him about the idea of starting a newspaper. He suggested that instead I take on a role in public communications on behalf of the Pentagon. I didn't give him an answer on the spot, but I went on to meet with a man named Gary Thatcher in an adjoining office. He is a veteran journalist and editor who had just been tapped to serve as director of strategic communications for the Coalition Provisional Authority in Baghdad. "I'm a freedom-of-the-press guy," he said, and he encouraged me to think of the work we might do together as a mechanism to foster real journalism in Iraq. I thought we might get along well.

It did not even occur to me to mention the incident at Customs to any of these people.

A few weeks later, the agents who had interviewed me in Cambridge found me in New York and told me I was under arrest.

What the hell?

My lungs stopped working.

Rather than try to dislodge the hockey puck from my trachea, they next taught me the trick of squatting over my handcuffed wrists for maximal comfort in the backseat of their unmarked sedan. The driver put on the Yankees game and warned me that nothing good would come of rooting for the Red Sox, now or ever.

Very funny.

I was so utterly shocked and confused by my arrest that even my big mouth didn't work en route to the federal holding facility in Brooklyn. A radio ad came on during our half-hour ride that momentarily offset my disorientation with a flash of encouragement. It was a public service announcement paid for by the Lubavitchers: "The people of Israel lives! As long as you have *emunah shleimah* (complete faith) and *ahavat yisroel* (love of Israel), the Lord will never forsake you! Blessed be His name!"

"You hear that, Joe?" one of the agents interjected. "What you got to worry about? I rest my case."

Having failed to safeguard the Iraqi Museum during the invasion of Baghdad, the Bush administration faced enormous international pressure to redress the situation but fell short of doing so adequately. The military launched a plan to recover relics, but a host of items remain missing to this day. Nor did the government succeed in apprehending the antiquities traffickers who were responsible for smuggling massive amounts of museum property out of Iraq. All they had in handcuffs was me. It might seem strange that one branch of government was trying to hire me while another was trying to lock me up—but as they say at the airport, welcome to the United States.

Prosecutors issued a news release insinuating that I had been involved in the looting of the Iraqi Museum and that I was an antiquities trafficker who sought to profit from the cylinder seals—

though the actual indictment made no such claims. The news release and subsequent media coverage pained me indescribably. For years I had been trying to build relationships of trust across the Middle East, in hopes of putting these relationships to constructive use. Now I had made a stupid mistake. The insinuation that I was a trafficker in the region's ancient relics was as heartbreaking as it was false—and I would have to wear it like the brand of Cain.

The customs agent who had hauled me away boasted to my lawyer that John Ashcroft himself had taken a personal interest in the case.

The agent was going to get a pat on the back.

A number of people less stupid than I was formed opinions about what was going on. One was a Harvard law professor with a history of fighting politically motivated prosecutions. He told me in substance that he felt my hyped indictment amounted to scapegoating; that in an insidious tradition, a faction of the government was exploiting my illegal act to deflect attention from its own failings. He told *The New York Times*, "I just got the sense that this kid was being railroaded. Why they're prosecuting it like a major felony seems like serious overkill to me."

I moved back to my mother's house in Providence, Rhode Island, because my legal defense was going to be expensive.

A prominent defense attorney took me on as an act of kindness, through the intervention of the Jewish community, at a fraction of his normal rates—though the price tag was still a hardship for my parents, who footed most of the bill. The lawyer felt initially that he might be able to persuade the government to drop the case. He tried to argue that given the dearth of Middle East specialists available to Americans in Baghdad, I'd be more valuable to the government innocent than guilty. He asked one of the Pentagon officials whom I had met a few weeks earlier to write a memo opining that I would be useful to their effort in Iraq, but only if I didn't carry the baggage of a felony conviction. The Pentagon official agreed to this request. The prosecutors were not moved by his memo.

When Ali found out about my indictment, he wept. He was traveling between Iraq and the United States then, still looking for his niche in Baghdad. He came to Providence to visit several times, always asking whether there was anything he could do to help, always sharing tidbits from the motherland. "It's not what I thought," he said one night. "They're making a bloody mess. The Americans are fighting each other even more than the Iraqis are fighting them." He told me to count my blessings, noting that in the emerging bloodbath, a young Jewish entrepreneur named Nick Berg had been kidnapped and beheaded by the Jordanian terrorist Abu Mus'ab al-Zarqawi. "Better your mother's cooking than Zarqawi's," he said. My mom signaled her agreement, kissing the air as if God's own cheek were hovering over her.

A few months later my attorney made a new proposal to the prosecutors: since recovering Iraqi artifacts was now a prime directive for the U.S. government, why not have me formally cooperate in that effort in exchange for a reduction of the charges? The prosecutors showed some interest. Have Joseph come in and tell us what he would do to help, they said. So I gathered as much information as I could. I called the man who had hosted me in Baghdad. I called Iraqi friends in neighboring Jordan and the Gulf states. I called Arab journalists who covered street life in their native cities. I told everyone that I was trying to assist the government and persuade them to drop the widely publicized charges, and I asked for contacts and creative ideas that could lead to the recovery of more artifacts and perhaps the apprehension of antiquities traffickers. Each contact offered some advice. And of course, I called Ali. "This isn't exactly up my alley," he said, "but I do have a cousin who owns an antiques shop in Baghdad."

I put the information together and presented it to the prosecutors and customs officials in a meeting. They listened and nodded as I went down the list of suggestions explaining how helpful all my contacts wanted to be, but their eyes lit up at the sound of only one name: Ali.

It seemed as if they knew who he was.

"He's a close friend of yours," one of them said.

"My closest friend in the world."

"So here's what we want you to do."

It turned out they had other interests besides the artifacts themselves. A customs agent proposed to hand me $30,000 in cash to flash in front of Ali's face. He seemed to understand that Ali was a graduate student with loans to pay off. *Tell him you have a buyer for Iraqi artifacts,* he said, *and try to persuade him to procure some, fly them home, and make the same mistake you made at Kennedy Airport.* If I did that and Ali was successfully apprehended and charged, the prosecutors offered, my own felony charges would be reduced to misdemeanors.

"Let the kid think it over," my lawyer told them, then walked me outside to a taxi and urged me to take a few days to reflect on the matter—but under no circumstances to discuss it with Ali, as that would compromise my position with the government.

I went home with an ulcer.

Over the next few days, my attorney advised me repeatedly that I should cooperate with the prosecutors: "I'm your lawyer, not your friend's lawyer, and this is a good deal." My rabbi, meanwhile, had another opinion: "No way," he said. "The Torah teaches, 'Do not put a stumbling block in front of a blind person.' Money can sometimes blind a man in debt, and for a Jew to betray his Muslim friend makes this ten times more nauseating."

I had brought this predicament on myself and Ali. My own hopes of working in Iraq were already shot—and now the good that Ali could do for his native country was imperiled as well. If I chose to cooperate against Ali, his son might grow up talking to his father through a window in a prison.

So I decided to bite the bullet: refuse to cooperate with the prosecutors and confound any attempt they might make to trick Ali into committing a crime.

Since my lawyer had warned me not to speak with Ali about the proposed plot to ensnare him, I asked a mutual friend to explain the situation to him on my behalf, as if that might make a difference. Then I called my attorney and told him what I had done.

"What was the one thing I told you *not* to do?" he said. "Now I have an ethical responsibility to report these actions to the government so they will not be blindsided." He also explained that this would compromise my ability to cooperate in a manner that would result in a reduced plea. He warned me to have no further communication with Ali until the case was resolved.

It wasn't long before the prosecutors came back to us with their reaction. *We might have cut the kid a break,* they said, *but now we're going to nail him to the wall.*

We were going to trial.

I survived in federal court for about a day and a half, including the time it took to select a jury. In front of the judge, my attorney and the prosecutors sparred about the interpretation of the law under which I had been charged. If we could persuade the judge that my motivation in importing the cylinder seals was relevant to the legal statute, then we would have a fighting chance: I could take the stand and tell the jury why I felt it necessary to bring the items to the United States and what I intended to do with them. A retired FBI agent had taken a train into New York at his own expense and was waiting to testify as a character witness on my behalf.

Unfortunately, a determination was made by the court to define the law narrowly, so that my intent was of marginal relevance to the charge I faced, leaving only binary questions such as whether I had imported the items and whether I had declared them on my customs form. My lawyer went on to explain that if the judge thought I was lying, it would only increase my punishment at the time of the sentence.

"I really want to take the stand," I told him.

"But your story won't help you even if the jury believes you," he explained. "Anyway, how would you explain not wanting Customs to have the seals?"

I looked up at the ceiling. "Remember that scene at the end of *Raiders of the Lost Ark* where the Ark of the Covenant gets stuffed away in some giant government warehouse?"

My lawyer rolled his eyes. "Thank God this wasn't the Ark of the Covenant."

"Hey, man," I said, "you want the Ark, I can get you the Ark."

He gave me a gentle pat on the back, and I entered a plea of guilty.

When you stick your neck out for a friend, you may end up a few inches shorter, but at least you still have your friend. That was what I thought as I left the courtroom a newly minted felon. I picked up my mobile phone on the other side of the metal detector and turned it on as I walked out the big glass doors. At last I had the freedom to call Ali. I rang his cell number, but there was no answer. I tried again several times later in the day; nothing. I called his house line and left a message on the answering machine. The following day, I tried him several times again.

"They're probably after him too now," my lawyer said.

"But he didn't do anything wrong," I told him.

"Maybe you don't know everything about him there is to know," he replied. "If he isn't talking to you, there's probably a reason."

I refused to believe Ali had done anything regrettable that he wouldn't share with me. Years later, I still don't believe it.

You could say I was lucky as the weeks went by. Prosecutors tried hard to persuade the judge to put me in prison, but friends and colleagues came through with letters pleading for leniency. To the consternation of prosecutors, former CIA director R. James Woolsey wrote to acknowledge that I had been "helpful to the United States in matters related to terrorism." The retired FBI agent who had wanted to testify as a character witness on my behalf wrote a letter as well, describing the nature of the work we'd done together against jihadist groups. "I feel some responsibility for his troubles," he wrote. "Even though I was not directing his actions, I should have taught him more about risk assessment and sound judgment." An Iraqi professor in the Gulf who ran the Arabic and Islamic manuscript archive where I had worked wrote in as well. The archive had been set up to acquire and preserve medieval manuscripts from war-torn areas of the Muslim world. He noted that I had been entrusted with access to all the archive's libraries and collections and was faithful to that trust throughout the period of my fellowship.

The judge made some special comments at my sentencing. She

observed that there had been no evidence nor any suggestion by the prosecutors of a pecuniary motive on my part; she acknowledged that I had made a valuable contribution to the security of the United States, and ultimately accepted my attorney's request that I be spared a prison sentence. In an act of compassion, the judge sentenced me to six months' house arrest. It could have been so much worse. I'm not the sort of person who gets cabin fever easily. Living with a bracelet around your ankle, though, is a painful experience. Long after it comes off, you remember that it was there—in your waking hours and in your dreams.

But so what.

What I wanted most was to talk to my friend.

Months went by and the silence grew colder. I tried sending emails to all his email addresses and passed messages to Ali via mutual friends. After I had served my sentence, I took a bus to the house where he and his family were now living and knocked on the door. His car was parked out front. I thought I heard footsteps and could feel someone peering through the door scope, but the door stayed shut.

He hadn't been arrested; I knew that much.

The informed conjecture of several lawyers I spoke with was that federal agents were now trying to use their legal victory against me to build a new criminal case against Ali. They had met with him. As they are not required to tell the truth to a man they are hunting, they had probably lied to him about what I had said and done after my arrest. They might have tried to fool him into thinking that I was cooperating against him.

It would seem that Ali, a Muslim American, was living in fear of his own government and had come to blame it on his longtime Jewish friend.

Years have passed. I have only shreds to go on now, gleaned from the Internet, mutual acquaintances, the odd stranger in our field of study. I know that Ali never managed to enter the fray in Baghdad as he had planned to do, and I wonder how he feels about the latest news from his native land. He divorced his wife not long ago, so I wonder whether he sees as much of his children—there are two now—as he would like to. I wonder how many of our inside jokes he still remembers, because I remember all of them. I wonder what dreams he has now, and whether he still daydreams about the future of Baghdad despite all the bloodshed of the past eight years. Weeks go by sometimes that I don't feel like a convicted felon at all. I've been through the trauma of a divorce myself, yet that wound, too, is healing. It's Ali I can't forget.

When I ask myself why our friendship was destroyed, vague notions form out of things my lawyer said, advice my rabbi gave, scenes in movies, and the Arabic satellite television I watch to go to sleep. One answer might come from the realm of karma—a short answer, though not so sweet. The other answer would be longer: a story with a beginning and an end, with details I know and details I don't know. Sometimes I feel the urge to prowl around for the part that's missing. I know how to prowl around, after all. But I never do. I just don't have the stomach for it.

TEN

Afierce wind through the backseat window of the taxi is messing up Bari's beard.

"The village where I'm from," he says after minutes of silence, "there were Jews there once. My father always told us that the Jewish butcher had the tenderest meat. Why is that?"

"One quick incision to the neck," I explain. "No time for the lamb to tense up."

"Ah."

Music blares from the radio. I hear the reverb-dampened twang of a fretless banjo meandering without rhythm along an Eastern scale called *rast*. It is a bright, sweet scale, though spicy to Western ears. A man's deep voice joins the banjo for a slow, wordless tour of the scale's bottom half: "*Waaaa,*" he sings at length, stitching long tones together with birdlike trills. "*Waaaa waaaa waaaa,*" he wails, tracing each interval with an air of longing. "*Woooo!*" He jumps an octave.

Bari forms the shape of the same sound with his lips and closes his eyes, hard.

"*Wooo wooo,*" the singer goes, "*wooo waaa,*" tumbling back to the tonic note where he began. There is aching in his voice, a prologue in raw emotion to the song's first words in Arabic: "Where are the people who used to gather around you, those people of good intent?"

"*Ohhh,*" a raucous chorus responds, "*Ohhh, siniya.*"

They are chanting their poem to a *siniya,* the round platter Moroccans use to serve food and drink to their guests.

"Where is my life? My home?" the leader sings. "Where is what is mine?"

"*Ohhh,*" they moan again. "*Ohhh, siniya.*"

The singer's dreams, a lost love, the fragrances of his youth, all refract in words off the polished round plate and its cups of steaming drink. The chorus assures him, leaping a fifth beyond the octave to the highest note yet, that they know the memories he means:

"Ambergris, mint, and wormwood!" they shout.

"*Ohhhh, siniya,*" he mourns.

The cabdriver in front of us joins the chorus with a wail of his own.

Bari chokes up, mouthing the lyrics unevenly.

Suddenly, in the dingy light of the street, I can feel his loss.

I can smell *za'atar* boiling in the busy yellow-and-orange-painted room. I can see the green herbs, the patterned blanket on the cot, the yellowing Arabic printed sheaf, the paper and Styrofoam scrawl. I can almost picture Bari sharing his stories, in the desolation of the warehouse by night, with the bearded man who lived there, his cherished friend.

The banjo's percussive strumming kicks into a four-beat groove, simple and insistent, breathing joy and life into the longed-for past. The groove feels bright, infectious—a heartbeat on air. The banjo is joined by a new sound: the funky paper-and-wood-thudded syncopation of a terra-cotta drum, known in Morocco as the *darbukka,* that homes in on the heartbeat, deepening the groove.

I am squinting in the moonlit darkness, struggling irrationally to conjure a picture of Ibrahim Dey.

"*Ohhhh, siniya.*"

Bari ends his lip-synching and looks over at me. He must be looking for a sign that I was stirred.

"This band," I tell him, shaking my head.

"Nas al-Ghiwan," he says. "The best band in the world."

The name of the ensemble registers.

"They are from right here, you know," he adds. "Al-Hay al-Muhammadi."

"The chief of Precinct Five offered to introduce me to them."

Bari smiles. "This music brings all Moroccans together," he says. "Even the police. Ibrahim Dey loved it, too."

Bari puts his right hand on my knuckles and presses it down. Then he curls his fingers around from underneath and clasps the whole hand.

It can be awkward for a Westerner to experience the intense physical contact that is so common in traditional societies. Tonight, I am intrigued by what I feel. Bari's hand is channeling his memories and his grief, the intensity of his connection to a man I never met. I know that sort of connection, so I wish I knew who this man was.

Baghdad is a place I tried to make myself know. I put together bits from books, the testimony of family members, recollections from Ali. When I got there, part of what I saw surprised me, but another part felt familiar, as if I had actually been there before. I ask myself what is easier to construct in one's head: a big city or a single human life.

The cabdriver flashes a question mark at Bari with his eyebrows through the rearview mirror.

"He's a Jew," Bari says. "An Iraqi Jew from America."

"Welcome, welcome," the driver volunteers.

We swerve onto a gritty asphalt clearing, an expansive open-air market of produce and smoke. Bundled-up women sift through wagonloads of avocados, oranges, sugar snaps, and bananas under a growling sky fleeced of light. The fatty smell of organ meat is everywhere. Bari leads the way on foot, zigzagging with a limp around the pumpkin seed, pistachio, and peanut tanks, past the barbecue grills, and across a parked procession of old white shuttle taxis pointing east. We turn off the concrete courtyard of a large mosque into a side street that ends in a wall. On top of the wall, I spy a cursive shadow with hairlike tendrils looping in the moonlight. It must be razor wire—the edge of the Jankeer barracks.

Bari inspects the looming wall. He draws a deep breath. I watch the blood flush out of his face. His cheeks are pale. I no longer see the longing for Ibrahim Dey in his eyes. He appears to be contemplating the darkness.

"Already we have found a link in this plot," he says quietly, pointing up at the razor wire. "Somewhere on the other side of this wall is the bunk where the soldier slept. And here, right next door, we find Attar's flat. Nothing is a coincidence. Not in Morocco."

He asks me to walk back toward the street, so that the first thing Attar sees when he opens the door isn't a suspicious stranger from far away.

Bari is banging on the apartment building's front door—black, encased in blue, ornamented by a finger-thin carving of white painted wood in the shape of a treble clef.

"Hasan!"

He waits awhile.

"Hasan!"

No response.

"He is afraid," Bari whispers to me in the distance. "He has problems with the police."

The door unlocks to a crusty pair of high cheekbones five feet off the floor, cloaked in a winter cap.

"Peace be upon you and the mercy of God and his blessings," the man says, fast-forwarding through the greeting in a squeaky pitch. He looks fearfully overhead for a lightning bolt or an asteroid or something.

"I have a friend with me," Bari says. "He's a good man."

Attar eyes me suspiciously as I draw near the door to his apartment.

"May we come in?" Bari asks.

"My wife she is sick," Attar says.

"God give her health."

The little man consents to join us at one of the benches in front of the nearby mosque. Stuffed into his coat and cap, he sits between us and stares dead ahead into the giant keyhole-shaped entryway of the sanctuary.

"This American is trying to understand what happened," Bari tells him. "What really happened."

"I don't know, by God," Attar replies. "I don't know I don't know!"

It is a tormented howl of a nonanswer. We might as well have shot him in the kneecaps for it.

"Forgive him," Bari tells me. "He has only just lost everything."

He tries to put his hand gently on the ex–warehouse watchman's shoulder, but it lands on him like a cattle prod anyway. The shock wears off and at length Attar appears to accept the gesture of consolation.

"We were like brothers," Attar murmurs. "No words between us. Just pure democracy."

Attar's idea of what democracy means appears to differ from mine. In some countries, the concept isn't taught particularly well— perhaps in part by design.

"Do you understand what it means to lose such a friend?" Bari asks. "And to lose your livelihood on the same day? Just imagine."

A Moroccan proverb seems apt, I think: *The weight of the burden is known only by he who carries it.*

"Twenty years I worked for the Jew," Attar says. "He was a good man. Then suddenly without any good reason he decides to get rid of me."

At this my neck fattens up with a primal rush of blood. "I thought there *was* a good reason, actually," I cut in. "I heard that 'the Jew' paid you to guard the place at night, but for five years you gave the work to your friend instead."

"And should he never go home to his wife and child?" Bari says, raising his voice. "For the few dirhams he was paid? With all respect."

Attar's grizzled little face slopes down toward his lap. He pinches the wrinkles at the meeting place between his eyes, and without a tone to his voice he begins to cry.

"I am sorry," he sobs.

Bari tightens his grip around Attar's shoulders. "He has a lot inside him now. Maybe too much. When he is ready, I know he will open up."

I feel bad now. For a long moment I hesitate to ask him anything.

"If you could say one more thing to Ibrahim Dey, what would it be?"

"Just 'God keep you,'" he whimpers. "'God keep you' is all."

The night sky overhead is sagging into an ocean of scattered city light. I survey Bari's shaggy coat, the oatmeal arm around Attar, the trickle of tears running through Attar's mustache and down his neck.

"You should help us," Bari tells me.

Attar just shuts his eyes.

"We need to know why our friend is dead," he goes on. "It's another secret, another terrible secret. But it's *not* just another secret. He's my best friend. We shouldn't have to live with it."

He is so sure that something sinister lies behind the killing. He is so sure, and maybe I believe him. But maybe it doesn't matter whether I believe him. He wants to find his own truth and peace of mind. I'm impressed by his determination.

"This secret," I ask, "you want to figure out what it is?"

He nods with all the muscles in his neck.

A chill runs down my spine. It doesn't come from the night air of Casablanca.

"You know, sometimes it's better not to know something," I tell him. "I mean, who knows, you might find out something about your friend that hurts you, or gets you into trouble. Or maybe he was hiding something from you and he wasn't as good a friend as you thought."

He looks at me as though I'd just insulted his mother. "How can you say that!" he exclaims. "I know my friend!"

My heart rate quickens. I know what he means. I know he's right.

"Imagine you were me," he says. "Wouldn't *you* want to know? Wouldn't you do everything in your power to find out?"

Bari's eyes are blazing now, and I try to avoid them, but I can't. "It's hard for me to put myself in your shoes," I tell him, though that isn't true.

"How could you go on with your life if there was something like this hanging over you?" he presses on. "What would you *do* with your life? Believe me, the secret would follow you wherever you go."

That's not true, I tell myself. *You can move on with your life. It's not easy, but I know I have.* Then I think about Jabri, Chief Sharqawi, Lieutenant Abd al-Jabbar. Bari is asking me to help him look for holes in *their* story. They wouldn't like it if we found some.

Then again, what's the point of being here, anyway?

"You're not scared?" I ask him.

"I am Moroccan!" he cries. "This is *my* country, and it should be my right to know what happened to my friend."

His back is straight now. The palms of his hands are facing the sky. For a moment he looks as if he rules the country.

"You wouldn't give up in the middle or something?" I ask him.

"I have nothing better to do," he assures me.

I look up at the smudge-grease cloud forms overhead.

"You know what?" I tell him. "Neither do I."

ELEVEN

S o this is the "social fabric" that the Judiciary Police presume to guard.

A poor man in Casablanca, weakened by hard times and ill health, wants to snatch back a secret from the security services—and do it in cahoots with a visiting Jew. He is not blind to the bloody history of the police in his kingdom, the continuing dangers of their war on militants and crime. To the contrary, he sees himself wading into the crossfire by tracing a conspiracy and cover-up that may involve terrorism or drug cartels or both. He deems these risks to be worth his trouble, because he cannot rest until he knows what really happened to his friend. He does not seem to doubt that the police have captured the man who killed him. It is the true story of what happened between them, and why it happened, that he wants to know—a story he feels has been concealed by the state for nefarious reasons.

Bari's proposition is daring and unusual for someone who lives in a part of the world under authoritarian rule. It is hard for me to picture a similar quest ending well in nearby Algeria or Libya, let alone Syria or Sudan—especially given a case of interethnic murder, particularly when the man who bashed the victim's skull in was an agent of the state. These are the sorts of fissures that can destabilize a wobbly regime, and none of the regimes I have named is particularly sturdy. They are states like Tunisia on the eve of its revolution. Their definition is not in history or culture but in lines on maps, drawn by foreigners over whiskey, held together ever since by fear. Muhammad Bari is not afraid, he says, of the consequences of launching a private investigation into state secrets on his native soil. "I am Moroccan!" he told me out loud, as if that was his license to brave a tyrant and redeem a lost soul.

Maybe he is a fool, or extraordinarily brave.

He is succumbing, in any case, to a hunger felt all over the world.

One of the interesting aspects of authoritarian states is that they have aspired not just to control the levers of government, but also to control the stories their citizens can tell about their own lives. They have censored artists and journalists because they know the power of stories and the power of truth. Autocrats are sometimes threatened by the truth, because the truth is often messy; it's human and specific and uncontrollable and subverts a simple ideology. A true story can be a threat to a regime that wants to govern according to its own myth. But even in the most repressive regimes, people have been willing to die to find out the truth. Consider the women in Argentina who marched against soldiers because they simply wanted to know the true story of what happened to their loved ones who had been "disappeared" by the state. In China's Sichuan province, enraged parents clashed with police because they wanted the true story of why schools had collapsed during a terrible earthquake. In country after country, writers and journalists have been jailed simply for seeking out the truth. In South Africa, postapartheid, the new leadership realized that more than prosecutions and prison sentences, the population just wanted to know the truth of what happened over those bloody years, and thus the Truth and Reconciliation Commission was established. The truth wasn't going to bring back those disappeared Argentineans, or the children who died in the earthquake, or the victims of apartheid; yet people were willing to risk their lives for it. We *need* it.

Westerners might not fully appreciate how prized a commodity a "true story" is in parts of the world where denial of the truth is a regular part of life. In the United States, we surely accept a certain amount of dishonesty from officialdom. But if your best friend dies in America, chances are the story will come out somehow. Detectives, medical examiners, judges, district attorneys—all are out to expose the truth in a public forum, which maybe we take for granted. But then something happens like, say, the tragic death in Afghanistan of football pro–turned–soldier Pat Tillman. His death was mischaracterized by the military as a hero's story. But his family did not want the official story. They wanted to find out the sad and mundane fact that he had been killed by friendly fire. The true story is what ultimately honors the individual, allowing him to live in dignity and die in dignity. It is human nature to pursue it, even at the risk of a painful revelation. Though not every woman who suspects her husband is unfaithful would care to know the truth about his indiscretions, a great many would—even at the cost of a ruined marriage.

But in much of the world, pursuing a true story can be deadly.

"I am Moroccan!" Bari cried. That was how he explained that he wasn't afraid. It was not, on its own, an expression of religious faith, and he has made clear already that it is no vote of confidence in the police of Precinct 5. He seems to believe in something that isn't God, the government, or himself. He trusts that his nationality will keep him safe in his pursuit of the true story of Ibrahim Dey's murder. He believes that the ties binding Moroccans to each other are not so fragile as police would have me believe. I wonder what it is about Bari's identity as a Moroccan that would imbue him with so much confidence.

Millions of people from different ethnicities, spiritual backgrounds, and clans do not easily come together to embrace a single national identity. Often enough, they do not manage to come together at all. The social fabric of Morocco was woven from roughly the same mixed cloth as neighboring Algeria's, for example, and stitched into a flag at around the same time. Both nation-states fought off the same Western occupier; neither has gone on to achieve democracy since then. But how many Algerians would invoke their nationality in the face of an Algerian police conspiracy, real or imagined? Fewer, I would guess, than the 150,000 who were killed by their government over a recent decade of civil war. Algeria is wealthier than Morocco to boot—yet it seems to be Moroccans, in their poverty and squalor, who have the greatest faith in their shared identity. Some would attribute this to the differing powers that rule North Africa. Though its modern history is brutal, Morocco is a monarchy with a three-hundred-year-old lineage in a neighborhood of young military dictatorships. Memory and tradition, in a traditional society, can go a long way.

But in getting to know Bari, I detect other reasons for the resonance of Moroccanness within him—reasons a little closer to the tin-roofed huts near his neighborhood in Precinct 5, reasons that might explain both his hunger for a true story and the courage he displays in wanting to pursue it. In the country's modern urban areas, in the shantytowns and slums where so many first learned to see each other as children of one nation, the social fabric was not woven by a king or a president. It wasn't woven by the French, the British, or the Americans, either. It was poor rural migrants, in fact, people like Bari and his friends—hurled together in the human cauldron of Casablanca's Al-Hay al-Muhammadi district—who negotiated the tapestry of postcolonial Morocco, fought it onto a flag, and spread the new identity far beyond their huts. They learned to believe in Morocco, having helped invent it. They invented it by weaving together an idea called Morocco out of the stories they told to each other. They continued to believe in the country they had dreamed up together, even after the man who ruled it let them down.

They came, on the promise of factory jobs, from corners of a map that had not been drawn yet: shifting sand dunes of Saharan desert to the south, tiny red stone villages on the trail out of Arab cities to the north, the green plateau of Bin Sulayman due east, the waterfall-gushing Atlas mountains cutting diagonally across to the northwest. Some of the newcomers were descendants of West African slaves who had been bought and sold centuries earlier by now defunct medieval dynasties. They still danced and prayed to a spirit world in which their ancestors watched over all life. For their skin color they were dubbed Gnawa—a Berber word for "black"— by Bari's people, the Berber mountain dwellers of the south, who came to the city thinking of themselves as white. Arab Moroccans, who migrated out of strongholds in the north, east, and center, claimed lineage from the Arabian conquerors, who had first spread the message of Islam to Berber and slave alike. But their progenitors long ago had lost control of how Islam was practiced, and now a thousand flavors of mystical dance, ancient magic, and freewheeling metaphor had been infused into the rituals of their faith.

These peoples, languages, and cultures met by the quarries, sweatshops, and production lines of Casablanca—over biscuits, butter, sugar, and glass; ironwork, wool, silk, and wax. In the filth of their ramshackle lodgings, they exchanged harrowing tales about their European taskmasters, prayed together in improvised mosques, and, on their one day off from work each week, listened to each other's memories of home.

Moroccan Jews, locked in their ghettos, were largely missing from this new melting pot.

Back in the early thirties, when "Hoovervilles" were cropping up in Depression-era America, the shantytown crowds of Al-Hay al-Muhammadi gathered around neighborhood performers in little circles called *halqat*—vaudeville without the stage and ticket windows. Every distant homeland had its local minstrel troupe. From the High Atlas valley, women shoulder to shoulder in multicolored robes would sway in rhythm, slowly picking up speed, to a Berber folktale sung in verse by drummer men. Some of their stories recalled the ancient hero Antaeus—strong as a rock while his feet were planted on his native soil, weak as water once lifted into the air. In the next show over, from the east, a one-stringed fiddle would join a trio of turtle shell mandolins to accompany the metered epic

of an Arab bard. He would sing torrid Arabian verses about the
star-crossed lovers Layla and Majnun, whose tragic story teaches
that love is the most powerful and irrational force in the human
soul. Meanwhile, just down the road, the oldest musical scale in
human history—the pentatonic—would give groove to a band of
whirling Gnawa dancers and their lead singer, wearing indigo blue,
in a seven-part Technicolor re-creation of the birth of the universe.
There were stand-up comics like the legendary Sheikh Ali, whose
terse little tales spoofed hearty Bedouin migrants getting outfoxed
by shifty-eyed city slickers. Herbalists and cuppers peddled cures
for every ailment; sorcerers saw the future and communed with invisible spirits across from prim Qur'anic preachers who railed
against this "pagan" magic. It was a thousand years of heritage and
storytelling in a slum—a trash heap of diamonds and gold.

Most of the audience, predictably, favored performers from their
own birthplaces; they gathered around the fables they knew, to ease
their longing for a far-off homeland. But a growing few, especially
the young, took to buzzing like bees from one folklore bouquet to
the next. In tasting from the various shows, they could digest something profound: that shared ideals of love, honor, and faith resound
across the dividing lines of color and language. It was one big racket
every Saturday, anyway, that boomed unnoticed by the other side of
Casablanca, where Sam played piano for Humphrey Bogart and
Ingrid Bergman. For those who listened in each week as the years
went by, it was possible to faintly hear the disparate tales of the
shantytown coming together.

Ultimately, the audience came together in blood.

After the Second World War, when Sultan Muhammad V spoke
out against French rule, the neighborhood of Al-Hay al-Muhammadi
rioted for his throne. They chanted slogans in each other's languages and threw bombs named after their respective primordial
heroes. French forces exiled the young sultan to Madagascar in
1951, but the ranks of his fighters across the shantytown only
swelled. The mosque preacher and the witch doctor railed as one
against a common enemy. The rainbow of Saturday *halqat* show-

cased new stories set to music—about the return of a king, freedom for a nation—the ancient prophecy of good over evil starring a modern cast of characters. A legion of dirt-poor dervishes fought for a land they had only seen in parts but had learned to conjure as a whole in costume, rhythm, and rhyme.

The king came home in triumph to rule and built a grand mosque named after himself at the edge of the slums. He put up a center for youth culture and a hospital with an emergency ward, and he promised democracy and prosperity to the people who lived nearby. Al-Hay al-Muhammadi, he declared, was the beating heart of a new, free Morocco.

Kings know better than anyone else, of course, that so many strands of storytelling and ancient truth can as easily recombine to serve another master.

Poverty and unrest never left the vast neighborhood, but more waves of rural migrants kept gushing in—a population explosion amid the turmoil of a newly formed state. In the 1960s and '70s, homegrown enemies of the monarchy emerged—socialists, Arabists, dissenters within the army—for whom the story of how Morocco came together was a useless myth, a fairy tale manipulated by a king to justify his monopoly on power. But they had stories of their own about what was right and just, and they tried to spread them. These dissidents came knocking for support on the same old tin-roofed huts. Whoever let them in did not survive in town for long; there were disappearances and summary executions by state security in the dead of night, forced dispersions of entire neighborhood blocks to far-off parts of the city and beyond. You might lose a best friend and face enormous pressure never to ask after him. You could watch a neighbor die and fear a similar fate just for telling others. New protests routinely met the rifle fire of the Royal Army, though the roots of discontent ran deeper than bullets could reach. In June 1981, a leftist coalition organized area youth against the government's price hike on basic foodstuffs, notably bread. Thousands of slum youth in Al-Hay al-Muhammadi rioted for three days and nights. This time police and the army put down the unrest with machine guns and tanks. Hundreds are believed to have been killed, thousands maimed.

If you were any kind of nationalist, you had to wonder what it meant to be Moroccan now, when killers and their victims all waved the same flag. So the shantytown capital, in its richness, dusted off the ancient treasures and found an answer.

Nas al-Ghiwan, Morocco's best-loved band, was formed on the turf of Precinct 5 during the bitter "Years of Lead"—the age of Vietnam and "flower power" on the other side of the Atlantic. Its early members were mainly children of the slums who had grown up wandering with open ears from one Saturday *halqa* to the next. Umar Sayyid, the son of Berbers from the mountain south, beat the *darbukka*. So did Arab songwriters Boujema Hagur and al-Arabi Batma. They were later joined by Abdel Rahman Pako, an esteemed Gnawa singer and instrumentalist. They practiced in the back room of a tailor's shop with a poster of Charlie Chaplin in the front window, sewing machines clacking—and emerged with a seamless fusion of their component parts in sound. They wrote songs about love, faith, brutality, and corruption, and they set out to deliver "a message to all Moroccans," Umar Sayyid recalls, "that would echo around the world." If four boys from Liverpool could do it, why not a crew from Casablanca? They hoped to resound with as much truth as any world-class rock band—as if differences over truth in Morocco could actually be aired without fear. Nas al-Ghiwan had the courage to try, though often, of necessity, they told stories in cryptic language.

A bee, for example—a queen bee, at that—flew off to see a human king one day. A favorite Ghiwan song about their conversation describes how honestly and efficiently her hive was run: "There isn't a single greedy official to deceive me," the queen bee boasts in verse. "I have students of justice in my service, and God protects me from every cheat." The king tells her in confidence that he is not so lucky, and she flies away sadder and wiser about human affairs: "The king is a doctor," she concludes, "and his people are wounded, yet there is not a single government official who will tell him of their plight." The song exonerates a monarch for the suffering of the population even as it takes a dig at his regime—a suitably ambiguous critique for a dangerous, conspiratorial establishment.

In a chiseled old Andalusian style of Arabic, Nas al-Ghiwan's lyrics gave new voice to the joy and pain of being Moroccan and made an epic out of the journey of rural migrants into the sea of urban living. "I've gone and left it all behind," a beggar sings in a blueslike Ghiwan verse. "I've gone and left it all behind, though my family and loved ones didn't want me to go. But I just know I did not fall into this ocean by chance." Even without translating the words, you can hear the edgy determination of a displaced newcomer in al-Arabi Batma's stinging lead tenor voice. You can hear Africa in Pako's pentatonic banjo riffs, Arabia in Hagur's terra-cotta drumming. They made themselves into one *halqa* for an entire nation. Their sound filled stadiums across Morocco, and won a fan base in the royal family itself, by preaching universal values to everybody, powerful or weak. "Oh, children of man," they sang, "why the lying? Why the slander? Why the fighting? Why the tyranny?" Their bootleg cassette tapes spread into Algeria, Tunisia, and Libya. Within a few years the band had played to millions in North Africa, the Gulf, Syria, and the Moroccan diaspora hub of Paris. Jimi Hendrix sought out Pako for a legendary jam session on his visit to the southern Moroccan city of Sawira. Martin Scorsese used the band's tribute to a founding member who had died, "Ya Sah," in the soundtrack to his film *The Last Temptation of Christ*.

None of these achievements, to be sure, have caused Berber, Arab, Sahrawi, and Gnawa to forget their differences, let alone transformed Morocco into an especially enviable state. In the twenty-first century, the turf of Precinct 5 is a more cramped, polluted place to live in than ever before. *Halqat* no longer gather crowds on Saturdays, either. Eyes are glued, indoors, to Al Jazeera news and sports instead, and the mythology that captivates cabdrivers and slum youth is the same shadow play of America and al-Qaeda, Palestinians and Israelis, that unnerves and polarizes the region. Left-wing militancy that was once out in the open has been supplanted by right-wing Islamist groups with underground explosives factories. There are vicious drug cartels in Morocco, as Bari seems to know, and the slums are filled with drug addicts and alcoholics, as I have witnessed myself. For all I know, it may be no less risky or foolish to open up a sensitive murder case in Casablanca than in Damascus, Tripoli, or Khartoum—whether the Moroccan police have actually been lying to us or not.

And yet Muhammad Bari wants to know the true story of why his best friend died. His desire resembles so many quests people have undertaken before to pry truth out of a regime that would lock it up forever. I think it's no accident that he ascribes his courage to pursue this quest to being Moroccan. He has seen the stories he grew up with come together to narrate a national identity. He has listened to the Ghiwan weave new stories out of the old to disparage the abuses of the man who ruled the country. Now Bari wants to uncover a new story, a story that reclaims a human life from the darkness; a particular life, apart from the collective, with all its preciousness and fragility. Whether this man's death turns out to be a piece of the larger tale of his people—like the stories of the *halqat* and the verses of Ghiwan—doesn't matter to him. Bari is willing to make this journey at great personal risk, and he is looking for someone to help him.

I believe in the power of a true story, too. I believe in the same kind of friendship, the same sort of memories of a lost loved one, that drive Muhammad Bari. And I believe in anybody who is willing to stick it to an authoritarian system in the name of transparency and truth. Perhaps, as I hope, the Moroccan police will respond kindly to a citizen inquiry of the sort Bari is proposing; it would be a sign of the hoped-for openness and progress that senior government officials have welcomed me here in order to show off. Of course, I'm nervous that they will not respond so kindly—and frightened about doing something that might aggravate the police in a foreign country, being shell-shocked from my prior experience with federal agents back home. Meanwhile, part of me worries that Bari would be better off not knowing the truth about his friend's untimely death, as secrets can be dangerous, or painful to contend with.

Yet I can't think of anything I'd rather do. I want to help this man uncover the mystery and honor the death of his best friend in the world, his fellow Moroccan, his brother in life, the late Ibrahim Dey.

TWELVE

Though my head and my heart have moved outside the precinct walls, my body still shows up for embed duty.

The police are hunting for a missing schoolgirl named Nidal—a runaway, it seems, from something that frightened her back home. At seventeen and a half, she made the fateful decision earlier in the week to have sex with her twenty-five-year-old boyfriend. Her mother found out, and now her uncle knows. Big mistake, Nidal: in underclass North Africa, the honor of a family still rests between its daughters' legs.

It's 10:00 P.M. and cold outside.

Officer Marzuq and a young subordinate stand in walkie-talkie vigil on a paved sidewalk in one of Al-Hay al-Muhammadi's mixed residential strips, under ice-blue lighting from an industrial parking garage across the street. Behind them runs a long white wall with painted-on slogans in Arabic exhorting all Moroccans eighteen or older to vote in the forthcoming parliamentary elections, which took place six months earlier. Behind the wall lies an elementary school. Its principal, sheepishly whispering into a policeman's ear, happens to be the father of Nidal's boyfriend.

"The name of this school is totally irrelevant!" Marzuq warns me, pointing to my notebook. "Consider it a secret."

All right, all right.

Ambient traffic, blocks away, melds into whirring white noise. Every voice on the sidewalk carries clear and sharp into the night air, well beyond the range of its intended audience. I can hear the concerned parties alternately bickering and suggesting possible hiding places for the missing girl. Her mother, bundled up in baby blue and a hot pink headscarf, sizes up the boyfriend, Elias—his hands jammed deep inside the pockets of his jogging pants—and lobs curses at him every so often with a raw onion rasp. He mutters meek, barely intelligible rebuttals into the pavement. The two cops, for their part, are peering keenly at the uncle. The nicks on his clean-shaven, pasty round face glisten ruby red in the pale light.

Hours have gone by. Every hubbly-bubbly bar—otherwise known as a hookah bar—and night café in the precinct has been searched. A call has gone out with the girl's description citywide. It's a waiting game now.

Wherever she is, Nidal has new worries tonight. Having lost her virginity, she has effectively taken herself out of the running to marry a Moroccan man—unless she can cover up her sexual history, as many young women do, or find the rare bachelor who would be willing to overlook it. A more pressing and terrifying concern, meanwhile, is the distinct chance that a male relative would try to murder her in order to redeem the family's good name. The scourge of "honor killings" still runs rampant in rural parts of Morocco and is not unheard of in sections of Casablanca like this one in which mostly rural migrants and their children live.

To help prevent such tragedies, police and the courts work especially hard to reward a girl's family for resorting to the law. Yet even this well-intentioned policy may pose further hardships for Nidal; because she was six months short of adulthood when they had sex, her boyfriend can be charged with statutory rape. The likelihood of his long-term incarceration is greater than it would be for a similar offense in Europe or the United States—and Nidal's legal guardians, not she, will decide whether to press charges. Her parents are divorced; her father, out of the picture. Enormous power, in this situation, lies in the hands of her mother.

"You piece of shit," she tells twenty-five-year-old Elias.

The young man's father overhears the comment and swallows hard.

It is the mother who took away Nidal's cell phone two nights ago. The hunt has been more daunting for its absence from the girl's purse. The police believe the mother also beat Nidal during a heated fight over her big news, and even threatened to kill her. "Kill" might only have been a figure of speech, however—hence the importance the police attach to sizing up the uncle.

There is an obvious, traditional solution to this crisis, assuming the young woman is found alive: marry off Nidal to Elias and turn the night's bickering assemblage into one big dysfunctional family.

"That's how this is going to play out," Marzuq explains into my left ear. "We'll find the girl, that is sure. Nobody can hide from us in this city and certainly not a girl. Next, the mother will simmer down a little. Then the boy's father will come to the house on his behalf and offer the girl a husband and a family. Of course he will. It's either that or the boy goes to prison."

"She doesn't look as if she wants to be his mother-in-law much," I observe.

Marzuq winks. "You just wait. I see her turning them down once, maybe twice, as a matter of pride. But I see a wedding in front of me, brother. I see a wedding like I see you."

The school principal won't talk to me and neither will his son, but Nidal's mother is available for comment. She shares a photo of her handsome daughter flirting into the lens. "The best little lady in the world," she says. "Pretty and God-fearing and smart. I'm not satisfied with that runt to marry her. But enough about him. I hear you are American."

I hustle away to the uncle. His somber gray eyes drag the rest of his head down, like round lumps of lead.

"Our family is a good family," he mutters. "We do not want her ever to see that boy again. He incited her to corruption. She stopped studying because of him and did badly in school. The right man should *raise* her status in this world, not lower it."

I look him over—short, stout, an agitated quiver to his lips—and wonder whether to put him down as a man who would kill for a medieval motive. On the one hand, his talk of Nidal's status "in this world" sounds like an indication that he wants her to live. The further away his musings are from the world to come, the better. He is even concerned for her grades. On the other hand, I don't like the woeful look of mourning in those eyes. For a modern man, there ought to be plenty to worry about tonight, but nothing to mourn.

"Are you saying Nidal's family would reject an offer of marriage from the boy?" I ask him. "Maybe they love each other."

He sighs, slowly. "There are many girls these days who lose their virginity out of wedlock. We know this, of course. For their families it is a test from God. What is needed now is for her to return to the house and obey her mother. I don't want to even think about anything else."

"This is a good man," Marzuq cuts in, locking his arm around the uncle's shoulders. "An honorable man. We are going to stay in touch with him, look after him and his family. We in the Judiciary Police are going to personally look after their dear girl as if she were our own sister. You understand? In Morocco, all men are brothers."

The uncle's posture crumples into the crush of Marzuq. His cheeks flush pink, and shyly he begins to cry.

"The tears of an honorable man," the cop adds. "A civilized man."

An hour later, the mobile unit is still combing the city.

I walk back to headquarters on my own and drop in on Lieutenant Jabri, busy with paperwork, who has been informed about the case.

"Where do you think the girl is hiding?" I ask him.

"A girlfriend's house, maybe. She'll go anywhere now. You—" he points—"if you offered to let her stay in your place, she would go. Ah, you know, these problems are very common. And it's never a good idea to get too caught up in any one crime, if you can help it."

I probe his eyes. He might as well be wearing shades.

He has reading glasses on. They are drifting down his nose. He pushes them back up.

"Marzuq told me he's sure that the girl's mother will agree to marry the two of them off," I tell him. "But honestly, it doesn't look that way to me."

He acknowledges, with a been-there nod, the possibility that Marzuq is mistaken. "The mother may be the type to abuse the power that has suddenly fallen into her hands," he says. "The power to send a boy she never liked to prison. We are familiar with such cases."

"You would let that happen?"

His eyes explore the sooty window beside him.

"Maybe God won't let it happen."

"Sorry?"

He twists his right hand ninety degrees, as if he were turning the knob of a very old machine.

"Perhaps we will discover there was some confusion with her national identification card, for example, and it turns out Nidal was eighteen after all."

His eyebrows leap and land and meet a new twinkle in his eye.

The police, I hope, will be too busy, too beleaguered by the continuous drama of Precinct 5, to bother about my slipping away for hours or days at a time.

Word will presumably reach them, sooner or later, that Muhammad Bari and I are snooping around their jurisdiction to reinvestigate the murder of Ibrahim Dey—and if they decide to stop us, they undoubtedly can. I am betting nonetheless that the goodwill I have accrued with Chief Sharqawi and his lieutenants will serve to soften their objections. I have praised their performance in the Dey case, after all, as "a model police investigation." They ought to indulge me a little space at least, if only so I can properly understand the context of their hard work. Should Sharqawi question me about the time I spend with Bari, I will try to justify it as research into the social impact of a poor man's death. In any case, I'm far from certain that anything we uncover would actually trouble the police.

Bari lives with his wife, eight children, and a litter of kittens in a $26-a-month clay and concrete flat, shielded here by a pockmarked ceiling and there by an ingrown pomegranate tree, off Shifshaouni Street near the roundabout of Ayn Sabaa. Pomegranate season is months away, and dry leaves are drifting slowly onto the cracked linoleum floor. The kittens, a recent addition to the household, were discovered by Bari's seven-year-old daughter in the back alley outside their entryway the night after Ibrahim Dey was found dead. Bari came home from a grueling day of police interrogation only to meet the girl's fervent plea to adopt the tiny creatures and their mother. Wearily, he stuffed some cushions into an old packing box. The five of them have been sleeping, nursing, and feasting on bones and scraps ever since. "I like sharing our home with another family," he explains. "It lightens my spirit to watch them grow."

His youngest girl, home from school, skips across the linoleum floor, thumbs tucked under the shoulder straps of her backpack. Bari sweeps her into his arms, his mouth open wide like a hungry bear, and she squeals into the air on liftoff. He parts her auburn hair and finds a kissing spot on her forehead, then releases her to skip away, like a fish too small to eat.

A meal is prepared by Bari's wife, whom modesty prevents from leaving the kitchen. Two of her boys lug the food out on a giant tin *siniya:* a plump chicken, stewed whole with seven vegetables, all piled over a gleaming mound of couscous. Bari flakes off pieces of juicy dark meat with his right hand and brings them straight to his lips, chewing in silence.

I twist off a wing. I watch his two young sons walk back into the kitchen and think of my brother when we were kids, and my mother's cooking.

"What caused those scars down your temples?" I ask after a while.

He is not shy about telling the story—not even over lunch.

As a nine-year-old in Tarudant, a sun-drenched village in Morocco's southwest, he suffered from an eye affliction that made bright light painful. The local remedy back then was to bleed the edges of the eye sockets by cutting into them with a silver knife, then rub the wounded area with various herbs. "My uncle, God have mercy on him, performed the operation," Bari remembers proudly. "He cured my eyes, and praise God, gave me the health and the courage to come to Casablanca and start a new life."

He was only thirteen when he made the journey north, on a bus full of Berbers with chickens in their laps. He did not know anybody in Casablanca until he arrived. Like most rural migrants in the 1960s, his only schooling had been reading lessons from a preacher, in the otherworldly Arabic of the Qur'an, along with the wisdom of Berber proverbs, quoted by parents to their children on a need-to-know basis. Yet Bari felt confident he had everything he would require for the big move: gumption, faith in God, and a strong young back. He was right: by the time American troops invaded Baghdad, forty years later, he had worked his way up from peddling baked goods on the street to operating an enormous oven that supplied bread to a dozen corner grocers. He had fathered six children by a Berber woman, divorced, married again, and raised a bunch more. He was far from wealthy, but he enjoyed the dignity of an independent living.

Ibrahim Dey, to him, was a humble man from the old country who had not been as industrious or as lucky—one of several to whom Bari gave a sack of day-old bread now and then and with whom he shared memories, in their mother tongue of Shilha, over a cup of wild oregano tea.

"Someone told me he was *majdub*," I point out.

"Yes, it is true. If you showed him generosity or kindness, God had a way of rewarding you. It was always a good idea to share something with him, and if you lived around here, he gave you plenty of chances to help him out. He would show up in the café and place his Qur'an, a mobile phone, a string of prayer beads, and some business cards on the table as if he were arranging a workspace. He crossed his legs like a real businessman, and he always tried to do real business, but most of what he did was watch people—watch them and wait for an opening in their conversation. In particular, I noticed that he liked to watch *me*. I used to wonder why."

"Did you ever ask him?"

"He told me on his own. We were sitting together and he said he had had a dream about me. I said to him, 'A good dream, I hope.' 'A good dream indeed,' he said. 'I dreamed that we were going to be close friends.' "

One spring morning, Bari recalls, he left the bakery to pick up his daily pack of cigarettes. Suddenly he felt a cutting sensation in his stomach—an unbearable, incessant pain that sent him wailing home to bed. A fever came next, and it wouldn't leave. "I checked in to the Muhammad V Emergency Ward and went through a series of tests," he explains. "The doctor told me I had cancer. It was going to kill me for sure, he said. They sent me on to Ibn Rushd hospital. The doctor there prescribed radiation therapy, but the cost was twelve thousand dirhams—far beyond our ability to pay."

Bari sighs, cradling his stomach. *In his heart a man may plan his course*, he recites, *but God determines his every step.*

"How did you survive it?"

"I didn't believe I would. I grew too sick to work. My oldest son was too lazy to run the bakery in my place. The business collapsed. We sold the oven. My wife had to take a job sewing jeans in a factory. And me, practically overnight I had a new life: my bed, the coffeehouse, the clock on the wall, and the company of Ibrahim Dey."

"His dream came true."

Bari just smiles into his food.

It was a friendship born of mutual need, he tries to explain. The two men filled each other's long hours of idle time. They discussed the local gossip, Bari's family, and Dey's get-rich schemes. They watched satellite television in the café and sifted through left-behind Arabic newspapers, trying to make sense of inscrutable things, like the inner workings of their political system and the mysterious lands beyond Morocco. Like the vast majority of Moroccans, neither of them had ever been outside the country.

"It must be difficult for a hardworking man to get used to sitting around and watching time pass."

He bites into the edge of a bone and chews off some marrow. "I had to relearn the concept of patience. I would tell this to Ibrahim Dey. He seemed to like it when I said so—as if he felt happy that at last there was something he could offer to *me*. Sometimes he would recite proverbs, like *Patience is the key of paradise*. He had a favorite verse of Qur'an on the subject of patience, too. It's the children of Israel speaking to Moses. 'Surely,' it went, 'surely we will stay here sitting.' "

"Is that a verse about patience? I thought it was about the settlement of the Holy Land."

"To us it meant that we were sitting in the coffeehouse and that was where we were going to stay."

His silly grin softens the wrinkled grooves along his cheeks.

"Our time together always gave me a feeling of relief. He took my mind off the fear of leaving this beautiful world too soon. What's more, I think he saved my life. He helped me find the cure to my sickness."

"The cure for cancer."

He nods solemnly.

"I didn't know there was one."

It was a few weeks into their daily sessions in the café, Bari explains, that Dey made a suggestion. For the price of a long bus ride, he said, Bari could go see his uncle, the mountain healer, and find a traditional treatment that might work even better than radiation therapy. Bari hadn't thought about his uncle in years—and in this city, it had become popular to dismiss the folk healers of his childhood as frauds. But he took the advice and rode home to Tarudant. He found the old man, who turned out to have retired from the field of health care and gone nearly blind himself. He hadn't taken a knife to a boy's temples since the early seventies, when the practice was banned by the government, Bari recalls. Anyhow, there was still an encyclopedia of ancient medicine between the old man's ears. Bari told him what was wrong and he listened patiently.

"He had a cure."

"My uncle was a very special man, God have mercy on him. He told me to get three dead owls from the market and burn them whole—feathers, bones, and all—burn them to a black crisp. Spoon the ashes three times a day, he said, swallowing a little and rubbing some more onto the tumor itself. So I went to the Jmi'ah market—"

"What's that?"

"It's an outdoor market that sells animals, living and dead, and potions and ointments and everything you would need. I went there and I bought three owls, and I burned them and I followed my uncle's instructions for a month. Praise God, it worked. On top of everything else we actually have a cure for cancer in this country, would you believe it, and the cost is practically nothing!"

I roll my eyes at his outrageous claim and spy a curved shard of peeling paint on its way down from the ceiling.

As if to volunteer hard evidence, Bari removes his trench coat and lifts three layers underneath. His soft, wrinkled belly shivers in the drafty sitting room. I see the remnants of a black wound the size of a prune, just below the navel. Having made his point, he pushes the layers of his clothes back down without bothering to tuck them in.

"The recovery was very slow, of course. There were many long months of prayer and weakness and fear."

"Once you were cured," I ask, "did you try to go back to work?"

His eyes twitch and the smile melts away. "I am too old now," he says. "Look around." He waves his left hand vaguely in the air. "The city is full of young strong men who are out of work themselves." He reaches over to tap my notebook with his index finger. "It will be nice to wake up in the morning with a sense of purpose again, praise God."

The chicken carcass is hauled away, and tall glasses of laban— pungent liquid yogurt—come out on a smaller tin siniya with slices of pound cake.

"Can I pay my compliments to the chef?" I ask.

"She does not visit with male guests."

"Not even in the presence of her husband?"

He shrugs. "It's just the principle I established when we got married. That's the way it has always been."

The way it's always been, I marvel—even now that she provides for Bari and all his children. In my mind I weigh a confrontation over this point, but decide to put it off.

Couscous-induced languor sets in for both of us, aggravated by a rooster crying out somewhere over our heads. For big-city poultry, it's always the crack of dawn.

"So how do we uncover the truth about this murder?" I ask.

Bari straightens his posture. He knits his eyebrows and stares hard into the wall. There are a few false starts as he struggles out loud to devise a plan of action. "We will cross-check every clue," he says. "We will question all the suspects. We will leave no stone unturned." Then he enumerates a few planks of yesterday's hazy conspiracy theory: "Lieutenant Jabri, we will find, cut off the investigation prematurely. The Jew Toledano, we will learn, has influence over the government. The army is corrupt and involved with the drug cartels, and so of course the soldier was for hire."

I am waiting for marching orders, and all I'm getting is cop show one-liners and Al Jazeera–inspired hunches.

"Think back," I suggest. "Did something actually happen to make you feel the murder was plotted by someone?"

He moves his jaws in contemplation, as if he were chewing gum.

"Ibrahim Dey had a dream a few weeks before he died," he says. "It sticks in my mind. It must have meant something."

I join him in sitting up straight. I think he is about to tell me something important. "Ibrahim Dey talked a lot about dreams."

"Not really," he says. "Not to me, anyway. That's why it sticks in my mind."

"All right."

"He dreamed he was with his uncle, who is dead, and his cousin, who has fled the country, in the coastal city of Jadida where they grew up together."

"The police file didn't say anything about another city. It said he migrated from the mountains with his parents and grew up in Casablanca."

He shakes his head. "Ibrahim Dey left his father's house when he was twelve or so and moved to Jadida. That's where he grew up, with an uncle and a cousin on his mother's side. He always had problems with his father. In this dream, anyway, there was a pot of money and a scale. The uncle measured out equal amounts for Ibrahim Dey and his cousin. Ibrahim said, 'May I have a little more?' So his cousin said, 'Here,' and gave him everything."

"How did he feel about this dream?" I ask.

"He wanted to know what it meant, of course. It confused him."

"What do *you* think it meant?"

He looks up at the pomegranate tree.

"Probably it was a warning to him from God," he says. "Probably something dangerous was coming to him from his past in Jadida. The scale—that's a sign of the Day of Judgment. You know what is the Day of Judgment."

I certainly do.

I'm moved by Bari's belief that God speaks through dreams. My biblical namesake, Joseph, would have agreed with him. A psychoanalyst, on the other hand, would be more interested in what Ibrahim Dey was trying to tell *himself* through the dream. If Dey had been a middle-class Westerner, he could have picked apart his night visions with a paid professional and tried to gain insight into his innermost struggles. I wish I knew what those struggles were. Now the trail of the dream has run cold—unless of course, as Bari believes, the source of the dream is the living God.

"Maybe the dream is a sign for us as well," he suggests. "We should go and see his surviving relatives in Jadida. It's only a two-hour train ride from here."

Like a drive from Providence to New Haven with a little traffic, I muse. What choice do we have, anyway, but to treat Dey's dream as our first clue?

The family may know something about a past travail that had been on Dey's mind toward the end of his life, we agree. Bari says the parents live a short walk from here. If we can win their trust, perhaps they can open doors to the more distant relatives.

"The parents will lead us to the relatives, and the relatives will lead us to the answer!" Bari exclaims.

He tucks the shirt layers back into his trousers and puts his trench coat on. He shuffles out the front door and up the alleyway toward the main drag of Shifshaouni Street. I tag along behind him.

Alas, we do not get very far. There is a man waiting for us on the corner. A big man.

"Baaariii. You are making a mistake."

Black coat, black slacks, and horn-rimmed gunmetal glasses off-set the glare of a golden tooth jutting out past his scowl. His triple chin jiggles between the syllables of Bari's name, but from the neck down his massive frame stands boulder still. At length he swivels his head, shutting one eye and aiming the other at me.

"You," he hisses in Arabic, drawing a deep asthmatic breath through his nose.

I feel the yogurt I drank burning in my stomach.

"Some secrets are best left unknown," he declares. "Both of you are entering a world that you have no capacity to deal in or understand."

"What are you talking about?" I toss out. I hear my own voice tremble.

His eyes narrow, and he whispers, "Ibrahim Dey."

Bari puts a hand on his meaty right shoulder and tries to warm him up a little. But the boulder man won't have it. He, too, quotes the Qur'an, pointing an index finger between Bari's eyes: *Do not take the Jews and the Christians as allies.* He points his other index finger at me.

Suddenly I remember where I am. I remember *who* I am. I can hear my pulse throbbing inside my ears.

With both fingers blazing in the air, the man turns his back to us and marches away.

I catch my breath. "Who the hell was *that*?"

"Around here we call him Muhammad of Ayn Sabaa. Nobody knows his last name. But it is generally agreed that he knows a lot of things."

"How does he know what we're up to?"

Bari shrugs again. "He knows."

"But we haven't even done anything yet!"

"Look, don't worry. He says things like that to people all the time."

THIRTEEN

My west Casablanca apartment is far enough away from Bari's neighborhood that I no longer feel spooked by Muhammad of Ayn Sabaa when I get home by taxi around midnight.

My mind returns to Ibrahim Dey's dream.

It's only 7:00 P.M. back in Providence, Rhode Island, my hometown. Julia, an old friend who is in graduate school for psychology and takes particular interest in the interpretation of dreams, would be just finishing her work for the day. It occurs to me to call her on her cell phone and ask for some professional advice on the dead man's behalf.

"Obviously we can't really do this without the participation of the dreamer," she says. "Tell me what you know about him, and tell me exactly how the dream was described."

We walk through the dream in light of what I've learned so far, sticking as close to Bari's telling as possible.

Julia observes that Dey's vision of a reunion with an uncle who is dead and a cousin who has fled the country suggests, on the face of it, that he yearned to be with family, especially given that a gathering with these two relatives was not possible. The fact that money figures prominently in the dream could simply reflect a constant pre-occupation with money—though what money means to a poor man in Casablanca would be different from what it means to a Westerner. She adds that Dey plays a passive role in the dream: he waits for his portion of the money to be doled out; he asks whether he can have some more. "He's not an active agent," Julia says. "He's waiting to receive. He could have said, 'I want it,' or just taken it, but instead he said, 'May I have a little more?' " The fact that Dey and his cousin are divvying up the money suggests that the two of them had a relationship more akin to siblings, she notes.

"What's the most striking thing to you about the dream?" I ask her.

"He's controlling this primitive urge to want more," she replies. "The ending of the dream where he gets it all is immature, like the child's fantasy that he's going to get every toy in the toy store. He's conflicted over asking for more, but there's this magical ending where he gets it all anyway."

I thank her for her advice and say good night.

So whatever qualities Dey and Bari might have had in common, it would seem that chutzpah wasn't one of them. I try to imagine a reverse situation in which it was Dey whom I met after Bari had been killed. If Julia was right that Dey harbored childlike hopes of attaining his treasure without demanding it, let alone seizing it, then it's hard to imagine him summoning the courage to investigate his own friend's death in the brazen manner that Bari wants to do now.

It's bedtime.

Lying under the covers, I continue thinking about my conversation with Julia. I remember that in recounting Dey's dream—she told me to do it as precisely as possible—I forgot to mention the image of the scales. Assuming I wasn't having a premature senior moment, I wonder why I would unconsciously withhold that detail from an old friend.

I fall asleep picturing a big brass scale, lopsided.

The great social imbalance of North Africa is the unjust division of power between Arabs and Berbers. The latter, as I have already noted, are the ancient indigenous inhabitants of the region. They predate the Arab invasions by three thousand years and today number 40 percent of the population in Morocco alone. I seem to be meeting quite a few of them. Muhammad Bari, Sharif the book peddler, Hasan al-Attar the warehouse guard, the ominous Muhammad of Ayn Sabaa, and the late Ibrahim Dey all share this ethnic identity. They grew up in a society in which the culture of their family and rural roots had been systematically marginalized. Even today, none of the three Berber mother tongues is recognized alongside Arabic as an official language in Morocco, and for the first fifty years of the country's history as a modern kingdom, the languages were not taught in schools. Human Rights Watch has reported that scores of Berber parents in the country who wished to give Berber names to their newborns were prevented from doing so by the civil registrars who processed their birth certificates. Local Berber advocacy groups have charged that their proud history, including their distinguished contribution to the spread of Islam in North Africa, has been deemphasized in Moroccan textbooks. Morocco is an Arab kingdom, a member of the twenty-two-state Arab League. As in some of its fellow member states that also are home to large non-Arabic-speaking indigenous populations, Moroccan dynasties have been waging a campaign to "Arabize" the culture for centuries. In fits and starts, Berber activists in modern Morocco have pressed for their own civil rights. But too much activism can turn deadly in an authoritarian state. In neighboring Algeria, for example, "uppity" Berbers have suffered lethal crackdowns by the army and security services. Whether in Algeria, Morocco, or elsewhere, this ancient population has faced the same agonizing dilemma that marginalized peoples do everywhere: risk pressing too hard for their rights and draw a backlash, or simply ask for them politely—passively, like Ibrahim Dey in his dream—hoping for a magical windfall.

Of course there's no way to be sure what a scale and a pot of money meant for Dey on one night of his forty-one-year life. But in the premodern world, these were the symbols of a merchant—and the particular Berber ethnic offshoot to which Ibrahim Dey belonged, the Shluh, have been a mercantile people for a long time. They come from a region called Sous, in the mountains of southwestern Morocco, where the barren, desiccated soil has always been difficult to cultivate. In small valleys here and there, the Shluh have maintained groves of almond, olive, and argan trees alongside modest fields of barley. But the farm yield rarely sufficed. To survive, they turned to the trans-Saharan trade route stretching from "black Africa" into Morocco and tapped other merchant traffic along the Atlantic coast. In years of drought and famine, entire communities of Shluh might desert their farms and head north to the coastal plains of the Atlantic, vying for work as small-time traders. Over the past seventy years, Shluh have migrated in large numbers up to Casablanca and the smaller coastal city of Jadida, where many, like Dey's family, have settled for good. Some Shluh have become wealthy, while a much greater number have found work as shopkeepers and peddlers.

Meanwhile, back home in the southwest, a mix of overfarming, state neglect, and global climate change has conspired to overrun the valleys of the Sous heartland with encroaching Saharan sand dunes from farther south. During each windy season, whether in times of drought or of relative plenty, the sands have circled up like swirling demons and swarmed old patches of green, imperiling the remaining farmers' livelihood. Across the African continent, in fact, this trend of desertification has pushed indigenous peoples by the millions far away from their farming roots and into big cities like Casablanca, Cape Town, and Dakar, where their cultures have spilled into the urban life, whether Arab-, Anglo-, or Francocentric. There has been a sameness to the result: while young people add their energy to the new ways of the city, the pristine memory of the old country slowly fades away. Between parents and their children, the magic of their ancient heritage dries up like the waters of the south—except for the families that strive to preserve their old traditions or maintain a semblance of contact with the homeland.

These are the big trends, anyway. But something remarkable has begun to happen in Morocco more recently: Berbers, sensing that their young king's regime has loosened its grip somewhat, are at last pressing hard for their civil rights. Witness the Amazigh Democratic Party—"Amazigh" being the indigenous term Berbers prefer to call themselves—whose members have boldly reached out beyond Morocco to Kurds in Iraq and Israelis on the basis of their shared status as "marginalized peoples" of the Middle East. The move toward strengthening ties with Israel, in particular, has inflamed Arab public opinion in Morocco, where Islamist and populist voices in the media remain dead set against a formal peace with the Jewish state. Other young Berbers have linked up with the World Amazigh Congress, a transnational advocacy group glued together by the Internet, to lobby against their own country in European parliaments, complaining of their marginalization by the state. These moves have been viewed as incendiary and separatist by Arab elites in the country. They even posed a political threat to the government's agenda in Europe, where Berber lobbying emerged as a potential wedge for European states to use against Morocco as a means of exerting political pressure.

In the face of gutsy Berber activism, the regime faced a dilemma: crack the whip the old-fashioned way, or make concessions to the Berbers that might placate them.

The king has lately chosen to do the latter. In a break with fifty years of educational discrimination, he has permitted the teaching of Berber languages in schools kingdomwide. He facilitated the launch of an all-Berber satellite television channel. He appointed longtime Berber activists to develop national policies to help promulgate the Berber heritage. He appointed new Berber ministers to his cabinet. These concessions may fall short of bringing about the equality between Arabs and Berbers that the latter seek, but they are testimony to the kind of change that is possible when an autocrat's population says "I want it" and even presses for it rather than merely hoping for more. One might say that Bari's quest to learn the guarded secret of his friend's death reflects a similar attitude, and that Dey's personality, as reflected in the dream, more closely resembles the resignation and wishful thinking of Berbers in generations past.

Who can blame a man for suppressing his "primitive instincts to have more," after all, in a system that is designed to deny him more? Brushing my teeth the following morning, I ask myself what happens to a person whose dream of a "magical ending" does not come true in real life. How do these dashed fantasies play out as he goes about the day? Does his resentment stoke the desire to punish those who deny him what he craves? Does he seek to escape the world by squatting in a private space alone? For that matter, if Dey had the opportunity to express himself now, what would he want his friends to do for him to mark his untimely death? Would he really want Bari to dig for the truth? Or would it comfort him more, perhaps, to fall back on the more traditional Berber redress for a murder? In the old ways of the Shluh, for example, there were strict rules for how the rural society would deal with someone who killed a man in cold blood. Five members of the victim's family would be officially designated avengers, with a free hand to track and hunt the killer, as quickly or as slowly as they saw fit. Whether the memory of this traditional system of justice survives among Ibrahim Dey's next of kin remains to be seen. The police, as I have already learned, are keen to see that it is forgotten.

Both parents and a sister of the late Ibrahim Dey share a thatched-roof home of parched red paint, not far from Bari's house, in a maze of matchbox housing called Timseet. The property lies a four-minute walk from the warehouse where Dey slept for years and died, and it has a spare room. Dey could have slept in it, I muse, rather than squat in a warehouse nearby. Perhaps the family didn't want him to. Or perhaps Dey had some special reason of his own for wanting to sleep in a dark, secret space.

Bari knocks on the brown metal door.

"Peace be upon you."

"Upon you peace."

A woman in her forties lets us in. Her headscarf wraps a pale, weary face with thick chapped lips and not a trace of makeup.

"The sister, Fatima Dey," he says.

"Your mourning and our mourning are one," I offer.

She brushes past a string of wet blouses hanging in the entryway and points us into a traditional sitting room. Over the thick, embroidered carpet, a rectangular formation of honeydew-and-white-striped cushions traces the inner wall. Shuttered windows lock in the smell of old age. The victim's mother, Khadija Barrada Dey, sits alone on one of the cushions, in a black veil and heavy brown robe. Three weeks have passed since the killing. A sustained pitch of lamentation flows from her diaphragm—the most tortured sound a mother can make. The father, an invalid who no longer speaks, is orbiting the little entryway in slow motion. His lower jaw sags as if it has been dislocated, and he pokes his head through the sitting room door on every round, looking but never venturing inside.

I watch Bari attempt to break the ice with Mrs. Dey. It's all in the Berber mother tongue of Shilha. She nods, shakes her head, cups her head with the palms of her hands, and returns to sighing.

At length Fatima emerges with translucent crimson cups of sweet mint tea.

"This young man has a relationship with the police," he explains in Arabic so I can understand, "but he isn't one of them. He is trying to learn what happened. What *really* happened."

Fatima nods her head vigorously. Her mother's eyes sparkle wet.

"Of all my brother's friends, Mr. Muhammad, only you have come to check on us, God keep you. Ibrahim had so many friends, God have mercy on him, but where are they now?" She pushes one steaming cup to the space near me on the coffee table and takes a seat across from her mother.

"I wish I could have met him," I tell Fatima. "I feel as if I have his whole life to understand."

Bari asks Khadija Barrada Dey to share some memories of her son, offering to translate from Shilha into Arabic. He speaks to her with his head down humbly and his hands wide open on his lap, as if he were addressing a tribal dignitary.

The old woman, upon request, conjures the scattered fragments of a mother's love and lays them out tearfully in front of us: how soft and sweet the baby was, how gently he played, how little he ate.

Her soaking nostrils flutter like gills in the water. His lack of schooling was not his fault, she insists, and her arms come alive. He lived
in two worlds from an early age—one year in Casablanca, the next
back in the mountains, on and on, back and forth. It was a common
arrangement for migrant families then, she explains; her husband
and his brother swapped turns minding the farm down south, and
their wives and children moved between city and country life along
with them. As a result, the little boy and his sister Fatima missed
every other year of public school in Casablanca, until both dropped
out around fifth grade. But the family held on to the land they loved,
kept it from going dry as long as they could, and took care of their
elders until they died out. And anyway, she notes with a finger in the
air, there are a few things the state does not teach in its schools,
which can only be learned in the mountains of Butabi.

Her eyes flash flame, and her words taper off.

A growl sounds through the door, clearing a throatful of phlegm.
It's the old man again. I spy the prickly white of his beard growth.
He peers inside and presses his hand against the outer wall. His
wife, through her tears, faintly lifts her neck and curls in her fingers.

Fatima makes a smile.

"So after fifth grade," I pretend to confirm, "Ibrahim Dey spent
the rest of his life in Casablanca."

Fatima peers across to her mother and the nearest cup of tea.
"There was a misunderstanding between my brother and our father
a long time ago," she says more softly.

"A misunderstanding," I repeat.

"They did not get on so well. My father was . . . strict." She lifts
her steaming cup of tea carefully by the rim. "Ibrahim worked for
him awhile, in his milk business," she explains. "He had a good
business, milking cows and pasteurizing the milk and delivering it
all over the city, but our father was disappointed in Ibrahim's contribution. He had older sons from a prior marriage, and he always
said Ibrahim did not stack up. Meanwhile we had family on our
mother's side, not far from here, in the town of Jadida. An uncle
of ours had a grocery store, and children Ibrahim's age—a son, a
daughter. We all used to spend time together in the mountains when

we were little. Ibrahim always enjoyed being with them, and so when the time came and he finished with school, that is where he went—to live and work with his uncle and cousin."

"How did he end up back in Casablanca?"

She scans the level of our cups. "You have not been drinking your tea."

"God keep you," Bari replies. "Long live the hands that brewed it."

There's the father again at the edge of the room, looking straight at me. He has mustered the strength to arrest his circular orbit and stand erect by the door. I wonder whether he understands.

Fatima smacks her lips. "Ibrahim spent fifteen years of his life in Jadida. But there was a woman there."

The remark provokes a spark in Bari's eyes.

"This woman drove the family apart," she goes on. "The grocery went bankrupt. I never understood what they were fighting over exactly. His cousin fled the country, to Tunis. Ibrahim came back from Jadida very sad, afraid—afraid of his own shadow."

"He used to speak of a woman to us at the café sometimes," Bari says. "Latifa—am I right?"

"Latifa." The mother nods.

"He didn't say much about her, you understand," Bari goes on. "But once he told me she was evil, capable of doing anything."

Fatima kneads her left hand with her right thumb. "The important thing is that he went there in peace and came back here in peace. Only he left something behind in Jadida, some part of himself that he never got back. That sense, you know, that anybody should have who is still healthy and young—that his whole life is in front of him. He came back and he told us that he was cursed, that someone had put a spell on him. Someone he did not dare to name. Of course we all knew who it was. He said that ever since he had been cursed, he was sick, and weak, and everything he put his hands to would fail."

The old man is growling again now, louder, and tapping on the wall. The mother gets up and marches toward him, closing the sitting room door behind her.

I try to reconcile Fatima's image of a broken, ill-fated man with the reputation Dey enjoyed around town as a hearty free soul, a trusted friend who brought good luck. I look at Bari and wonder whether the same account jars his own memories. He does not seem to register surprise. Then I think of the wishful nature of Dey's dream. It seems to incorporate both facets of his personality.

A boom box blasts an ersatz tune outside. The faintest draft through the window brings the crude smell of poverty into the stately sitting room.

"Do you have a photo of him?" I ask.

Fatima proceeds toward the hallway, leaving the door slightly open and Bari and me alone.

He hunches toward me. "Latifa is the secret to it all," he whispers. "She must be. She knows magic. *She* put the curse on him. You see how Fatima looks so angry when she talks about that woman? We have to go there to Jadida and find her, confront her. It's *very* urgent."

His arms are jittery and sweat is forming around his collar. I can hear a sort of religious fervor in his voice, and I wonder whether to place my faith in it. His theory about Dey's death has suddenly shifted from a grand conspiracy involving drug cartels or terrorists to the realm of family beefs and supernatural powers. I resist any knee-jerk dismissal of his new hunch. In a traditional society, the tangled roots of clan and family are deeply enmeshed in public affairs as well as private lives. For that matter, I could say the same thing about my hometown of Providence.

From a countertop in the hallway, Fatima Dey returns with the only extant photographs, she says, of her brother in life. Two are identical passport photos, snapped against a glossy background of make-believe clouds and a make-believe sky. "These were taken a few years ago," she explains. "He had a dream at that time of visiting Tunis."

I look the passport photo over carefully. A sharp black beard, jutting straight up to the sideburns, primly brackets the wide brown eyes of Ibrahim Dey, lengthening his narrow face. The twin sickles of his mustache meet an olive skin clearing at the ridges below his nose. The hairless region extends around his lips, which appear to be as full and forbidding as his sister's. His eyebrows frame an off-kilter stare into the camera, a combination of beguilement and suspicion. As a foreigner in Morocco, I can hardly imagine putting such a man at ease. I produce a digital camera from my briefcase and snap a picture of the photo.

"Did your brother actually make it to Tunis?" I ask.

"Only his cousin did," Fatima replies. "The circumstances were not happy ones. But he has been there ever since. I think he has traveled from there to Libya a few times, but his new home is Tunis, God keep him."

The mother finds her way back into the room and gently reclaims her seat. Her husband, wherever he is, has stopped circling the door.

There are two more pictures, which I also photograph with my camera, of a younger, happier-looking Dey minding a corner grocery store alongside a beardless man with a warm smile, apparently his first cousin, who clasps two small children between his burly arms.

"The cousin had his own family?" I ask.

"Of course," Fatima replies. "He was married to Latifa."

Khadija Barrada Dey looks down into her lap.

I try to draw the mother out on her recollections of Dey's adult life, but through Bari she tells me in Shilha that the tragedy rubbed away her memories like an eraser on a chalkboard. "Everything is gone," she says, putting her hands around her head again as if it needed to be held down.

I ask Fatima instead what she can tell us about Dey's years at the warehouse.

"He had such a sad life toward the end," she recalls. "We knew less and less about it as time went by. He was living here at first, after he came back from Jadida. Slowly he tried to rebuild his life, doing odd jobs, errands for people, hoping to be paid something. 'Find me a used car for this price.' 'Help me license my new store.' 'Get me through the motor vehicles registry.' He waited for his friends to pay him for his hard work, and often they did not, and he just went on about his business, saying, 'Praise God for what I have.' Years went by and his situation stayed the same."

"But about the Jew's warehouse," Bari interjects.

She appears to demur at first. "The Jew." She smacks her lips. "We don't really know. It started out that he would fill in for the guard there once in a while, and he was proud of that. He had been staying here in our spare room and he would leave for the night to keep watch in that place. 'I have work tonight,' he used to say. Soon he was guarding the warehouse every night, and we almost never saw him again."

Bari puts his hand around my wrist, signaling an opportunity.

"Well, we believe something happened there that police do not want Ibrahim's loved ones to know," he tells them. "We think they are hiding the truth. We are trying to understand why he was killed, and we wonder if you can help."

The mother's sobbing swells. Fatima speaks for the two of them: "We would be so grateful, Mr. Muhammad. We are not powerful people who could hire a lawyer to press our interests, but we would very much like to know why he died."

Within moments, an address is handed us on a piece of orange paper for Ibrahim Dey's family in the coastal town of Jadida, together with the promise of an introduction by phone.

We finish our tea and Bari initiates the ritual of pleasantries that will lead us gradually out the door. Ibrahim Dey's mother whispers something to her daughter as our departure draws close, vaguely grinning. Fatima steadies her mother with a wrist to the arm.

"She wonders, will you be paying a visit to the family of the man who killed Ibrahim, in the same way that you are visiting us."

I look to Bari for a cue. He seems to expect the same from me.

"Is there something you would have us pass on," I ask, "if we do manage to meet them?"

The old woman summons another regal flash from deep inside and lifts her arm at a stiff right angle without trembling. Her reply comes out in Arabic: "I would tell them we are weak, but our Lord is a God of vengeance and He is the strongest of all."

Bari straightens his back. "We will tell them, my sister. And we will do what we need to do."

That comment frightens me. I worry about the consequences of our quest.

The weakest man in the house, Dey's ailing father, groans as if he had something to add.

FOURTEEN

Casablanca is a city of smokers, and the central train station reeks of cheap cigarettes. I find Bari fumbling a Cleopatra between his lips when we meet the following morning, by a magazine kiosk, for our ride southwest to the town of Jadida. He ought to quit, I think, especially since by his own account he stands only three burnt owls away from death by cancer. I weigh delivering a grave health warning to him but decide against it. Which is typical, alas: as a Jewish boy in a Muslim capital, I would like to see many things change that I rarely breathe a word about. I would like, for example, the freedom to thumb my nose at yesterday's ominous stranger, Muhammad of Ayn Sabaa, and tell him to mind his own business about Bari's propensity for "befriending Jews and Christians." But a cautious voice usually gets the better of me. It is preferable not to stir controversy in a dicey environment, I reason; better to stay quiet when a rare cohort like Bari emerges, and let him keep his smoking habit. He is showing himself to be a man of courage and a deft communicator, after all. I may even have to lend him some money next time he wants to buy a pack.

The grubby-windowed train we ride cuts past lush eucalyptus groves and textured farmland on the two-hour route to Jadida. It has new, upholstered seats in the first-class cabin but an old-fashioned urinal that spills onto the train tracks beneath. We have a whole car nearly to ourselves. Bari hunts the other seats for leftover newspapers and comes back to our table with the yield, beaming into the sunshine and basking in the thrill of his first-ever field expedition. "Now I feel like Columbo," he says, referencing a popular American TV detective series of the 1970s. The last time he visited Jadida, a popular weekend getaway for Moroccans in the coastal center of the country, was years ago. He adds that he started watching *Columbo* decades ago when reruns of the program with Arabic subtitles reached Moroccan national television. Cops I have met in Casablanca have also credited *Columbo* as their inspiration to join the police force.

"I don't feel like Columbo," I tell him, "but I do feel a little like I'm on vacation."

Bari smiles, admiring the cloud-cloaked sky through the window. "See how mysterious is the will of God," he says, raising a cupped hand into the air in triumph. "I lost my best friend, and for asking God to redeem his truth I have met you. Perhaps this is a gift of God's fate."

We slow into a coastline of rough-hewn beachfront cordoned off by white concrete. A few dozen teens in jerseys play soccer along the frothing shore. Behind them, a white-paved town of broad sidewalks hugs a centuries-old medina with looming outer walls the color of the sand.

Jadida, which means "new," is a three-hundred-year-old city built around an older Portuguese garrison town. The original purpose of the latter was to defend trade vessels between Asia and Europe from Morocco's terrifying coastal pirates, who plundered in the name of jihad. It was the dynasty that rules today that co-opted the pirates into a more purposeful Muslim army and wrested the town back from the Portuguese. The modern city is a hodgepodge of elegant French façades and younger, drabber buildings sandwiched in between—a place of relaxation for the people of Casablanca, free of shantytown squalor and the pressures of politics and commerce. It also happens to boast the second-largest community of rural migrants from Butabi, the Berber mountain hamlet from which Ibrahim Dey's family hails, after Casablanca itself.

Wading into the street, Bari borrows my cell phone and dials the number off the orange slip we received from Dey's mother and sister. "We are here," he mumbles, ambling across the street to the garden café of a French hotel.

A thirtysomething woman in a tiger knit head scarf rises to greet us: Aisha, she introduces herself, the younger of Ibrahim Dey's maternal cousins. She smiles broadly, in contrast to her relatives in Casablanca—like a woman who has never seen a ghost. "We wouldn't have expected someone from so far away to show an interest in our beloved cousin, God have mercy on him," she says, extending a hand toward me. "It is an unexpected privilege for us," she tells Bari.

I thank her in advance for her willingness to talk. We join her at the table and order tea.

"*I* would be grateful if you could help us," Bari declares. "We are trying to understand the life Ibrahim led as a young man in Jadida."

She pats down the air bubbles in her headscarf and tightens the knot from behind. "But your concern for my cousin," she asks, "is it . . . is it a humanitarian issue?"

Bari lowers his eyes toward his lap, then lifts them up again to lock into hers. "He was my best friend," he explains, "and he had a dream about this place not long before he died. We need to know what it meant to him to be here, so we can understand the meaning of his dream."

Now it is Aisha who lowers her eyes. She begins to fold her arms on the tabletop, which is bad luck in North African folklore, only to release them and let her hands fall slowly from view. "What I know," she offers, "is that he came here a boy and grew up to be a man. And I for one owe a lot to him."

"You were close," I throw in.

"It's not so much that we were close," she says. "He was the kind of person who could do things, even little things that nobody hardly even noticed, that changed the path you were on. Maybe some of the things he did were not so important to him, but they were life-changing for others, including me."

A gentle sea breeze ruffles her headscarf and she tugs at her winter jacket.

"He was barely a teenager when he came here to live with us in the seventies, and my father, God rest his soul, put him to work in the grocery store. He was so grateful to be here. He loved working in the store with his cousin Muhammad, my brother, and he was a hard worker. He took instructions very well. I was a little girl and I used to love just going in there to visit. The way he hauled the boxes in and broke them down outside with so much enthusiasm. The way he served anybody who came in with so much dignity and respect. He had a bright future, Ibrahim. You gave him a structure to sweat in and he could thrive."

Bari nods. "Once he told me he used to be called 'the prince' in Jadida."

"Oh yes, 'the prince,' " she recalls, chortling. "After hours he would smoke a pipe and walk around town like a full-on Saudi prince. Only he *earned* his princely status, unlike the royals from the Gulf who come here to drink. I remember that."

Mint tea arrives with a brick of sugar, which Aisha drops into the pot and stirs vigorously. Bari pours the syrupy green liquid into and out of our little glass cups from on high, foot-length streams of hot tea steaming in the salty air.

"By his twenties he was turning into a real businessman," she goes on. "My father was slowing down, happy just to maintain the grocery store, but Ibrahim took the initiative in suggesting we open a bakery nearby. He wanted my brother to be his partner in the new business, and meanwhile for *me* to take over the grocery store. Would you believe it? Me! It was quite unusual back then for a woman to manage a business in Jadida, but Ibrahim said I could do it. I was a girl in my twenties. He insisted, over the objections of my father, and that is when I started working. In truth, that is when I started to have my own life. I've been working full-time ever since."

"In the grocery store?" Bari inquires. I can tell he is being sly and I'm impressed.

Aisha shakes her head. "We don't own the grocery store anymore. The grocery store and the bakery are gone."

"What happened to them?" I ask.

She samples her tea. "What happened is that my brother got married. He married a woman named Latifa who had ambitions of her own. She is still with us, but my brother Muhammad is gone now and Ibrahim is long gone, and both the businesses have been sold off."

Her bright smile wears thin, and she stares across the street, past the sputtering cars into the ocean and horizon.

"Still with you?" I ask.

"She is the only one in our home with children," Aisha explains. "And she has boys—three of them, from Muhammad. My brother meanwhile has left the country for Tunis. So she is the caretaker of the household now."

"Why did your brother leave?"

Aisha lifts her hands and levels them in the air, then shrugs. "Conflicts, you know? Personal matters that are beyond me. And you know how it is to try to explain a conflict. I could tell you what I understand from the outside, but only God knows all and sees all. You'll meet Latifa, I am sure, and she'll tell you her own stories. But they are just her point of view, and only God knows the complete truth."

"Try us," Bari says.

The woman lowers her gaze to Bari's beard and rubs a finger on the table, as if to erase something quickly. "Well, Latifa, she disliked Ibrahim almost from the beginning. And she had her own designs on these businesses. She wanted to bring her blood relatives into the bakery and force Ibrahim out of it. She got involved in the friendship between the cousins, and fighting started over money. Within a few years the businesses were almost bankrupt. Thank God we had saved enough to keep the house, but we held on to little more than that. Years later my brother is gone and I work for other people."

"This must have been very difficult for Ibrahim," Bari observes.

"When you give your blood for something," she replies, "it's hard to have the reward taken away. The experience was bitter, and it changed him. He looked for comfort in other places. Toward the end of his years here, for instance, I noticed that he was becoming more religious. Once during the last few months of his time with us I saw him listening to a tape on his Walkman and I asked what it was. It was a sermon of the blind Egyptian preacher Abd al-Hamid Kishk. He wanted me to hear it. He was growing more isolated, more lonely, and that tape kept him company for a while. But he needed more than that. Eventually he went back to Casablanca, I guess to try his luck somewhere else."

"Is that the time in his life when he first grew a beard?" I ask.

Aisha nods, a little awkwardly. "But he was never an extremist."

Bari moves his lips as if he were about to join the conversation but apparently changes his mind. His fingers reach into his coat pocket for a cigarette, which he tosses back and forth awhile between his hands.

"You are welcome to come and see our home if you wish," Aisha adds. "I can show you where he lived with us all those years. Would you like to?"

I pay the bill, and we set off.

The late Abd al-Hamid Kishk was one of the most popular Muslim preachers in the Arabic language in the 1980s and '90s. His sermons spread on cassette throughout North Africa and the Middle East. He fiercely opposed peace with Israel and the "normalization" of relations between Muslims and Jews—as if warm relations between the two should normally be abnormal. He railed as well against secular music, which he believed should be banned; Arab secular elites; and the liberalization of women's status and family law in Muslim countries. At the same time, Kishk and his colleagues were voices of piety who exhorted their followers to avoid envy and excess, be kind to their Muslim brothers and sisters, and shun various abominations such as adultery and rape.

I wonder what Ibrahim Dey would have been listening for in his Walkman. Why would a native speaker of Shilha, anyway, pick a voice that spoke to him about God and politics in Arabic? Abd al-

Hamid Kishk would seem a strange choice of spiritual adviser, moreover, for a man who had only a few years earlier inspired a female cousin to run the family store. Then again, perhaps that type of guidance was not what Dey was seeking.

In the late twentieth century, cassette tapes played an important role in radicalizing the Middle East. They first proved their value as a powerful tool in the 1970s, when Iran's Ayatollah Khomeini was still a dissident exiled to Paris by the Iranian monarch. Khomeini used his time away from home to deliver stem-winding sermons against the ruler of his country into the microphone of a tape recorder. The cassettes were smuggled into Iran and duplicated by the tens of thousands. Students and supporters of Khomeini's message avidly sought out the latest recordings. The cassettes indoctrinated a generation, forming the ideological core of the Islamist movement that came to power after the Iranian Revolution in 1979.

A few years later, in the eighties, it was clerical elites in nearby Saudi Arabia who caught on to the trend. The Saudi kingdom was staunchly allied with the United States at the time in supporting the jihad against Soviet troops in Afghanistan. In addition to providing substantial financial support to train and arm the Afghan mujahideen, the Saudi government enabled Arabic-language preachers to reach out to Muslim populations, urging the faithful to join their Afghan brethren on the battlefield. A generation of so-called Afghan Arabs drew inspiration from recorded sermons that were dubbed and distributed in most Muslim countries. Preachers raised the prospect of a divine reward in the afterlife for those who died a martyr's death, and they told stories of glory on the Afghan battlefield. Listening on their Walkmen, young people learned, for example, that the dead body of a holy warrior never decomposed. While Russian corpses gave off a putrid smell, one cleric claimed, the mujahid in death would gracefully fade away—giving off the scent of *misk,* an aromatic oil the prophet Muhammad used to wear when he prayed. Listeners heard the story of a Russian tank that tried to run over a Qur'an in the desert sand. The holy book exploded like a land mine, blowing the tank into a thousand bits.

Some of these recorded sermons did more than hype the war in

Afghanistan. They made the case for a jihad without borders. It was incumbent on the believing Muslim, they preached, to struggle against secular regimes across the Arab and Muslim world and beyond—from Palestine to the Philippines, from Algeria, Tunisia, Morocco, and Egypt to Iraq, and indeed as far west as Europe and the United States. These ideas flowed from the ideological movement that coalesced into al-Qaeda. Thousands of devotees of the strident sermons were inspired to leave their native soil and converge on Afghanistan for training in weapons and bomb making, only to return and wreak havoc back home—or farther afield.

The Afghan battlefield attracted mostly Arabs and Pakistanis, along with smaller numbers of other Muslim ethnic groups. Berber populations in North Africa were among the least swayed by these cassette tapes. As far as I know, Berbers were altogether absent in Peshawar, the Pakistani border town that the so-called Afghan Arabs made their headquarters during the Afghan jihad. I once heard a tape of a Moroccan jihadist cleric bemoaning the absence of Berbers there. Given long-standing ethnic tensions between Arabs and Berbers, their lack of interest could be attributed to a discomfort with a movement that was led predominantly by Arabs. The polemics of jihad would also seem to run against the peaceable style of Islam taught by most Berber preachers to their flocks. In the bloody 2003 attacks in Casablanca for which an al-Qaeda offshoot claimed credit, none of the suicide bombers was a native speaker of a Berber mother tongue like Ibrahim Dey—though some had mixed Arab and Berber roots. On the other hand, there is evidence that in the melting pot of Casablanca, attitudes are shifting these days, and the call of jihad may be more compelling to Berber youth than in the past.

Could a younger Ibrahim Dey have developed an interest in a radical strain of Islam that most of his coethnics didn't care for?

Cassette tapes like those of Kishk led some followers in a different direction: toward the international Muslim Brotherhood movement, which in several Arab countries has purged its armed elements and focused on nonviolent political and social action. Morocco is one such place: the Brotherhood-affiliated Unity and Re-

form Movement, which aims to preach its way to power, has a pragmatic offshoot political party that in 2007 became the third largest
in parliament. In contrast to the armed groups from which Berbers
have been largely missing, the URM and its political offshoot claim
many Berbers as members.

It is hard, on balance, to be an Islamist in Morocco, and many
Moroccans who sympathize with Islamists express their views in secret. The king claims direct descent from the prophet Muhammad
and hence a special leadership status over Islamic affairs. For this
reason, among others, the state does not take kindly to any man
who believes in a rival Muslim ideological claim and has consis-
tently worked to undermine and marginalize the country's Islamists.
On the other hand, it isn't easy to oppose Islamist movements in
Morocco, either. They are very large. They feed on the unpopularity of the government's foreign policy—its alliance with the West, its
support for Palestinian-Israeli rapprochement—and win enormous
sympathy by railing against government corruption and brutality.
The radical ideas about Islam that once penetrated Morocco via
cassette tape now spread more easily and broadly via interactive
websites and satellite television. Even if they are embattled inside
the Moroccan kingdom, Islamist activists enjoy inspiration and solidarity from their brothers and sisters across the Muslim world. Efforts to counter their radical ideas through a more moderate,
homegrown brand of preaching are now at a fairly junior stage,
while the cassette tape revolution is evolving and flourishing.

Ibrahim Dey may have allowed himself to be influenced by the
radical teachings of Abd al-Hamid Kishk, or he may simply have
turned to the cassette for a dose of moral inculcation that he felt he
needed—though I still know of no moral flaw in Dey that would
have justified a guilty conscience. There is a third possibility, too.
He may have listened to Kishk for the same reasons I did earlier in
life. As an American Jew studying Arabic, I have listened to hundreds of hours of Islamist preaching. It was part of my education, to
be sure, but it also stemmed from intense curiosity—wonderment,
even—at this powerful transnational movement with the hearts and
minds of so many Arabs and Muslims in its grip.

So Dey may have been a secret Islamist. He may have been a seeker of knowledge. He may have had a dark side that he sought to excise with a little fire and brimstone. Or he may have been a combination of all three. But it's hard to see how any of these possibilities squares with the passivity that Julia, my psychology graduate student friend, ascribed to Dey in thinking through his dream. Something doesn't add up here, and I worry that what we don't know yet is dangerous.

Down palm-tree-lined Boulevard Muhammad VI, sunlight bares the chalky peeled paint of an old French theater building and the yellow-and-orange-framed windows of a glistening post office. We turn onto a dense commercial strip of popcorn pushcarts, restaurants, and sidewalk cafés, then turn again onto a quieter residential street called Al-Faqih. It is the name, in formal Arabic, for a Muslim legal scholar—but for the people of Morocco, *fqih* with the first vowel dropped also has the colloquial meaning of a man who can work magic.

Aisha's family home is shielded from the street by tall, pink-painted stucco walls and a black steel gate. She unlocks the gate, and as we walk into the vine-shrouded inner entryway, I produce the camera from my briefcase and begin to snap pictures.

At just the wrong moment a buxom woman in a lilac cloak walks in. The heavy scent of *misk* trails behind her as she struts past Bari and me and accosts Aisha in a corner. She whispers something into the younger woman's ear and gesticulates with her right arm. Aisha's smile expands even as her ears and face flush pink.

"No no no!" the woman in lilac calls out to us, shuffling in our direction. "No one gave you permission to take pictures here!"

My fingers turn squishy around the camera and it almost slips to the ground.

"Forgive him," Bari says, venturing toward her. "He is not from here." He examines the faint wrinkles around her lips and surveys the stray strands jutting beyond the bulk of her kinky black hair. Her eyes, in contrast to her olive skin, run a deep shade of blue.

Bari's next few words come out in the Berber mother tongue of Shilha, with a mischievous smile on his face.

The woman thaws ever so slightly and smiles back at him.

"This is my sister-in-law, Latifa," Aisha explains.

I apologize for the camera and restore it to my briefcase.

Latifa loosens her chin and nods. "We can talk," she assures me in Arabic. "You can even come inside. Just no pictures."

Indoors, Aisha disappears into the kitchen while Latifa guides us into a sumptuous, cardamom-scented living room. She makes a quick review of messages scribbled on sticky-pad memo slips on a corner rolltop desk, then sits to face us on an easy chair opposite the couch.

"Why are you so curious about the deceased?" she demands.

"My friend Bari," I offer apologetically, "he cannot rest until he understands why Ibrahim has been lost to him. They were very close friends. And me, I would like to be helpful. He believes that something happened in Ibrahim's life to lead to his murder that night—that it wasn't a simple matter of an anonymous man who wanted his pocket money—and we are trying to figure out what it could have been."

Latifa twirls a tuft of her hair and puts a forefinger gently between her teeth. "You want to know about Ibrahim? He was a homewrecker, for one thing, I can assure you of that."

"No, he wasn't," Bari protests.

"You want to know or you want to know?"

I put a hand on Bari's nearest shoulder and he quiets down.

Latifa crosses her right leg over her left, inclining toward us, and heaves a heavy sigh. The front door jostles open and a schoolboy shuffles in, followed by two more. She claps her hands at them, and the trio line up for a fingernail inspection. Working her way across thirty nails with a connoisseur's eye for detail, she is eventually mollified and sends the three upstairs.

"I can tell you everything about Ibrahim," she continues. "Not in this house, though. We can meet later, just the three of us, and I'll tell you more than you would even want to know. But first you tell me something: you knew him all these years in Casablanca, so, did he ever talk about me? What did he say?"

Aisha emerges from the kitchen with a plate of cut-up cake. Latifa moves an index finger hurriedly over her lips, staring at Bari, then drops her hand and smiles at her sister-in-law.

Aisha joins us on the other easy chair. Hunching over the cake, she points to a slice and looks upward into her sister-in-law's deep blue eyes. Latifa declines.

"Mr. Bari and his friend," Aisha says, "they were inspired to come here by a dream Ibrahim had, God have mercy on him— a dream about Jadida not long before he died. Would you believe it? He never stopped dreaming about us, God have mercy on him."

Latifa widens her eyes and probes Bari more intently. "Tell me about this dream."

"He told me he was back here with his uncle and cousin Muhammad, sitting in front of a scale to divide up some money. The two young men got equal portions at first, but then Ibrahim said, 'May I have a little more?' and his cousin took his own portion and handed it all to Ibrahim."

"You want to know what the dream means?" Latifa says. "*I'll* tell you. It shows that when Ibrahim came here, his family gave him *everything,* without even thinking about the consequences. They gave him money, more than he ever earned. They gave him a place to sleep, they gave him all their love, and what did he do? He squandered it. My husband, he loved Ibrahim more than his parents, more than his sister, more even than his own wife. In the end he fled the country for passing bad checks, he left a trail of debt behind him, and Ibrahim is to blame. My husband never came back."

Aisha massages her thumbs uneasily and compresses her frame, like a schoolgirl held after class.

Latifa rattles on about her estranged husband's failings as a bookkeeper, then rails against Ibrahim Dey's profligate spending. If not for her own intervention to sell the businesses, she boasts, the debt would have escalated and the family would have been forced to sell this house. Whatever it is she wants to tell us in private later on, it doesn't seem that it will be about money. I marvel at the freedom Latifa apparently has to sound off about the family she married into in their own home, in the presence of her sister-in-law. I wonder whether her license to criticize the family comes simply from her having mothered male children. Perhaps, on the other hand, she earned the run of the place by actually saving the household from ruin, as she claims. I remember Ibrahim Dey's warning to Bari about Latifa, that she is "evil, capable of doing anything"—a view essentially shared by the murder victim's mother and sister in Casablanca. Perhaps it was not any wickedness on Latifa's part but her strength as a woman—her willingness to step in and shoulder a man's responsibility—that has been causing a traditional family to speak ill of her behind her back. I wonder, in short, whether I should dislike her or develop a crush on her.

Aisha puts cake slices in front of us on little plates, and a faint smell of wormwood or some other pungent herb wafts in from the kitchen to the angry tone of a whistling kettle.

The question resurfaces in my mind whether Ibrahim Dey might have had the gumption to join an Islamist organization. I think back to the supposed tell-all line in his dream: "May I have a little more?"—rather than "I want more" or simply taking more. Well, now I know more about Dey's life in Jadida, courtesy of Latifa. The family gave him everything he wanted, she says. Maybe all he had to do was ask for more. Maybe in the dream, Ibrahim Dey was being sly.

Around twilight, Bari and I wait for Latifa after a hefty snack of deep-fried smelts at a sandy beachfront café called Les Quatres Dauphins. Ruffled clouds floating briskly into the horizon blush orange and pink between the sunset and a faint crescent moon. Only a handful of soccer players remain to kick their ball around the blustery shore. The Britney Spears song "Hit Me Baby One More Time" blares, distorted, out of stereo speakers in the distance. Bari is sucking his third cigarette for the hour, and the cold ocean wind brings its fumes straight at me.

"I keep remembering that terrible morning in the warehouse," he says in a subdued tone. "The blood all over the stairs and the police everywhere. I just can't get it out of my mind."

Looking into his forlorn eyes, I suppress an urge to cough up the secondhand smoke. "Do you think what we're learning here might actually shed some light?" I ask.

"I don't know. But I tell you, something about Latifa really bothers me."

"Okay," I reply, "but remember not to let it show."

Half a cigarette later, Latifa hustles across the concrete promenade toward us in a thick blood-orange cloak, shepherding an oversize handbag. "There you are," she calls out, and greets me with a peck on the cheek.

Bari stands up, cigarette in hand, and bows his head.

"You know," she says, "that is a disgusting habit and it's going to kill you if you don't quit."

He glares at her mouth without saying a word.

"She's right!" I tell him suddenly, surprised at my own outburst. It doesn't stop: "You have a wife and children to live for! What is this you're doing to yourself?"

He nods vaguely. "Let me finish this one, anyway."

I look to Latifa for another cue, but she just takes a seat at our table. She flips open a laminated menu and puts it down without having read a word. A wave crashes hard along the shore, and we watch Bari take a long drag and put out the cigarette at last. *Now what, Latifa,* I ask her with my eyes. She doesn't even notice that I'm homing in on her. She has hung me out to dry, and I'm crushed.

"Thank you for coming out to see us," Bari mumbles.

She catches the waiter's eye and asks for *nus nus,* Moroccan slang for hot milk and a shot of espresso. "I did not have to come out here, of course," she says, "but I saw you wanted to know the truth about Ibrahim and I knew that nobody in his family was going to tell it to you straight. They are all covering up for him, you see."

Bari positions his long-empty coffee cup symmetrically between himself and Latifa on the table and rotates it slowly in place. "We're interested in knowing the truth, of course," he says.

"Well, the truth is that he was corrupt," she explains, "and he corrupted my husband."

"How so?" I ask.

She clears her throat softly. "Every night for years, he was out with girls," she says. "Girls and drinking, drinking and carrying on late into the night. My husband became his partner in these adventures long before we met, and he never stopped throughout the years of the marriage. With the money from the bakery, they rented an apartment of their own for their escapades. I used to follow them there in secret and watch them coming in and out. I tried to get my husband to stop. I told him the drinking and sex was sapping their energies and doing damage to people's lives, not to mention that it was wasting a fortune, not to mention that it was devastating *me*. But Ibrahim had this power over my husband, and there was nothing I could do."

I think back to the police report's description of Dey as a "good, stable man who performed his religious obligations punctually and did not smoke or take any intoxicant or narcotic."

"Do you know what it means to seduce even one girl out of wedlock in this country?" Latifa asks me. "It's like playing with fire."

Bari reclaims his empty coffee cup from the center of the table and lifts it halfway toward his lips as if there were something left to drink. He puts it down again, smoothing his beard with the other hand. "In all the years I knew Ibrahim Dey in Casablanca," he recalls, "I never saw him with a woman."

Latifa just smacks her lips.

"Do you know some of the girls they slept with?" I ask her. "Who are they? Where are they now?"

"You find those kinds of girls everywhere," Bari cuts in dismissively. "You find them in the coffeehouses, in the nightclubs. In every city in Morocco we have girls looking for adventures. We have prostitutes. It's not a question of who they are."

"Not for you, maybe," Latifa says. "It's different if they're your daughters, or the man after them is your husband. Are you questioning the truth of what I'm saying?"

"Latifa," I interject, "I think he's just trying to square what you said with the picture of the humble, pious man he knew in Casablanca. We even heard that he was listening to cassettes of Abd al-Hamid Kishk while he lived here. Something doesn't fit."

"Listen," she proclaims, "I would travel with you to the mountains of Butabi if you like, to show you the truth about Ibrahim Dey. I am divorced now, and my boys say I can do whatever I want. If you want me to go with you, I'll go."

Bari furls his eyebrows at her, then lifts one well above its rightful place beside the other. Perhaps he is remembering that Latifa's boys are in grade school.

"Maybe everything you're telling us is true," I offer, "only he changed his ways toward the end of his time here."

She stares into the smoldering clouds. "I agree there was a period when he slowed down from his wild nights and became very isolated—the last year or so. I know he used to sit alone in his room at our house for long periods of time. I think he started to regret things when we ran out of money, maybe. That's what always does it. But as for his reputation in Casablanca, I wonder if you know everything there is to know."

Bari steels his eyes at her. "What would *you* know about his time in Casablanca?" he demands.

"Maybe a little," she says coyly. "My brother is a beat cop there."

A soda-and-snack cart rolls by our darkened cabin every few stops on the night train back to Casablanca, and long pauses intersperse an attempt by Bari and me to review the day's yield of information. The fits and starts to our conversation might be a sign of deepening friendship, our having dispensed with the formalities of chatter. More likely, however, they are an indication of discomfort—since each of us has learned something in Jadida that is personally unsettling and awkward to talk through with the other.

What seems to trouble Bari is the impression of a wild, pleasure-seeking side to Ibrahim Dey, which stands at odds with his memory of the ascetic man he knew. He falls short of denying Latifa's claims outright; it was a time in Dey's life, after all, of which he has no first-hand knowledge, and he knows I hail from a culture that is permissive of alcohol and extramarital sex. Instead, he confines himself to casting aspersions on the source.

"I suspect Latifa," he declares.

"Of what?" I ask.

His mouth forms several words that do not come out. "Of what? Look at the way she behaved with us. She has three sons at home and she went out to a café with two strange men. And she offered to travel with us alone to a faraway place. In my country, these are not the actions of a trustworthy woman."

"But her husband left her years ago," I point out. "She has the right to a cup of coffee."

"That doesn't matter; she is still the mother of his sons, and they are still very young. Imagine her traveling far away and leaving them behind for days. And remember what Ibrahim Dey said about her, God have mercy on him—that she is evil, capable of doing anything. She despised him, obviously. I think the family is right that she put a curse on him, at least. And consider that her brother is a cop, while the man who killed Ibrahim Dey is also involved with the police. I suspect her of something, for sure."

"That's pretty thin," I tell him, although I picked up on the same clue. "And besides, is it so hard to believe her claim that Dey had a wild past?"

Bari weighs the possibility, stroking his beard. "I think she is exaggerating about his adventures, for sure," he says. "But yes, why not, everyone has regrets about their past. I already knew that he smoked a pipe, and I think I heard he used to drink, and so I suppose he did these things and eventually he repented. As for the sex, every man can be forgiven a little experience with girls here and there."

It is Dey's "repentance," meanwhile, that worries me. His reputed religious awakening has sirens going off in my head. The repentant sinner is the most likely zealot.

"It didn't disturb you to hear that he used to listen to Abd al-Hamid Kishk on cassette?" I ask after a long pause.

Bari puts a reassuring hand on my forearm. "I know my friend," he declares. "He was no terrorist. He would have taken the good from those cassettes and discarded the bad."

I would like to believe that Bari is right. I do believe that an intimate friendship can enable two people to know things about each other without needing to ask or tell. But in the rumbling darkness, it hits me again that Bari may be risking more than he knows. If he uncovers a secret about his friend that violates his memory of their friendship and mutual trust, he may lose his peace of mind.

FIFTEEN

There are several ways an Arab government can counter jihadism within its borders. One is to address the corruption, poverty, and social ills that seem to underpin the popularity of Islamist groups. Another is to compete with Islamist preachers and militants in an ideological struggle over Islam. The third is to unleash the security services in an all-out war against the militants. States across the region, confronted with terrorism as well as the growing challenge of Islamist political parties, have experimented with all three approaches. Unfortunately, the first necessitates a war against high-level corruption and bureaucratic dysfunction that most Arab governments are ill equipped to wage. The second, while promising, takes time to bear fruit. The third, a security crackdown, though typically brutal, yields results immediately. Pro-Western Arab regimes in particular have had the backing of the United States and Europe in clamping down hard on Islamist militants. Even their own populations, angered at civilian carnage wrought by terrorists, have lent their support, at least at first, to harsh security measures.

As a journalist, I have made a study of Arab government responses to terrorism and Islamist politics. I have traced the toughening of antiterror measures in Jordan, followed Egypt's recent antipoverty campaigns, and watched governments in the Gulf states reshuffle their own clerical elites. Nowhere in the region have I seen a more comprehensive response to a terrorist provocation than in Morocco. King Muhammad VI announced an ambitious plan to implement all three approaches to fighting jihadism within weeks of the May 2003 suicide bombings. He has followed through on all three fronts, with mixed results. Predictably, the most urgent and incessant of his actions was the ratcheting up of security measures to counter Islamist militancy. As I have already noted, there have been unpleasant side effects to the crackdown.

One of the many indirect outcomes was the murder of Ibrahim Dey.

The first plank of the king's prescription against Islamist militancy was to declare war on poverty, because so many of the terrorists who blew themselves up in 2003 hailed from the squalor of Casablanca's shantytowns. The government made plans to eradicate the shantytowns, gradually resettling slum dwellers in new housing projects. Tens of thousands of homes were built each year beginning in 2006, breaking off the vast population of the shantytowns one large clump at a time. The deeply impoverished neighborhood of Sidi Moumin, where several suicide bombers grew up, has been all but cleared. But years lie ahead before the half-million shantytown dwellers of Casablanca alone, to say nothing of millions more kingdomwide, are all resettled. Meanwhile, the latest crop of terrorist plots has demonstrated that poverty by itself does not explain the allure of Islamist militancy. In the 2008 Belliraj conspiracy, for example, university professors, teachers, and successful businessmen were implicated in the plot.

The second plank of the king's prescription was to flush out extremist preachers from the kingdom's mosques and streamline Muslim leadership in the country. In one speech, the monarch made a disparaging reference to foreign ideologies from "the East"— alluding, apparently, to the puritanical Wahhabi ideology that had been blowing in from Saudi Arabia for years. To combat it, the king introduced new rules for the training of Muslim clerics: they would have to attain a bachelor's degree and acquire knowledge of psychology, communications, and foreign languages to complement their study of the Qur'an and Islamic law. The king's Ministry of Islamic Affairs introduced female religious "counselors"—a first in the Arab world—to share in the oversight of male mosque preachers. A government fatwa council was established to assert monopoly control over the issuing of fatwas—religious edicts—by clerics. And a Moroccan Islamic satellite channel was launched to compete with foreign channels, widely viewed in Morocco, that promulgate the Islamist values of terrorist groups like Hezbollah and extremist ideologies like Wahhabism.

In seeking to reclaim Muslim culture from the extremists, the kingdom has a rich religious heritage of its own to draw from. For centuries, Morocco has been a stronghold of Sufism, the mystical strand in Islamic culture, which emphasizes the purification of the soul and promotes harmony and peace among religions and sects. Among the vanguards of Sufism in Morocco are the Gnawa brotherhoods. As noted earlier, these mystical troubadours carry on a spiritual and musical tradition with roots in sub-Saharan Africa, from which slaves were imported to Morocco centuries ago. For generations, the Gnawa have brought healing and spiritual elation to Moroccans through séances and musical rites. Yet Islamists, in recent decades, have sought to marginalize them, railing against their belief in magic and the African spirit world. Now Morocco's government has begun to reinvest in the Gnawa brotherhoods as a counterweight to Islamists, sponsoring festivals and conferences to highlight their importance and reinvigorating Sufi *zawiyas*—the equivalent of mosques—with more generous funding. Policy think tanks in Europe and the United States have touted these steps, suggesting that other Arab countries should take an example from Morocco in promoting the mystical strand in Islam.

These maneuvers probably sound cynical to Western, particularly American, ears. Isn't religion supposed to ebb and flow on its spiritual merits, without manipulation by a government? Welcome to the history of Muslim societies, where a ruler's assertion of authority over Islamic theory and practice dates back to the Abbasid empire in Baghdad in the eighth century. Even the prodding of outside powers such as Europe and the United States has its historical precedents in the age of European colonialism. Nor is Islamic history unique in this regard. Consider King Henry VIII's invention of the Anglican Church in England, baldly for the purpose of political gain. Witness northern Europe in the age of the Protestant Reformation, where local German princes backed a new Masonic stream of Christianity known as Protestantism for political gain in order to neutralize the influence of the Catholic Church from Rome.

In any event, such initiatives will take time to affect the religious culture of Morocco, just as extremist trends wrought by Saudi petrodollars took decades to seep in.

Meanwhile, the government has also seen fit to crack the whip.

The wave of arrests and harsh interrogations that followed the 2003 attacks—three thousand detainees in all—came along with a series of new security reforms that have largely been in place ever since. An elite new unit of the Judiciary Police was formed with special training and a gloves-off mandate to pursue jihadists and those who support them. New technologies were introduced to more thoroughly monitor email and Web browsing. An irregular army of informants were recruited to keep tabs on politically active young people, from the university to the mosque to the privacy of their homes. Journalists critical of the counterterrorist campaign faced crippling fines and, in some cases, jail. These aggressive steps, among others, enjoyed the cover of new antiterror legislation.

There was a further step in the struggle to reestablish security in Morocco that was as much a demand from the citizenry as a government initiative. Early on in the state's response to the 2003 attacks, the people of Morocco's cities demanded more security on the streets. The perception that jihadists could strike anywhere at any time, and that too few police were available to stop them, led to a grassroots consensus that more boots should be placed on the ground—a special unit, ideally, primed to squash any terrorist threat.

The man in charge of security at the time, Hamidu Lanegri, was a worldly top cop. He had spent years in the United Arab Emirates, a regional hub of intelligence and security cooperation, as a senior security adviser to that country's president. As chief of the intelligence services in Morocco in the nineties, he had worked to strengthen the security alliance between Morocco and the United States. Under his watch, the kingdom became an important pit stop in the CIA's "extraordinary rendition" program, in which American detainees suspected of terrorism could undergo harsh interrogation or torture on foreign soil in secret. His prescription for Morocco's streets, by contrast, was plain to the naked eye.

Confronted with the demand for heightened public security in Morocco after 2003, Lanegri determined that the kingdom needed a robust new physical presence in urban areas, loud and recognizable, to break down the perception of insecurity together with the reality. He deployed six thousand men to the streets in armed convoys—typically two or three motorcycles flanking a Toyota Prado—to deter terrorism and other forms of crime and vice. Most of these officers were gleaned from the ranks of the uniformed police and the Judiciary Police; about a third were fresh recruits. The new division was officially called the Urban Mobile Units, but Moroccans, in their fashion, gave them a couple of nicknames. The first, during the brief period of their honeymoon with the population, was "wedding convoys," because that is what they looked like. The second nickname, which stuck, was "Croatians"—because their orange-and-white-checked uniform reminded sports fans of the Croatian soccer team, and perhaps because, over time, they came to wear on the population like a foreign occupying force.

But some of the "Croatians" themselves had been influenced over the years by the dogmatic Islamist ideology of Wahhabism. Given a free hand to secure public order, many saw fit to function more like Saudi Arabia's guardians of public virtue than a counter-terrorist unit. They stormed brothels and rounded up prostitutes and their clients. They walked into discotheques, nightclubs, and cafés and demanded proof of marriage from young couples. They also abused their power for personal gain, angering the population. When a woman in a nightclub explained, for example, that she had left her wedding certificate at home, some "Croatians" would demand a bribe. "It got to be excessive," a security services source tells me, "like a cross between Tony Soprano and the Saudi religious police. Once my daughter was at a respectable café and the 'Croatians' barged in and frightened everybody, extorting money." Their abuses grew heinous: in 2005, a member of the nascent force was tried and convicted of stealing from a pair of thirteen-year-olds in Marrakesh who had run away from home. Later that year, several more were found guilty by a Moroccan court of torturing two men to death while in custody.

Moroccans learned the bitter lesson that guardians of public safety could as easily be among its worst offenders. By May 2006, when "Croatians" marched in front of King Muhammad VI in a military and security service parade, the public booed and hissed. Their architect, Hamidu Lanegri, meanwhile faced a public scandal of his own when one of his senior deputies was indicted on charges of collusion with Moroccan drug traffickers. In 2007, Lanegri was demoted to commander of the Auxiliary Forces, and the "Croatians" were unceremoniously disbanded.

Despite the unpopularity of the "Croatians," Moroccans had grown accustomed to their noisy presence on the streets. No sooner had the disliked unit vanished than their deterrent power was missed—and perhaps with good reason. Crime rates went up, and two suicide attacks were perpetrated in Casablanca in 2007. The incoming director of national security, Sharqi Darees, determined in response that a new unit should be deployed to Casablanca to fill the gap left by the "Croatians"—only with built-in restraints. He arranged to draw four thousand privates from the Moroccan armed forces, give them a crash course in urban policing and counterterrorism, and send them out, equipped only with clubs, not to rove the streets on their own but to assist and take orders from the regular police. This is how the Rapid Intervention Forces were born.

Every security innovation has its drawbacks, alas. The remilitarization of urban areas is a sensitive issue in Morocco, because the bitter memory of tanks suppressing riots in Casablanca and Fez as recently as the eighties and nineties, respectively, remains fresh among the population. Moreover, the subtleties of policing an urban society are hardly a soldier's stock in trade. Moroccan soldiers typically hail from poorer rural areas of the country and lack firsthand knowledge of the complexities of city living. Trained to kill on the battlefield, the Rapid Intervention Forces have only a few months of police training to shore up their civilian relations skills before their deployment to Casablanca. Not surprisingly, there has been more than one altercation between an RIF soldier and a civilian that turned lethal.

The first of these happened in December 2007 in broad daylight, in the vast courtyard of the seaside Mosque of Hasan II in Casablanca—the largest mosque on the African continent. A teenaged girl walking home from school found herself surrounded by five RIF soldiers, who catcalled and began to touch her. She cried out to a classmate for help. Sixteen-year-old Hamza al-Yafi rushed to the scene and made a valiant attempt to defend her. He was alone that afternoon—a gentle teen who loved his home soccer team, Widad, and had just made the honor roll in the Mulay Yusuf secondary school nearby. The soldiers beat and kicked him, though Yafi resisted, until one of the five pulled out a knife and stabbed him in the stomach. He expired at the gates of the nearest hospital. Yafi's slaying sparked neighborhood protests against the Rapid Intervention Forces and a rash of negative publicity for the nascent security unit. A lead kicker for the Widad team marched in the funeral procession to show his solidarity.

A few weeks later, the second act of murder perpetrated by an RIF private, al-Raddad Murtaziq, was the gruesome killing of Ibrahim Dey.

I return to Precinct 5 and find the first-floor entryway cluttered with used furniture and machinery, like a rummage sale. Four mattresses, three rolled-up Berber carpets, a wooden table and some chairs, and two crates full of old sewing machines line the long linoleum bench built into the inner wall.

"What is this?" I ask the guard.

"Thieves' garage," he explains. "There's more upstairs with Lieutenant Jabri, along with the boys who stole it all."

I navigate beyond the mess to Chief Sharqawi's office and knock a little nervously on the leather-padded door.

"Come!" he calls out. I open the door and he cries, "Welcome home!"

Sharqawi motions me to join him opposite his oversized desk. An aide walks in with a pile of documents for him to sign. He takes a pen to the top sheet, hands it over, and puts the rest of the papers aside with a curt frown. The aide vanishes, and I fear there is nothing left to stand in the way of his interrogating me now about my time away from his supervision. *Might as well get it over with,* I think.

"So, how have you been?" he asks.

"Praise God."

My mobile phone rings. I remove it from my pocket, notice Bari's number on the caller ID, and send the call to voice mail.

"How was the excursion yesterday with your new, er, friend?" Sharqawi asks.

I make myself smile. "Uneventful, but important for me to begin to understand the social context of the crime you solved."

The chief chortles generously. "If you should learn anything we don't know," he says, "I hope you'll tell me. We're always interested in learning more about our cases. Maybe we'll turn up something new."

That was not so bad, I think. *Might as well try to talk to him about the case.* "I did learn something that might be of interest. Ibrahim Dey had an in-law who didn't like him much, and her brother is a beat cop in Casablanca."

Chief Sharqawi's eyebrows make a wide-open V shape. I mention the man's name, and he makes a note of it. "By the way, I have a little surprise for you later on today, in the evening," he adds. "I promised you I'd do this. The band Nas al-Ghiwan is going to meet you. They're the heart and soul of our neighborhood and the nation."

I take a deep breath and let it out slowly. "Wow," I tell him, "that would be an honor."

"Anything we can do, you know," he says. "Meanwhile, you can go upstairs if you like. Detective Amin is trying to get to the bottom of an assault case. You might be interested."

I make my way toward the stairwell with a sigh of relief.

The case upstairs concerns yet another soldier from the Rapid Intervention Forces. The brawny private is seated opposite a wiry teenager half his size named Safwan bin Suda, whom he accuses of picking a fight with him the day before. Detective Amin, a beefy man in his thirties cloaked tight by a black leather jacket, stands between them like a gruff TV talk show host. A potbellied liaison officer from the armed forces sits off in a corner observing the interplay as a matter of protocol. The soldier tells Detective Amin that he was walking down the road off duty, minding his own business, when Safwan attacked him from behind with a rock to the head.

Safwan moves uncomfortably in his chair.

"What?" Amin demands.

Safwan faces the detective, peering at me from the corner of his eye. "May I say something?"

Amin sighs. "You are free to speak your mind," he mutters. Registering my presence as well, he adds, "You know we have human rights in this country."

The teen clears his throat modestly. "Everything that soldier is saying is a lie! I never touched him with a rock or anything else. He attacked *me*."

"By God Almighty I swear," the Rapid Intervention Forces private cuts in, "I was walking down the street with my friend and this kid hit me totally unprovoked."

"There he goes!" Safwan says. "Yesterday he told you he was alone and today he says he was with a friend, so already you've caught him in a lie!"

The private clenches his teeth as his face reddens.

"You threw me in jail for nothing!" Safwan calls out bitterly.

"Enough," the detective says. "Boy," he tells Safwan, "I warn you I am going to get eyewitnesses, and we're going to get to the truth here. And if you're lying to me now, that is a crime in itself."

A typist walks in, and Amin summons me outside. "Just the way the kid Safwan is talking," he whispers, "there is something ugly about the way he communicates. I don't trust him. This is not a serious case either way, and maybe we'll just drop it. But before we drop it we are going to get to the bottom of it. Nobody should ever cross one of our soldiers. They are here to help us maintain order."

My mobile phone rings again—Bari.

"Excuse me," I tell Amin.

"What do you want?" I whisper into the phone. "I'm busy."

"It's urgent," Bari says. "I was summoned, for questioning."

A bolt of adrenaline shoots through my stomach. "Summoned," I repeat softly.

"It happened this morning," he adds.

"Meet me at the café," I suggest.

On my way down the stairs, three women block me—perhaps a grandmother, a mother, and a daughter—and the youngest clasps my hand, shoving a name and phone number into it. "We are Safwan's family," she says. "We want to thank you for being there for our son just now. If not for you . . ."

"If not for me, what?" I ask. "I'm just an observer here."

"Let us call you and talk about it," the youngest of the three says. She hands me a pen and paper and I scribble my name and number. "That soldier is lying through his teeth and my brother is totally innocent. Now they're going to send him back to jail. Maybe there is more you can do to help."

How serious a matter it is to be "summoned for questioning" in an Arab country depends on who you are and where. I have been questioned, officially and unofficially, by several governments in the Middle East in the course of my travels. None of them has ever mistreated or demeaned me, and we typically enjoyed a few laughs in Arabic along the way. Egyptian security once barged into my apartment at night when I was spending the summer as a language student in Cairo. On the coffee table they discovered my collection of old taped speeches of the late Egyptian president Gamal Abdel Nasser—I had put them there for a reason—and flashed their approval. "American?" they asked. I nodded and smiled. "Very good," they replied. I made them tea, still in my pajamas, we shot the breeze awhile, and they left without demanding a bribe. When there's trouble, moreover, it clearly doesn't hurt, in the outlying autocracies of the Pax Americana, to be an American citizen. The asset of a U.S. passport even trumps the disadvantage of a man's Jewish background in some ways—particularly when dealing with officialdom. It is the local population, not outsiders like me, for whom the gloves come off. Thus I am especially worried about Bari now that he has been "summoned." Though I have fears of my own, he is vulnerable in ways that I am not.

I find him chain-smoking at his favorite perch in the Tizi Ousli Café, looking out at his panoramic view of the noisy Ayn Sabaa roundabout.

"Who was it?" I ask.

"The Qa'id of Ayn Sabaa called me in."

That title denotes the powerful senior Interior Ministry official in each of Casablanca's seven precincts—a different hierarchy from the Directorate of National Security, which oversees my relationship with Precinct 5.

"What did he want?"

"He said, 'What are you doing, investigating a murder with this foreign man? Aren't you afraid that you will find yourself in danger?' I said, 'Danger from what?' He said, 'A criminal gang, a terrorist group. *Who knows what else.*' "

"So you feel it was a warning?" I ask.

"It felt like something between an unfriendly warning and a friendly threat."

The machinery of power weaves its magic, I marvel. I ducked Sharqawi's censure, but now, without directly blocking my own efforts to dig into Ibrahim Dey's past, the Interior Ministry is apparently moving to make Bari quit the pursuit that matters to him so much. Bari would be a brave man to buck the Qa'id's warning. As a stranger in town, I can offer him no assurance of protection should he face some form of retribution.

"What did you tell the Qa'id?"

Bari raises the palm of his left hand and steels his gaze into the air. "I told him it is my right to know what happened to my friend—that everything we're doing is legal, and it is a private matter that concerns me and my loved ones."

Wow.

"That was very brave of you."

"It was the only thing for me to say!"

"So how do you feel about it now that you've done it?"

Bari takes a fierce drag. "You know we hadn't even gotten serious about this yet. All we did was talk to the poor man's family in Jadida. We haven't even started looking into the killer's family. How do I feel? Angry. Scared. I go back and forth."

He blows smoke in my direction, and I don't even care.

"I want to think about this some more, on my own," he says, and walks away with the beginnings of a swagger, leaving me to linger at the table he used to share with the man whose memory started all this.

There's no shortage of reasons why authorities might want Bari to quit poking around. If Ibrahim Dey was a radical slain by a soldier, suppressing that fact spares the government the creation of a martyr. If he was involved in, or even simply observed, something he shouldn't have in the warehouse—some form of organized crime, for example—then his death at the hands of a soldier might have been a sign of government corruption, linked to a wealthy Jewish family, at that. It all hinges on who this man Ibrahim Dey really was—and apparently there are forces that don't want us to find out, that want Ibrahim Dey's true identity buried with him. The man and the memory, together annihilated.

It hits me that if it was worth the trouble for a faction of the government to try to squelch Bari's investigation of Ibrahim Dey, maybe it is only a matter of time before somebody tries to send me a message, too. I wonder who might be tapped to do so, and how.

In the evening I walk back up the stairs to Precinct 5 and find Rashid Batma, a member of the venerated Moroccan band Nas al-

Ghiwan, in the leather-padded head office waiting to greet me, at the behest of Chief Sharqawi—opposite the regulation photographs of the late King Hasan II and his son, the present monarch.

Batma rises awkwardly to say hello. With a baseball cap on backward, his round head of black woolly hair meets a chiseled, mustached face in Lennon specs. His zebra-striped coat would warm a New Englander in winter.

Chief Sharqawi grips Batma's right shoulder and pats his back. "The Ghiwan is the beating heart of all Morocco," he says. "You can ask them for advice, ask them to show you around, ask them even about your murder case if you like. Their wisdom will help you understand."

"Thank you so much," I tell the chief.

"My brother," Batma says in my direction, "we are at your disposal." He lifts his arm in a welcoming gesture. "Umar is in the car waiting outside," he says. "We'll take you around a little if you want."

We head across the street to a worn-out sedan with the engine running. The back door creaks as Batma opens it for me. The driver, smiling Ghiwan lead singer and elder statesman Umar Sayyid, sports a French beret over his curly gray hair. Sayyid is the Bob Dylan of North Africa, but his car is no stretch limousine.

Sayyid drives slowly south, past the body shops and warehouses of Rosh Noir and toward the teeming innards of Al-Hay al-Muhammadi's Martyrs' Square. The smell of grilling skewered meat billows out from underneath a flashing neon pharmacy sign across the street, where crowds of robed men stand and eat, warming their hands over a couple of outdoor grills.

"I understand you are a man with many questions," Sayyid says. "Morocco, the police, the society they protect. As artists we care about these matters, too. Security is a difficult business to manage in a poor country, and we depend on our kingdom to protect us from the worst instincts of humankind. King Muhammad VI, praise God, is a man to meet these challenges, and his police are dedicated servants of the people."

An authoritarian state has the power to reach the public through many proxies: government officials, pro-regime intellectuals, compromised journalists, next-door neighbors. Even the voice of a vocalist sometimes carries a message from the man who rules the country.

Which is not to say that the music is not good. In the Arab world, to the contrary, the best-loved singer of all time was nurtured by a military junta. I have in mind Egypt in the mid-twentieth century under the rule of Gamal Abdel Nasser, and the country's immortal diva Umm Kulthum. Arabs across North Africa and the Middle East tuned in to her weekly radio broadcast, the live recordings of which have been deservedly aired in every country, every day, ever since. She was the mother of Arab song, but also the voice of Nasser's Egypt—the emissary of his specific brand of nationalism to her fellow citizens and Arabs everywhere. She played the latter role deliberately and proudly, backing the regime as much as the regime backed her, even though the reality of Nasser's power wasn't as pure as the image of it that she conjured in song.

Umm Kulthum lived and sang into the 1970s, never amassing anywhere near the wealth of performers of comparable stature in the West. She had built her career in a part of the world that did not recognize the concept of a copyright or treat music as an industry per se. But she had other kinds of treasures: the power of the state to see to her every need, and legions of followers who treated her like a queen. When she died, her state funeral was attended by millions.

I have already observed that the Moroccan band Nas al-Ghiwan, which hit it big around the time of Umm Kulthum's death in the 1970s, came to represent the voice of the Moroccan people—though not the politics of the king. Their audiences believed that, by contrast to renowned vocalists in other countries, the Ghiwan sang with an independent voice. Their cachet as poor boys from the human cauldron of Al-Hay al-Muhammadi in Casablanca lent them the freedom, it seemed, to speak truth to power in song. The band's lyrics have been interpreted by fans as lamenting the worst injustices of the time, including those perpetrated by the very regime that ruled them. When lead librettist Umar Sayyid sang, "I worry for men when they disappear, when they are lost to us," the line was widely understood as a gutsy dig at the policy of state kidnappings and assassinations of left-wing political opposition figures under the reign of Hasan II. Some fans remember that in concert the band sang its famous lyric, "We are living the lives of fleas in a sheep's hide," while looking up at a portrait of King Hasan on the wall behind them.* The band has taken pains to deny this, always maintaining that its message transcends the politics of the kingdom. But they have long been revered for telling it like it is, albeit cryptically.

It is of course harder to maintain an independent voice than to live umbilically connected to a regime. Like Umm Kulthum, Nas al-Ghiwan performed and cut records in a legal environment that did not recognize or enforce intellectual property rights. But unlike the great Egyptian diva, they held their government at arm's length. Thirty years after Ghiwan's meteoric rise, most of the Ghiwan players still lived in and around the underclass Al-Hay al-Muhammadi neighborhood where they got their start. The vocalist Pako was ill, drummer Hagur had passed on and left his children strapped for cash, and lead singer Umar Sayyid, though still performing, was afflicted with rheumatoid arthritis. They were a rare twenty-first-century hybrid of world famous and poor.

One night in 2006, an emissary of the young king surprised vocalist Umar Sayyid with a knock on the door. He announced that His Majesty would assume financial responsibility for the livelihood of all surviving Nas al-Ghiwan musicians and their families for the rest of their lives. A cynic might say that in guaranteeing the band's sustenance, the regime effectively "instrumentalized" them, ensuring that their highly respected voices would sing the king's praises at every turn. A more charitable perspective on this act of philan-

*Elias Muhanna, "Folk the Kasbah: A Conversation with Omar Sayyed, Leader of Nass el-Ghiwane," *Transition* 12, no. 4 (2003): 132–149.

thropy would simply give credit to the monarch for a magnanimous gesture toward the arts. The truth, perhaps, lies somewhere in between.

The Arab world today produces fewer artists who presume to channel the voice of a nation or a state. Most of the dictatorships have loosened their grip on culture and the arts, while the youngest crop of vocalists have become pop stars in the Western sense. Lebanon's Nancy Ajram has amassed a fortune filling soccer stadiums, selling music downloads on iTunes, and making TV commercials for Pepsi-Cola. Along with heartthrob Haifa Wehbe and a slew of other sexy singers, she has achieved a vast regional following through new MTV-style music video networks that are not owned by any government, but blare in living rooms and coffeehouses from Casablanca to Baghdad. Sooner or later I think the region will find its own Justin Bieber—a techno-savvy teen who leverages the immense popularity of YouTube in the Arab world to break through barriers of censorship in a given country or nepotism in the region's music industry.

Nas al-Ghiwan remains a vestige of a different time. The players do not have Twitter feeds. They haven't done any TV commercials. And it is perhaps indicative of something, I'm not sure what, that they would be called in by a policeman to help manage the perceptions of a writer.

For me, anyhow, meeting the Ghiwan is the greatest honor of my trip. It is not often that one encounters the heart and soul of a country in the flesh.

While Umar Sayyid's car is stuck in traffic, a bearded street person saunters toward us to try to wash the windshield. He looks inside. "Umar Sayyid!" he cries, bowing his head to the driver. "Umar Sayyid, God keep you and protect you! God reward you a thousand times!"

Like a Sufi mystic, Sayyid blesses the man, cupping the beggar's oily forehead with the palm of his right hand, and hands over a couple of dirhams from his pocket. The man bows again and promptly moves on to another car.

"It's not easy to be an artist," he tells me. "Everybody expects you to play a certain role for them, always to be the person they know and love from your songs, but meanwhile inside we are hurting, we are aging. Our hearts are young and our bodies grow old."

We park near an open-air clearing framed by a few one-story buildings of worn white concrete. "These are the old cultural centers where the Ghiwan was born," Batma explains. "They were built after the country's independence from France, by King Muhammad V, God have mercy on him."

We duck into the House of Youth, a sparse performance space with a little stage inside, and catch three teenagers break-dancing eighties-style to some house music playing on a boom box.

"It's Western music," Batma says dismissively, "not the kind of thing we used to do with the space."

We walk outside and cut diagonally across to a smaller building, a stark practice studio called the House of Music. A teacher behind a small desk cradles a thirteen-stringed fretless oud in his arms, cueing a student with a black violin to play in unison with him. Off sheet music, they work through a melancholy thirteen-beat *samma'*, or wordless song, by early twentieth-century Egyptian composer Riyadh al-Sunbati. In my mind I can hear the orchestra that debuted it in Cairo on a record my mother used to put on when I was a teenager. The boy's violin screeches occasionally, but he has the complex rhythm down, and the brooding mood of the song hangs over the little space like a pregnant cloud.

"Only one month he has been studying violin," the teacher observes after one run-through. "You see, Morocco has talent."

It is a short walk down a bustling commercial street from Martyrs' Square to the social headquarters of Nas al-Ghiwan—the back lot of a tailor's shop with a poster of Charlie Chaplin in the front window. Umar Sayyid leads the way. A curtain shrouds the space behind the counter, where stitching machines clack softly to a sixteen-beat rhythm and the walls are lined with clippings of the band: a concert poster from France, a show bill from the tourist city of Agadir, postcards and photographs, a newspaper article about their stadium gig in Libya.

"Fill me up," Batma says to a plump, mustached friend working one of the machines. He dutifully rolls the singer a *kufta,* a paper cigarette of hashish. Batma lights it and takes a deep drag. Umar Sayyid does not partake. I'm surprised: drug use in an Arab capital by a state-supported band, in a country devoting its resources to fighting the hash trade? Artists are forgiven the vices that inspire them, I suppose.

"So tell us about your project," Umar Sayyid proposes. "This murder you are following."

I deliver a brief synopsis, to the best of my knowledge, of the life and untimely death of Ibrahim Dey.

"Ibrahim Dey was a victim *before* he was a victim," Batma declares out of a purple haze.

I look to Sayyid for an interpretation.

"He means he was a victim of poverty, illiteracy, lack of opportunity—of the Moroccan predicament. Ibrahim Dey was all of us. He lived his life like all Moroccans, he drank of our sadness, he lost his life to the same tragic phenomena that afflict us all. King Muhammad VI, God grant him long life, his whole heart and all his soul are concerned with alleviating the poverty of the Moroccan people, and God grant him success."

I rest my hands on one of the workshop tables and feel the rhythm of the stitching machines pinging my fingertips repeatedly. It's a funky groove, only waiting for someone to break into song.

"But my friend and I are investigating Ibrahim Dey not for what makes him the same as all Moroccans so much as for the things that made him unique," I tell Sayyid. "I am trying to recover the past history of one man, because we feel he deserved better and want to understand why he is lost to all his friends."

"The past is dead," Batma announces, and takes another drag.

"The past is dead," Sayyid repeats. "The past is gone, so let it be. It's a song we wrote. Let me share a few lyrics with you."

Against the backbeat of the stitching machines, Sayyid's breathy tenor voice savors a couple of lines from a Ghiwan classic:

O you who are concerned with the past, it is already dead.
O you who are concerned with the past, it is already dead.
The eye has shed tears for a past and a candle that are long
*　extinguished.*

"Umar," I cut in, "to my unfledged ears it sounds as if you are giving me a piece of advice."

Sayyid eyes me coyly. "The Ghiwan delivers its message, and it is up to the audience to find what meaning they wish to find in it. Go out and talk to any Moroccan about 'The Past Is Dead' and you will hear hundreds of interpretations. We are artists."

The whir of heavy traffic outside dulls the meticulous machinery groove, and a vague shouting in the distance from one of the denizens of Al-Hay al-Muhammadi clips the evening's calm.

SIXTEEN

Call me Jewish, but I just don't believe in forsaking the past.

I do not know what drove a local Interior Ministry official to warn Bari to back away. Maybe it was simply his discomfort with a private citizen, in an authoritarian society, poking into other people's private lives—in partnership, at that, with a foreign man. I cannot fathom why the band Nas al-Ghiwan might have been enlisted to expound on Ibrahim Dey, either, and sing me a song about the past being dead. But whoever may have put these people up to trying to talk us out of what we're doing is starting to piss me off—not that I would ever dare to show it if we actually met.

Independent of Bari's yearning to know the truth about his friend, I have questions of my own about the contradictions inherent in the dead man's life, and I wonder whether they connect in some way to the controversy we appear to have courted. Here is a man who during his youth enjoyed a few glory years in a seaside town. He earned a reputation as intrepid, successful, and outgoing— a playboy, even. Yet after he returned to Casablanca, over the last fifteen years of his life, he could not even make a living. His mother and sister say he came back from Jadida emotionally wounded. My psychology grad student friend found evidence of passivity in his dream about the division of money between Dey and his cousin. Yet by day around town, Dey kept up appearances as a ubiquitous small-time entrepreneur. He told his loved ones he had been cursed, growing ever more mysterious and distant from them. Yet to the new friends he made, including Bari, he found a way to bring good luck and inspiration. To a female first cousin, he was the feminist voice who inspired her to join the workforce. Yet the voice in his Walkman was an Islamist preacher who believed that a woman's place was in the home—and that Islam had many enemies who needed to be destroyed. Ruminating about Ibrahim Dey in the tailor's shop, Ghiwan singers Rashid Batma and Umar Sayyid seemed to want to link the dead man to a broader national predicament: "a victim of poverty, illiteracy, lack of opportunity," they said, who "lived his life like all Moroccans." Yet for a victim of poverty, Ibrahim Dey had known something of wealth—and for a Moroccan everyman, he picked a secluded storage facility, detached from the rough and tumble of the shantytown or the city, to live out his last years as an enigma. What kept him there each night? I keep asking myself. Did he have something to hide from other people, to safeguard in an obscure location? Who were the people who visited him at night whom his best friend Bari never met?

I want, in short, to hold on tight as Bari and I continue to pursue the mystery of Dey's life and death, despite having unsettled somebody for beginning to try. Bari is angry and scared, he says. I'm concerned about his emotional state. The situation is volatile.

It is Friday, and the dust in the streets of Ayn Sabaa is dancing in the January sun, swept up like glittery cursive writing in the chilly breeze. Across from the twin lions' roundabout, youths crowd around the double-decker kiosk of pirated American DVDs. Older men gather around a cauldron of *harira,* boiled vegetable and lentil soup, that steams a sweet-scented fog into the brisk air. I walk down the road and knock on the worn-out door of Bari's flat. One of his sons opens up and points to the starkly furnished sitting room, where his father sits alone under the hanging lightbulb in a pearly white gown, nervously fingering his prayer beads.

"There is no way," he says, as if we were in the middle of a conversation. "No way that soldier would have climbed into the ware-house just to steal a few dirhams. There is nothing to steal in a ware-house like that, unless you want to haul away a freight truck. That soldier had to know where he was going. He had to know who he was targeting."

I take a seat beside him.

"I tell you what makes me angry about the Qa'id warning me to stop what we're doing," he says. "All we were doing was talking to people, the family of my friend, God have mercy on him, and they wanted to scare me after we did that. But there are laws here, and I didn't break any of them."

I flash a thumbs-up.

"And now that I think about why I was warned to stop, I think that it is proof," he says, pointing an index finger in the air. "Proof that what the police say happened is make-believe."

From the shut-away kitchen on the other side of the flat, Bari's eight-year-old daughter emerges with two tall glasses of *laban,* liquid yogurt, on a tray.

"When am I going to finally meet your wife?" I ask.

Bari smiles. "We have been talking about it."

I take a sip of the pungent drink.

"You know we are going to need some more help," he says after a gulp out of his glass. "Now that we have been warned by the system, we need someone who knows the system better than we do. Muhammad of Ayn Sabaa."

I put down my glass immediately. "That big man who came up out of nowhere and told you not to befriend a Jew? To hell with that!"

Bari shushes me. "You have to get a little used to not taking every word people say so seriously around here. Muhammad of Ayn Sabaa is gruff, I grant you, but he knows how to work the system. And now that the system is uncomfortable with us, we need an ally. Furthermore, I understand he has his own interest in the murder."

"I don't even know what he does for a living."

"Relax," Bari says, "I don't even know his last name. But as for what he does, I hear he makes a small fortune cooking books. People find him around the courts getting involved in all kinds of in-trigue with the police and the legal system on behalf of paying clients. He is an agent of corruption, and in this country, everybody who wants to get a job done needs a man like him."

"Corruption sounds like trouble," I tell him.

"It's the kind of trouble that might get us somewhere," he says. "He's a barterer. You'll see. He'll want something from us and offer something to us in return."

"I don't know."

"Come to the mosque with me for Friday prayer," Bari says. "We'll find him there and talk to him about it. Come, let's go. Maybe someday you'll take me to a synagogue."

So even the search for a lost friend's truth requires an "agent of corruption."

Though common in every society, whether democratic or au-thoritarian, corruption is the great curse of developing countries, and Morocco is no exception. You find corruption in all walks of life here—from the petty to the powerful, from the private sector to the state bureaucracy, in everyday transactions and during national elections. Business leaders, internationally and at home, cite it as their primary reason for avoiding direct investment in the country. Young Moroccans aspiring to go to school or get a job encounter it as the greatest obstacle to their advancement: some reportedly have to pay a bribe for a seat in college or a passing grade; others find they have to know someone to secure an entry-level government job. Indeed, 60 percent of Moroccans surveyed in 2006 reported having found it necessary to pay a bribe during the previous year. Transparency International, which ranks the perception of corrup-tion in countries worldwide, has never been kind to Morocco in its assessments. But between 1999 and 2005, its ratings for the country fell from 45th best in the world to 78th. This suggests that after King Muhammad VI ascended to the throne in 1999 and promised to break with the country's corrupt past, his people steadily lost faith in his pledge. Nor has the country fared particularly well among Arab states, all of which have unclean reputations. Morocco came in eleventh out of seventeen Arab countries on the corruption index in 2006, and though it had risen slightly by 2011, God only knows whether this was a sign of improvement or evidence of more rapid deterioration among its sister Arab states.

For many years, Morocco has been one of those countries in which corruption is not merely a common social disease, it's a kind of state policy emanating straight from the top. The late King Hasan II made secret payoffs a core strategy to consolidate his hold on power. He used graft to buy off political opposition and win loyalty in the army and security services and among the bureaucracy. As the state's preeminent trendsetter, he created a culture and a hierarchy of graft descending to the lowest rungs on the socioeconomic ladder. Down at the bottom, the sprawling informal sector of the economy—rife with drug deals large and small—has long been a space in which people take their cues from the upper echelons, constructing smaller patronage pyramids of their own to hold business deals together.

Any information we might be after is small change, of course, in the universe of Moroccan graft. In an era of privatization of state enterprises, the royal family has transferred much of its authority over the economy to the private sector and turned the economy into a corporate oligopoly. The king and his relatives control ONA-SNI, a business juggernaut that dominates financial services, mining, and agribusiness. More indirectly, the family has its heavy hands in real estate, banking, insurance, and retail distribution. Friends of the family own many of the leading enterprises themselves, ensuring that competition beyond a limited social circle is virtually impossible. This informal consortium commands unfair advantages in business deals large and small, inhibiting the sort of entrepreneurial grit that can actually grow economies. Meanwhile, for most of the population, the culture of patronage pioneered by the king's late father continues to dominate daily life.

This is one of the surprising causes of ordinary Moroccans' embrace of Islamist movements—surprising because it's not about the siren call of ideology or religion, but something more pragmatic:

good, transparent governance. Islamists, living humble lives and preaching the Qur'an's message of egalitarianism and social justice, present themselves as the vanguards of clean government. Even as the state struggles to rid the country of the terrorist threat, its own corrupt behavior feeds into the anger and desperation that fuels extremist groups.

According to Bari, Muhammad of Ayn Sabaa reputedly makes his living greasing palms in the city's judiciary. This specialization would not altogether surprise me. For an "agent of corruption," the Moroccan courts are a cornucopia of opportunity. The country's judges are notoriously susceptible to pressure from the executive branch of government and business interests as well as from more humble petitioners with handshakes full of cash. A number of celebrated scandals illustrate the problem. In 2007 the Moroccan press was filled with reports about the "Rkiya affair," in which judges admitted on tape that they had accepted money in exchange for skewing their verdicts. A broader scandal came to light a year earlier in the northern city of Tetouan, where seven lawyers published an open letter slamming the city's courts for dealing in graft every day. They complained of rampant complicity between area drug lords, judges, and city magistrates. Rather than earn accolades for coming forth, the lawyers faced legal proceedings initiated against them by magistrates in Tetouan that led to their disbarment.

Struggles against corruption have been successfully waged in countries even worse off than Morocco, so there is hope for the kingdom. Witness Hong Kong, noted for its gangster "triads" in the 1970s that dominated business, government, and the general culture. Hong Kong managed to transform into one of the cleaner working environments in Asia within two decades. Its tool of transformation was the Independent Commission Against Corruption, a powerful body with a mandate to pursue and prosecute corruption in government and the private sector as well as to educate citizens about the perils of paying into the culture of bribery. Vaguely along these lines, the Moroccan government in 2007 inaugurated a Central Agency for the Prevention of Corruption. Alas, it lacks independence, a clear mandate, or any significant authority. The body has begun to make headway in stigmatizing small-time corruption within the society—part of the reason, perhaps, that Muhammad of Ayn Sabaa sees fit to conceal his last name from the general public. But this baby step forward barely registers against the long, hard road toward clean government and business.

Meanwhile, if the true story of an individual's life and death is kept under wraps by Moroccan authorities, it is understandable that a man like Bari who wants to know that story would hope that it is up for sale. And if it isn't available at any price, perhaps an "agent of corruption" will know how to help a man like Bari chase after it anyway, or at least keep him out of trouble while he tries.

At Bari's suggestion, we make for the neighborhood mosque.

Long ago I used to feel uncomfortable joining in Muslim congregational worship. I think about my friend Ali, who changed all that, as we enter the keyhole-shaped gate of the Uhud mosque in Ayn Sabaa, a crowded working-class sanctuary of cool blue stone graced by a tall white minaret. Ali helped me see that the substance of Muslim prayer is close enough to its Jewish and Christian antecedents that a believer in God, even if he isn't Muslim, can squint his way through the bits about the prophet Muhammad and experience some spiritual nourishment. Granted, in many Arab countries the Friday sermon goes straight for my jugular—a bloodcurdling talk about the perfidious Jews and the need to do away with them, for example. But this afternoon, at a government-controlled mosque in Casablanca, I feel reasonably assured I won't have to stomach anything of the sort. As I have already noted, after the suicide bombings of 2003, a concerted effort was waged by the security services to tone down pulpit rhetoric. Radical clerics were rounded up and replaced by quietists, with informants appointed to monitor each mosque. Now every preacher knows he is being watched, and if he veers into the realm of extremism, his salary and license to preach will be on the line. In other words, my tribespeople and I are the beneficiaries of a censorial policy that we would probably oppose if it were directed somewhere else. Nor are we the only ones who appreciate it when Arab states crack down on extremist rhetoric. We pay a price for endorsing these repressive tactics, however—and the people who live here pay a lot more.

I ask myself what Ali would feel about the situation if he were here with us.

Bari and I deposit our shoes in cubbyholes at the foyer and enter the sanctuary. Blue-and-white honeycomb geometry adorns the inner walls, and along taped-down white lines on the carpeted floor, several hundred men are lining up in tight, narrow rows, trailing sweat. We arrive just in time. The cleric, robed in black and gold, stands before the frontmost row and begins to chant in the mystical singsong style of the northern walled city of Fez. His cadence is angular, ethereal, punctuated by gutturals and heavy consonants. He opens with "the Key," the Qur'an's opening passage: *All praise is to God, the Lord of Creation . . . You alone we worship and from You alone we seek help.* Next he offers verses from chapter 23—a famous assurance, to those who suffer, from the God who reigns over humankind and the spirit world: *We do not burden any soul beyond its capacity, and with Us is a book that speaks the truth.*

Bari joins the worship on trembling knees. I spy him whispering "the Key" to himself and making his body move in ritual unison with the congregation, which I mimic:

Bow ninety degrees.
Stand tall.
Drop horizontal, forehead to the ground.
Kneel upright, one kneecap steadied in the palm of each hand.
Bear witness to the oneness of God.
Repeat.

After the second prostration, I notice that Bari's knees have stopped trembling and he is breathing more deeply. I know that he hasn't slept well since Ibrahim Dey was killed, but, as the muezzin chants from the minaret every morning at dawn, "Prayer is better than sleep." His posture is straighter than I've ever seen it. He looks as if he is drawing strength from the power of his worship.

We sit and listen to the cleric deliver a sermon about charity. No one except the very poor is exempt from the mandatory alms tax of *zakat,* he reminds the congregation; all should give according to their ability. At the sermon's conclusion, the crowd begins to stream out of the sanctuary. We reclaim our shoes and wander into the busy courtyard, past a line of elderly and disfigured beggars and into the realm of fruit stands and carpets full of knickknacks for sale. "Ibrahim Dey used to pray here every day," Bari tells me, "almost every day. We would come here together and leave together, on to the café."

He greets several friends with kisses on both cheeks, sifting purposefully through the crowd. At length the biggest man in the courtyard emerges from the hubbub, golden tooth and triple chin first, and takes Bari's hand. Bari greets him formally with twin kisses to the cheeks. The man is bundled up in a giant bomber jacket, a Muslim skullcap warming his head.

"What's *he* doing with you in a mosque?" he asks Bari, pointing to me. *"Haram!"* he declares, an accusation that someone has violated Islamic law.

"He came here to greet *you,*" he replies.

Muhammad of Ayn Sabaa takes a thumb and index finger to his stubbly chin and squints in the icy sunlight, apparently making a quick calculation. "He wants to sit down somewhere with us?"

"Both of us do. Why don't you join us for coffee at Tizi Ousli?" Bari suggests.

"Are you kidding?" the man replies, hunching in closer. "That's why everybody knows what you guys are up to. A microphone in every ashtray over there, the waiter listening in. We go across the street if you want to talk, and we consider switching locations if people get curious."

The café on the other side of the roundabout is slightly ritzier, with cushioned chairs, softer lighting, and tables topped with glass. Muhammad of Ayn Sabaa chooses our seats strategically: off to a corner, no mirrors nearby. He orders *za'atar* tea and mumbles something in Shilha to Bari.

"So you think you're going to get to the bottom of what happened," he says to me in Arabic. "I think you won't."

I feel my pulse quicken.

"I have the police file," I tell him. "That's a start."

"You have the second draft of the police file," he says. "What you don't have is the original version, before it got redacted and rewritten for your consumption. You've got nothing."

I watch him grin slyly at me.

"I've got nothing? You know I won't even dignify that with a response."

"Now, brothers," Bari says, his arms hovering over us both as if he were Bill Clinton and we were Yasir Arafat and Yitzhak Rabin, "it's important to me that the two of you get along. We all have common interests here."

"That's true," Muhammad of Ayn Sabaa goes on, a trace of brightness in his gravelly voice. "I am also interested in the murder of Ibrahim Dey. There is money in it, you see. I want to hold the Jew Toledano legally responsible for the death on his premises. It's like in America when your dog bites the mailman. If you're a real Jew, you should side with me on this as a matter of social justice."

I can feel my voice thicken as I hasten to stick up for Toledano, a man I have never met and who might not be especially worthy of a defense: "You don't have a case against him because Ibrahim Dey wasn't his salaried guard. He shouldn't have been there in the first place. In the eyes of the law he would be a trespasser." I don't even know what I'm talking about.

"Not *our* law," the big man replies. "I've been looking into this. Legally, either Ibrahim Dey was a thief or he was a guard. There is no third option. And if he was guarding the place in practice, Toledano owes damages. I swear, after I build this case I am going to have Toledano by his neck." He looks into my eyes. "There's no shame in it, you know. The Toledanos are a gangster family."

Bari puts a comforting hand on my shoulder and keeps his eyes on Muhammad of Ayn Sabaa. "What would you need from us?" he asks.

My heart is pounding.

"I need plaintiffs," the big man says. "You know the victim's family, and they are the bereaved party. I need to line them up against the Jew in court. Sworn affidavits. Your friend the night watchman, what's his name, Attar. He lost his job when they found out he had been entrusting the place to Ibrahim Dey every night without the boss's permission. I need him to testify that he was underpaid to begin with, and that he deputized Ibrahim Dey to do his job at night. You should help me line them up. There's going to be money in it for all of us."

Bari finds his reflection on the glass tabletop beside his teacup. "The quest we are on is not for money," he declares.

"Then the quest you are on is for nothing," the big man retorts. "Work with me and take the money. Now's your chance. God knows you haven't earned for your family in a long time."

Bari flushes pink. He doesn't say anything. I can see that despite the courage he has been mustering for our quest, he still has a weak spot.

"Step one," the big man goes on, "help me win the trust of the guard Attar. He's your friend."

"You won't get anywhere with Attar," Bari says, a little weakly. "He would never betray Toledano because he has been working for him for twenty years and he hopes to get rehired, despite the bad blood. Also, he's terrified of getting into trouble again ever since he got beaten by the police."

I remember Lieutenant Jabri's claim that no one had been beaten in the course of the Dey investigation. So much for that. But Bari never mentioned this detail to me before.

"How come you never told me they beat Attar?" I ask him.

Bari grins. "The sun comes up every morning and I never mentioned that, either."

"What happened exactly?"

"The usual," he says. "They blindfolded him, and about four men kicked him and punched him all over for about fifteen minutes. They tried to make him confess to Ibrahim Dey's murder, God have mercy on him. When he wouldn't, they started the beatings all over again."

Muhammad of Ayn Sabaa taps Bari with his index finger. "So how about it. Be my bridge to the family of Ibrahim Dey."

I'm digesting the foul image of Attar's beating, but the two Muhammads are on to something else.

Bari takes a deep breath. "It won't be easy, you know. Maybe meanwhile you can help us a little."

"What do you need?"

Bari hesitates. "You know I met that soldier once," he says. "They brought him into the lieutenant's office while I was being questioned. When I looked at him I was numb. It hadn't even sunk in that Ibrahim Dey was dead, God have mercy on him. But now that I've thought about it all, I need to know more about this soldier. I want to know why he did it. I know it wasn't over pocket change, so I need to know what it was really about."

"Any secret the soldier has is buried," Muhammad of Ayn Sabaa mutters. "You won't get anywhere near the soldier, and he's the one who really knows. He has guards surrounding his prison cell, with microphones everywhere."

"Why would that be?" I ask. I'm almost sure he's making this stuff up.

"By the time the reason why he killed him comes out," he replies, "it won't even matter anymore."

"I just need to understand who the person was who took Ibrahim's life," Bari declares.

"I thought you just wanted to know *why* he did it," Muhammad of Ayn Sabaa says.

Bari knocks on the table as if it were a door. "All these things are connected somehow."

Anyhow, they're connected in Bari's mind, I think, *and for me, that's what matters most.*

"It would be hard for me," he goes on, "but I would like to make a trip to the village he came from, this killer. I want to meet the people who brought him up and made him what he is. You can help us."

Muhammad of Ayn Sabaa lifts his head slightly and makes a *tssk* sound—a North African way of saying no. "I don't know what you'll find there. Your answers are here in Casablanca."

"There is something there," Bari says.

"You know what may help you? Have this Jew friend of yours pay a visit to the Jew Toledano. He probably knows something from the police, from his own employees, and he's a Jew. He's completely outside of our system and institutions, so he can say anything he feels like, especially to another Jew."

Bari returns to his modest request. "There is something waiting for me in that village, I just know it."

Muhammad of Ayn Sabaa puts his hands on the glass table and slowly nods his acquiescence. "Next week I'll be free," he says. "We can plan an excursion to Bin Sulayman for then." After a quick swig of his *za'atar* tea, he stands up and rumbles away like a slow-moving freight train.

"I can't believe we're going to help him make trouble for Toledano," I tell Bari. "I can't believe he called them a gangster family."

"Don't worry," he says, "it may all be so much talk anyway. These kinds of schemes get dreamed up one day and forgotten the next—always a new scheme, always a better one. Even if he does try it, the odds are always in favor of the Jew in our courts. Always the Jew wins in Morocco, no matter what. Why is that, and this is a Muslim country?"

I shrug as if I have no idea.

"Anyway," he goes on, "I doubt that he's actually going to take Toledano to court, and meanwhile, we'll try to get something of value out of him when we make our trip to Bin Sulayman. This is important. Just learn to play the game. That's the way it is here."

I walk up to the second floor of Precinct 5 that night and find Jabri holding court with a trio of young looters. Their confiscated garageful of pickings still clutters the office. The lieutenant is wearing his trademark charcoal gray blazer and jeans, peering down at his three catches through gold-rimmed bifocals. One of the youths is smiling at him; the other two sit grimly.

"What young Mustafa has done in confessing to the crime was an act of courage I would encourage you two boys to follow," Jabri announces. "It was an act of manhood. It will reflect well on him when the judge pronounces his sentence, and it will reflect well on him in the world to come." He snaps his fingers and the stenographer walks in lugging his typewriter and sheets of carbon paper.

"My dear brother!" Jabri calls out to me. "Where have you been?" Turning to the youths, he adds, "Our distinguished brother is visiting from America, a wondrous land. I have been there. Tall buildings. Kindhearted people. Universal Studios. Disneyland!"

The young men appear to forget their troubles for a moment.

"*Pa pa pa pa,*" he exclaims, "you ride through waterfalls and see sea creatures, flying monsters, movie stars. A land of miracles! By God, it is a godly place!"

Jabri puts his arm around me and whispers, "You see, my brother, our youth are bombarded with so many negative images about America in the media—of killing and violence and war. Whenever I have them in here I always take an opportunity to say something positive about your country."

"Thank you for doing that, Lieutenant."

He promises me his undivided attention in just a few minutes.

I watch him charm and cajole the other two boys to join their friend in confessing to theft, and I try to imagine the same genteel man presiding over the beating of an innocent. He appeals to their patriotism, plays down the gravity of the circumstances, and makes small talk about their shared love for the soccer team Widad, one of the home teams. The first of the two boys relents, offering to tell his story to the typist, and Jabri rewards him with a shoulder massage. Now both boys apply peer pressure to the third, and Jabri takes a step back and lets the circle complete itself. He stands over the typist's shoulders and watches the incriminating prose fill the page, correcting a pronoun here and a verb form there. The boys watch him tend to their confessions, eager to be helpful. Within twenty minutes they are ready to be arraigned.

"You see," Jabri tells me, "over nineteen years in the Judiciary Police I have learned that the best way to extract a confession is to treat the suspects with the utmost esteem. Now"—he switches briefly out of Arabic into slow-moving learner's English—"let us drink something hot, no?"

The typist distributes his two copies of the criminal complaint to Jabri and a young detective, then makes his exit. The detective escorts the three boys out to a National Security van parked down-stairs, headed for court, leaving Jabri and me alone in his office.

"So," he says, "you have been busy these days."

"I've taken an interest, you know, in your homicide investigation of last month."

"Ibrahim Dey," he says solemnly. "But I think by now you have learned a lot about it, maybe as much as you would ever need."

He is trying to discourage me from pressing on, and I begin to worry what will happen if, instead, I keep at it.

"We miss you around the office."

"I miss you, too," I tell him. "I still look forward to meeting your wife and cubs."

"They are waiting for you."

I came here for a reason.

"Lieutenant Jabri, I want to ask you a couple of questions. Are you sure that the killer Murtaziq went to Toledano's warehouse that night looking to steal something?"

"Absolutely. Ibrahim Dey, tragically, happens to be the man he found."

"And in arriving at this truth, in questioning everybody, you used the same gentle techniques I always see you using here in the office?"

The lieutenant moves the sleeve of his jacket slightly, enabling him to smile at the gold watch underneath.

"Was there some reason for the question?" he asks quietly. "Somebody say something?"

"About Hasan al-Attar, somebody said something."

Jabri buries the watch under his sleeve again and probes my eyes with a full-toothed grin on. "My dear brother, we in the Judiciary Police are working on these cases every day, and after all these years I think we have to show for our sweat a certain consideration with the society, a certain respect for our integrity. Not that we don't make mistakes, of course, but we are the institution that protects the public from harm, day in and day out. What you probably heard about Attar was street talk—and the talk of the street is always cheap. Much like Moroccan newspapers and the lies they print. Does that make sense?"

I stare a moment into my lap and return with a grin to match his. "Your word is good enough for me."

"God keep you, brother," Jabri replies. "So, where are you going next?"

"We're planning a visit to Bin Sulayman, where the soldier was born."

He smiles faintly and looks out the dusty window. "Bin Sulayman. You know, that's where I'm from."

I walk down the nine steps out of Precinct 5 and ask myself whether I should have told Jabri where we're going next.

Street talk in an Arab country is easy enough to dismiss when the talker is a blowhard, a bluff, an anti-Semite, and a stranger. So I don't need Jabri's help in laughing off the claim by Muhammad of Ayn Sabaa that the Toledanos are a "gangster family"—an obvious slight to my fellow Jews. But the man who alleged that Attar was physically abused is Bari, and what Bari says isn't street talk to me.

A gangster family, I think on my way home that night. What a bald-faced canard, leveled by a corrupt man against one of the few remaining indigenous Jews in Morocco. They are a wealthy family, I presume, and despised in a poor country for their material success. Why can't 31 million Muslims just leave three thousand Moroccan Jews alone to live quietly in peace? And what chutzpah for Muhammad of Ayn Sabaa to expect my cooperation in his campaign against the Toledanos.

That night in my apartment I turn on my laptop and Google the Jewish family name. My jaw drops.

HASHISH, GOLD AND SILVER, crows one Moroccan headline. THE SON OF YOSEF TOLEDANO IS IN TROUBLE. AND WHAT A MESS!

A COLOSSAL AFFAIR OF CORRUPTION, chimes another—JEWISH BUSINESSMAN OF MOROCCAN ORIGIN INVOLVED IN A MAJOR DRUG AND MONEY LAUNDERING CASE IN FRANCE.

MOROCCAN BUSINESSMAN JACOB TOLEDANO IS BEING HELD AT

<small>THE</small> F<small>LEURY</small>-M<small>EROGIS</small> <small>PRISON IN</small> P<small>ARIS ON CURRENCY AND GOLD</small>
<small>TRAFFICKING CHARGES, LEGAL SOURCES SAID IN THE</small> F<small>RENCH CAPI-</small>
<small>TAL</small> T<small>HURSDAY.</small>

The reportage notes that Jacob Toledano was arrested at Kennedy Airport before his extradition to Paris on smuggling charges.

Good grief.

Call me a hypocrite, but I hate it when Jews break laws.

Skepticism kicks in: I don't believe everything I read in Arabic newspapers, especially when the subject matter is a Jewish family in trouble. What Jabri told me about street talk and lies in the Moroccan press sounds comforting all of a sudden—even coming from a cop. Then I Google some more, and I find a story in the French press about the Toledanos with similar claims. There might be something off in the reportage, but it sure doesn't look like fiction.

I reread the headlines: hashish, gold, silver, trafficking. I remember my visit to the warehouse the family owns, the place Ibrahim Dey slept in for five years—the freight canisters, the tractor, the convenient isolation of the place. If someone were moving canisters of contraband in and out at the dead of night, Ibrahim Dey might well have caught a glimpse. Maybe Bari's early instincts were spot-on.

SEVENTEEN

The following morning is Saturday, the Jewish Sabbath. In Casablanca that still means something to fifteen hundred people in thirty-one functioning synagogues across the city. I put on a suit and walk toward a street address in the upscale neighborhood of Anfa that a Moroccan congregation back home in the States pressed into my hands before I flew east. Sunshine drenches the sparkling sidewalk. Barely a white tuft crosses the powder blue sky.

I turn off Anfa Boulevard onto a dusty side street lined with old French-style houses, a juice stand, and a snack shop specializing in deep-fried shrimp. Above a pair of locked steel gates, I spy twin stone tablets cloaked by an overhanging thicket of purple blossom vines and can just make out the engraving in Hebrew. It's a statue of the Ten Commandments. Just below it, three policemen and two soldiers from the Rapid Intervention Forces stand guard.

Tapping on the metal door, I feel my heart pound.

Nearly a million Jews used to live in Muslim cities and towns, from Tehran in the east to Tangier in the west, as recently as the 1940s. They were teachers, doctors, musicians, merchants, even civil servants in those countries where the government allowed them to serve.

An old man in a crimson fez opens the metal gate an inch and asks me to slip my ID through. He unlocks a tight chain, and two more uniformed policemen nod me into the graceful historic sanctuary of Beit El, one of the largest surviving congregations in Africa.

"Is everything well?" one of the cops inquires in Arabic. *"Shabbat shalom,"* he adds in Hebrew.

Inside the sanctuary, white-mustached old-timers weigh down the front seats and hold the fort for the first hour of prayer. They chant psalms to warm the hall while the young and the lazy trickle in. I look up to find a complex geometric design in bronze and silver skipping symmetrically up the walls and across the ceiling, gilding the grid of chandeliers. Arched stained-glass windows blaze highlights from the Bible in sunlit color. Above each translucent pane, time-honored advice to the congregation flows in black Hebrew block print—a selection of Jewish proverbs that resonate with North African and Arab values, uncannily uniform across the sectarian spectrum:

WHO IS BRAVE? HE WHO CONQUERS HIS TEMPTATIONS.
WHO IS RICH? HE WHO IS HAPPY WITH HIS PORTION.

And this ancient golden rule:

DO NOT SEPARATE YOURSELF FROM THE COLLECTIVE.

One congregant who seems to take the latter phrase to heart is an adolescent I notice clinging to his family for dear life. By midmorning it is obvious what frightens him: the imminent ordeal of his own bar mitzvah ceremony. His hands tremble and his ears burn red as the Torah scroll, hoisted by relatives, makes its way out of the holy ark by the eastern wall and heads straight toward him.

"Ma tkhafsh, ya'bni," I hear his father say. It means, "Don't be afraid, my son."

The temperature in the hall seems to rise as the rabbi lifts the scroll by its wooden handlebars, holding it up as high in the air as his arms will reach. Worshippers, now a swelling crowd of two hundred, raise their wide-open palms toward the scroll in ritual reflection of its invisible rays and wipe their faces with the godliness, slowly, from the forehead down. The cleric rests the scroll on the pulpit, hands the boy a silver pointer with a tip shaped like an index finger, and calls on him to read.

Gossipy voices quiet down.

The boy's hands quake as he aims the pointer at the start of his reading on the scroll. He takes a deep breath and begins to chant:

"A new king arose over Egypt who did not know Joseph."

To make it through a passage he has to run the cracks in his pubescent voice like a minefield. He labors to home in on the angular quarter-tone intervals of the Nihawand—a musical mode of the deepest blue dating back to antiquity and altogether absent from modern music in the West. Through the prism of his cantillation, an image more powerful than the boy or his voice flows from his lips:

"An angel of God appeared to Moses in a blazing fire out of a bush. He gazed, and there was a bush all aflame, yet the bush was not consumed."

Five times a day one hears the same haunting melodic intervals calling the faithful to prayer from mosque minarets all over town. Yesterday the same scale was used to chant the Qur'an in the mosque I prayed in with Bari. No faith owns the scale, but every faith's holy texts draw life from it. The cracks in the boy's voice smooth over as the passage approaches its climax and he winds his impeccable Hebrew diction around the fringes of the scale with mounting confidence. By the time he reaches the home stretch, Israel has had enough of Egyptian bondage, Moses has received his marching orders from God, and the boy seems to have lost his fears in the brooding, ethereal mood he has conjured in quarter tones. He steels his olive eyes into the parchment scroll and every syllable rings clear. At thirteen he is a man now, joined by Jewish law to the collective conscience of his people.

Women cordoned off in the balcony overhead lend wild ululation to the chorus of men and boys downstairs and pelt the bar mitzvah boy with candies, as if to shock him out of his modal reverie and back into the physical world.

The ancient call to action, the ululation, the outpouring of love for a child's rite of passage—rolled together here and now—touch my heart. I feel at once transported to my childhood in Hebrew day school and firmly rooted in Casablanca. But when I start to well up, I think it's for a different reason: this sweet manifestation of Jewish calm in a Muslim metropolis is partly illusory. A substantial security detachment is necessary to safeguard the place—a measure no mosque requires—which is only part of a broader policy by authorities to invest enormous resources in protecting the Jewish community. But for the shield of an authoritarian state, Morocco's three thousand Jews would probably have to leave in a hurry. I try, for the moment, to put this sad fact out of my mind. I have found my own place in a Muslim country now—a murky mission, granted, but one that has enormous meaning for my new friend Bari, and for me. I feel I have a role to play here. However gray our quest may be, it represents the fulfillment of a dream for me.

The service concludes with rhyming praise to the Master of the Universe. After the final Hebrew words, the congregation's unity breaks into factions and two new languages—Arabic and French— and I am alone again, a stranger to this place. Not for long, though. The boy's family invite me to celebrate with them outside without even asking my name.

The sanctuary empties into the courtyard, where a fleet of waiters have place-set two dozen tables, black and white and swarming with the color of old-fashioned North African salads piled on tapas plates of tin. I come close enough to hear the waiters' voices. They speak to each other in the Berber mother tongue of Shilha, and I think of Bari's cigarette-stained voice, a jarring image in this place that I quickly shake off. Its tapered, murmuring timbre drones softly, in stark relief to the strains of peppery gossip all around them: the Abitbul boys have been holding out on their donations to the synagogue, a graybeard declares. Azulay in Rabat is too full of himself to visit his ailing cousin, notes a man stuffed into a tux. A Perez is sleeping around again, so watch it. The Waknins have a bar mitzvah party coming up that will make the food here look like a snack.

It was a comforting sound, this standard synagogue banter—blessedly profane.

"So what are you doing in Morocco?" the bar mitzvah boy's mother asks in fluent Hebrew. Blond and buxom, she has been ordering the waiters around in Shilha and chatting up all the guests but me in French spiced with Arabic. Judging from the linguistic currency of her Hebrew, it probably rubbed off on the beaches of Tel Aviv.

I give her the elevator pitch.

"Interesting," the mother says. "But are you single?"

I tell her that I'm not.

"Oh, I see," she says, "*not* so interesting, then," and winks. "You know, we have girls to marry off around here." She waves her right hand.

On each table, eight tin plates are aligned in a central circle: smoke-salted olives, cumin-spiced carrots, vinegar-soaked fennel greens sliced paper thin, sautéed eggplant wedges, fire-roasted chilies, citrus-marinated avocado quarters, fava beans stewed in cumin and garlic, fried perch with sweet tomato sauce. While guests pick at the plates, waiters come around to fill every glass from a flask of rose-red liqueur. It is *mahiya,* Arabic for "Water of Life," the Moroccan Jewish moonshine—an anise-flavored spirit much like ouzo, clear as vodka until it meets an ice cube and clouds milky white. The *mahiya* on hand has been sweetened and colored with fresh cherries and a mellow birchlike root called *araq sus.*

I am already buzzed by the time the rabbi makes his benediction over the wine.

The man to my left is a seventysomething who still runs a family textile shop in the old city's *mellah* district, where the Jewish ghetto used to be. In pearly classical Arabic he says he is pleased to know that I rented an apartment in town: "Tourists pass through from Israel, America, Canada, but it is sadly seldom a Jew comes to live here, even for a few months."

"Why is that?"

He fumbles. "No good reason."

"Maybe the anti-Jewish talk scares people?"

"Yes, well, it is scary. But more often than not it's just talk around here. Our Muslim neighbors, they want to blow off steam. So they vent, and then we all go on with our lives."

My next glass of *mahiya* turns all of Casablanca a rosy shade of red.

"Still," he adds, "watch yourself."

On silver platters come mountains of *dafina*—a distinctive overnight-simmered Sabbath stew of beef, potatoes, and chickpeas suffused with cumin, olive oil, and honey. It is succulent, and it is going to be a slow walk home.

"Tell me," I ask the old man, "do you know the Toledanos?"

"Who doesn't?" he replies.

"I'm looking to get in touch with them."

"Why would you want to get in touch with *them*?"

I fumble a moment. "I have some information from my work that might be useful to them."

The old man shrugs. "But they don't worship here," he says. You'll find them at David Ha-Melekh, the new synagogue, the chichi one."

"Thanks." I stand up and begin to move in the direction of the front gates.

"Remember to take off your skullcap as you walk out the door," the old man warns.

Fear shoots through my stomach, mixing with the *mahiya* and all that food. I stuff the skullcap into my pocket, afraid of myself for having almost forgotten it was on my head.

After nightfall I wake up from a long *mahiya*-induced nap and pull the covers tight. An Atlantic storm has blown inland and hosed down the view out my bedroom window. I make it out of bed into the living room and turn on the TV. I switch to the evening news and catch Israeli aircraft firing missiles into Gaza. I switch again and find Gazans describing civilian casualties of the Israeli attack. I switch again and find a cleric prescribing vengeance for the Israeli attack. I switch again and find a cleric prescribing vengeance, without any reference to the Israeli attack. I switch again. I switch again.

EIGHTEEN

I t's not going to be easy to investigate the confessed killer of Ibrahim Dey, Rapid Intervention Forces private al-Raddad Murtaziq.

Ahead of our planned excursion to the village where he was born, I try to work the official channels to gain access to Murtaziq in his prison cell. The chief of Precinct 5 says he cannot help me, because authority over arraigned prisoners is in the hands of the Ministry of Justice. So I ask a senior justice ministry official for permission to visit Murtaziq and get rebuffed; pending the prisoner's eventual court-martial, he explains, control over his visits is in the hands of the army. I pursue the matter with a military liaison officer, who tells me I might as well be asking for a visit with the king. Only Murtaziq's family, he adds, have the right to see him once per week. Perhaps you should try to ingratiate yourself with them, he suggests. I recall that we have the name and phone number of the killer's father, thanks to the police file, but I doubt he would want to be helpful to us. The entire Murtaziq family would be wary of any inquiry into their accused son, fearing that information they provide to anyone they don't know might be used against the young man in court.

Nor are we clear on precisely what we're looking for in the place where Murtaziq was born. I have been nursing the hypothesis, based solely on a cassette tape Dey once owned, that the victim was a secret Islamist, possibly murdered by the soldier as part of a clandestine campaign to snuff out militants. If that's true, then the instruction to kill presumably would have come from a government office or an army base to which we do not have access, not the boy's hometown. Bari's initial theories that Dey was targeted by jihadists or a drug cartel, though they sounded improbable to me at first, might make more sense: the warehouse was owned by Jews and therefore an obvious target for an Islamist hate crime; and there have been criminal accusations against the powerful Jewish Toledano family itself, inviting the speculation that Dey saw something he shouldn't have among freight canisters in the dead of night.

But if Murtaziq was a jihadist, or a gun for hire, it's more likely he found these affiliations in Casablanca than in his small hometown. Maybe police are honest and correct in alleging that Murtaziq simply killed Dey over pocket change. On this score the boy's native soil may offer a clue—a hint of his character, or any prior entanglements with the law. I suppose Bari was right when he said, after Friday prayer the other day, that all our theories flow from the more basic question he craves most to answer: What kind of a man would kill Bari's best friend? Since our investigation is fueled by Bari's burning emotional need to know, we might as well trust his instincts. We went to the coastal town of Jadida, after all, on the strength of a dead man's dream. Maybe what we are looking for in this village is similar to what we found in Jadida: a slice of personal history. It's unfortunate that we don't have a dream to go on this time. And it's deeply regrettable that we're mixed up with an "agent of corruption," that big fat mug Muhammad of Ayn Sabaa.

The killer's native soil is a small farming village at the edge of Bin Sulayman, a lush agricultural plateau in the heart of a historic coastal region known as the Shawiya. An hour by car from Casablanca, the Shawiya is a stronghold of Arab Morocco in which few of the locals speak Shilha or any other Berber language. The lion's share of rural migrants to the big city hail from there, as do scores of young recruits to the military and security services each year. Among jihadists from Casablanca who have been identified or caught, numerous young men are the descendants of rural migrants from the Shawiya as well. So this green, fertile plateau is also a field of warriors, contributing human fodder to both sides in Morocco's war on terror.

With Muhammad of Ayn Sabaa, Bari and I cram into the backseat of a white shuttle taxi from Casablanca. The ramshackle housing at the fringes of the big city dissipates with the dusty smog and gives way to a long, whispering promenade of trees along the road. Eucalyptus groves are the first; their low-wavering shrubs shimmer in the sunlight. Then weeping willows crop up, followed by the *arar*, a cone-bearing tree with whorls of scalelike leaves, and finally a grove of *sidra*, a round shade tree that, according to the Qur'an, imparts divine knowledge to those who sit under it. Through the open car window, I savor the cleanest air I have breathed since arriving in Morocco. As we near the township of Bin Sulayman, a long white fence stretches for several miles. Behind it lie a military airport and training academies for the Royal Gendarmes, the Auxiliary Forces, and the air force. Next comes the Royal Golf Course and a few stately homes, followed by the humble town itself—a clean little Arab stronghold, insulated by the foliage and the brass from a surrounding sea of mixed ethnic cities.

We disembark by the town's main drag, Hasan II Avenue, where coffeehouses, professional offices, grocery stores, and the odd cybercafé line up flat against the street under arched wooden façades of pink, orange, and green. Two boys on skateboards narrowly miss us as they race down the sidewalk. Three veiled girls in jeans pass by arm in arm, giggling. Across the street, meanwhile, dozens and dozens of men and women are all walking purposefully in one direction.

"What's going on over there?" I ask.

"The weekly market," Muhammad of Ayn Sabaa explains—not looking at me while he talks, just muttering into the ground. "It's down the road a kilometer or so. Every family sends someone there for food and so on and to learn what's new. And all the farmers have their boys there or sometimes wives selling the produce for the week."

Bari shows no interest. "Let me have the phone number of Murtaziq's father," he tells me. "I want to talk to him and get a good look at him." He clenches his teeth.

Muhammad of Ayn Sabaa takes Bari's right hand. He looks into his eyes with sympathy—the first sweet gesture I've seen from him. "Why don't we sit down a moment," he says.

We find a table at a sidewalk café. Bari finds a cigarette in his pocket and lights it off the last match in a worn-out matchbook on the table. "*Nus nus*," he tells the waitress; hot milk and a shot of espresso. Muhammad of Ayn Sabaa asks for tea with fenugreek—*wiza* in Arabic.

"You see, my brother," the big man says, "Murtaziq's father is not going to be pleasant to talk to. You know that, of course. But he will make it harder for us to ask questions in his village. We should probably talk to him at the *end* of the day, after we've tried other things—not the beginning."

"He's right," I concede.

"I disagree," Bari says. "I think I can pretend we want to help his son and talk him into working with us, telling us everything he knows. Leave it to me, brothers; I know I can do it."

Muhammad of Ayn Sabaa and I glance at each other, but only for a moment. I make a nosedive for my briefcase, pull out the police file, and hand Bari my mobile phone. He has to dial it twice; the first time, his fingers move sloppily and he presses the wrong buttons.

"Hello, Murtaziq? I'm from Casablanca. It's about your son Raddad." Bari shakes his head. "He hung up."

"Hit redial."

"Murtaziq?" Bari repeats. "Yes, from Casablanca. We are in Bin Sulayman now. Can we see you? Yes. Where?"

Now he snaps his fingers and I hand him a pen and notebook.

"You see?" Bari says. "This is the way to do it."

We are to meet Murtaziq's father in a coffeehouse called the Sons of Haddu, deeper in the town. The locals who give us directions ad-vise that it is a social club of sorts, frequented by farming clans from the surrounding villages. A short walk from Hasan II Avenue, it lies off on its own, away from nearby homes and businesses in the middle of a grassy field. We peek inside and find robed men playing dominoes over hookahs and coffee. There is nowhere left to sit except outdoors. We take the table nearest the door and wait.

A waiter approaches us with a furtive glance.

Bari eyes him with suspicion. To me he whispers, "They are all one tribe around here. They keep close to each other, and we are the outsiders. They don't like Berbers here, and they can't stand foreigners. To them we might as well all be Jews."

Fifteen minutes later, there is no sign of Muhammad Murtaziq. Bari taps his watch and shows it to Muhammad of Ayn Sabaa. The waiter makes another round.

"Still nothing?" he asks.

"Maybe you can help us," I suggest.

Bari frowns.

"Do you know a man named Muhammad Murtaziq?"

The waiter looks down at his empty serving tray. "You are looking for him?"

"We came from far away to see him and he said he would meet us here. Maybe you know where he is?"

The man disappears into the smoky café. Three minutes later, he comes back. "What do you want with Murtaziq?" he asks.

Bari hesitates. "Perhaps to help him with his son."

The waiter makes a faint show of recognition, and leaves us again.

Eventually a tall, thin man in a green robe emerges—mustached, with grizzled concave cheeks and forlorn olive brown eyes. He saunters about the outer seating area as if he might pick one of the empty tables, and finally finds his way to ours. The waiter comes out to check up on him.

"Juice?" the man in green asks us, as if it were the last word in a long, exhausting speech.

We nod our heads.

"Mr. Muhammad Murtaziq?" I ask.

The question only makes him more uncomfortable. It doesn't help that Bari has his arms folded, or that Muhammad of Ayn Sabaa weighs 325 pounds and breathes like Darth Vader.

"We're here from Casablanca," Bari says, "because my friend here is a writer and he's taken an interest in your son's case."

That was dumb.

Murtaziq peers into my eyes, quaking a little. "Why you want to write about my son?" He speaks Arabic with a farmer's lilt—slow, twangy, hard for an outsider to understand.

Muhammad of Ayn Sabaa shakes his head at Bari, a gesture the father appears to notice.

"He wants to *help* your son," Bari tries to explain, affecting a smile. "He can write something good about him and it will help him get a lighter sentence."

"Sentence!" Murtaziq cries, standing up.

Muhammad of Ayn Sabaa shakes his head, looking helpless.

"What are you, Israelis?" the father goes on. "You're Israelis." He wags his finger at Bari. "You are a Zionist traitor, God destroy your house. Do not ever talk about my son, scum!"

"Please excuse him," I plead, "an unfortunate figure of speech."

"Get out of here," Murtaziq says. "Never come back. I have a big family, and I warn you if you stay on our soil it will be very bad for you. You might be killed!" He clenches a fist and raises it above our heads. "My whole family will come after you!"

The three of us get up and walk off fast, snatching glances behind our backs at this irate gentleman, who continues spouting until we are beyond earshot, perhaps even longer. We keep hustling down the road. Eventually we reach a large black clearing with picnic benches surrounded by hanging cow carcasses, scales, and men in white with cleavers. The atmosphere does not cure our jitters. Beside each meat stand lies a long iron grill, and thick bags of onions and tomatoes ornament the massive suspended flesh.

"Lunch," declares Muhammad of Ayn Sabaa, pointing at the nearest bloody carcass.

He's got a sense of humor.

We take a seat at a picnic bench, unsure whether to actually order something.

"I'm sorry, brothers," Bari says, still panting from the long, hurried walk. "I let my feelings get in the way of strategy."

A teenager wearing a black leather jacket walks by looking at us, shaking his head ever so slowly.

"What do we do now?" Bari asks.

"Tell me what you want us to do," Muhammad of Ayn Sabaa replies. "I'm here for *you*."

Bari stares into space. "Well, maybe we try another way," he tells me, tapping my hand with his index finger. "You're American. How would the FBI handle this?"

Fuck. I wish I didn't know the answer to that question.

Muhammad of Ayn Sabaa grants me a little smile for the first time. I'm not sure why. Maybe he can see my head racing. There is an unexpected look in his eyes of familiarity, almost collegiality.

Maybe we're thinking similar thoughts? Maybe not. I'm still jittery and he doesn't look scared at all.

"Ma tkhafsh, ya'bni," he says. Don't be afraid, my son.

What a strange and unexpected thing for him to say.

Now what I'm thinking, actually, is that the killer's father shouldn't have threatened us. Maybe he deserves something in return—something from Muhammad of Ayn Sabaa, Muhammad Bari, and me.

The big man nods at me with a sort of criminal solemnity.

"We're going to need a lot of cigarettes," I volunteer.

Some death threats are serious and others are empty talk. One of my FBI handlers used to assure me that when they're serious, it usually takes at least a few days to organize a team to carry out the hit. Which suits us fine this afternoon: Muhammad of Ayn Sabaa and I agree that we need only two days to suck this town dry. He and I determine to collaborate as if we were best friends, and we use every trick in the book to piece together al-Raddad Murtaziq's short life in order to try to give Bari what he came here for. Our objective is as pure as Bari's heart, even if our tactics prove not to be. We also decide that the killer's father, for having threatened to deploy his large family against us, deserves some poetic justice: we are going to take our information directly from his family, friends, and neighbors. Muhammad of Ayn Sabaa and I both know that the bigger the family, the more bad blood one finds among the relatives. Having met the father, we posit that Murtaziq has cousins, aunts, and uncles—maybe even brothers and sons—who are disenchanted with him, let us say, and would be only too happy to tell us all about his branch of the family, including and especially the one who is in trouble.

And we know how to find disenchanted relatives.

Muhammad of Ayn Sabaa meets with a crony of long standing in the local police station and offers a pack of Cleopatras for every criminal complaint filed against one of the Murtaziq boys. Sure enough, the killer's older brother Abd al-Nabi is the subject of a complaint filed by his own aunt. We photocopy it. Abd al-Nabi, it turns out, wanted very much to marry his first cousin Asiya. Asiya's mother refused, whereupon the young man threatened to kill himself. When that didn't work, he threatened to tie Asiya's right leg to a rope, tie the other end to a horse, and drag her at top speed several kilometers in the dirt. Partly as a measure of protection, Asiya married someone else a few weeks later. Abd al-Nabi showed up uninvited to the wedding, dancing as if it were his own and sticking a camcorder in the face of the beautiful hennaed bride. So reads the complaint, anyway. I visit the home of the woman who filed it. The fact that I'm an American writer—with an international audience, she presumes—appeals to her somehow. She dutifully shows me the part of the wedding video in which Abd al-Nabi is filming the bride at close range, and she proceeds to talk me through everything she knows about the Murtaziqs. She introduces me to a nephew who trained with Raddad in the army, who has his own stories to share, and a great-aunt who watched Raddad and his three brothers grow up. She picks up the phone and calls one of Raddad's disgruntled maternal uncles. And so on.

Meanwhile, we've sent Bari to the large outdoor market with instructions to pose as a produce shopper while actually shopping for something else. Tasked with specifics, he proves to be a quick study. Bari ambles around the vast market, tasting strawberries and sugar snaps and cucumbers, until he finds the Murtaziq family's stand. The killer's mother is standing right there. Having learned his lesson, he does not attempt to engage her in conversation. He just takes note of precisely what she is selling, then goes around looking for her competitors. Several of them say they despise the Murtaziqs and claim to know something about them. Some offer information in exchange for cigarettes; Bari has been equipped with plenty more than he would need to smoke himself. One young man says he knows a lot of secrets but wants a thousand dollars. Bari decides that his demand is so exorbitant that the only reasonable price to pay him is absolutely nothing. He's getting really good at this.

The following afternoon, Muhammad of Ayn Sabaa and I converge on the tiny village of Ayn Tizgha, on the outskirts of Bin Sulayman, where the Murtaziq family lives. There's a small new mosque there. We go inside and work the crowd. The big find: a onetime lecturer at the University of Pennsylvania whose roots are in this township and who happens to live 180 meters from the house where Raddad grew up. He and the killer's father have been talking regularly for the past two years. Muhammad of Ayn Sabaa judges that I'm the better suited to befriend and debrief the good professor, given our shared experience of American academic culture. I tell the man I'm conducting a sociological study, which is sort of true, and the ruse works just fine. Meanwhile, Muhammad of Ayn Sabaa talks to the other neighbors—"good ole boys" from the farm who love to smoke cigarettes as well—not the cheap local stuff, mind you, but the American imports. He has acquired plenty of Marlboros for just this kind of bigmouth.

"You know, you're really corrupt," Muhammad of Ayn Sabaa tells me after the stars come out on the second night of our collaboration.

I take in the cold, clean night air. "Muhammad, I think this is the beginning of a beautiful friendship."

So, let me review what we managed to learn, beginning with the Murtaziq family's legal defense strategy for their son Raddad. They want to bust him out of prison. Raddad's father has little faith in the young man's court-appointed lawyer and suspects he may even be working against Raddad. He does not place much faith in the country's legal system in general. He more readily trusts that cash can be used to bribe prison guards into letting his son out under an assumed name, and he is willing to sell off a piece of the family farmland to raise the requisite funds. The plan would call for a newly sprung Raddad to lie low for a while, moving from one rural area to another, until the murder case blows over and he can quietly return home. In Muhammad of Ayn Sabaa's expert opinion, this is an unrealistic plan. Having visited the Murtaziq property, he feels that even a large chunk of it would not fetch the money such a bribe would require. "Bear in mind we're talking about a military court-martial here," Muhammad of Ayn Sabaa observed. "They don't mess around." The ex-lecturer from Penn who lives nearby has been trying to talk Raddad's father out of the bribery strategy, but the family's distrust of government in Morocco appears to run deep.

In a sense, it goes back centuries.

Both Raddad's parents hail from the largest tribe in Bin Sulayman, the Ziyayda, who share a tradition of holding God and country at arm's length. When it comes to Islamic practice, for example, the Ziyayda are regarded as somewhat wayward: many of them have been brewing wine for generations, a blatant contravention of Islamic law; and they tend to join in congregational worship less frequently than most rural Moroccans—which might be one reason we were able to mingle in the mosque near the Murtaziqs' home without incident. As to their regard for the monarchy, it has had its highs and lows, but the lows are epic history. Centuries ago, the Ziyayda were among the last to submit to the authority of the three-hundred-year-old dynasty that rules Morocco to this day. They fought fiercely for their independence and had to be subdued by force of arms. This is not to say that all their fighting targeted the establishment, to be sure. In the nineteenth and early twentieth centuries, some of the tribesmen famously battled each other, as well as smaller tribes, over various personal disagreements, turning Bin Sulayman into a land of family blood feuds, unsafe for travelers. These conflicts subsided in the early twentieth century when the Ziyayda and most other tribes came together in a struggle against the new French occupiers. Years before the urban centers of Morocco had organized to resist French forces in earnest, the Ziyayda were stockpiling weapons in caves and ambushing foreign troops in the dead of night. Yet in the decades following Morocco's independence from France, some of the Ziyayda went back to opposing the new Moroccan government. The most notable example was a son of the Ziyayda named Mahdi bin Baraka, the most popular socialist dissident in the history of the country. He brazenly called for an end to the monarchy of King Hasan II, until he was kidnapped and probably murdered in France in 1965.

From one Moroccan establishment to another, the Ziyayda have been consummate fighters. But their historic opposition to the state is more a distant memory today, and it seems at once fitting and unsettling that so many members of the tribe now serve in the Moroccan army. The distrust the murderer's father shows for the Moroccan legal system appears to have a tribal pedigree—though, on the other hand, many Moroccans across the kingdom also feel the same way.

Al-Raddad Murtaziq, in his childhood, manifested the honor and generosity to which all Arab tribes aspire, but neither the militancy nor the prickliness of his fellow Ziyayda. Friend and foe of the family agree that he was the sweetest and most honorable of his father's four sons. You could hand the child a fistful of candy and expect all his brothers to receive their share before Raddad ate a piece himself. "It was the other three who stole carpets from the mosque," one neighbor observed, using a figure of speech peculiar to the village of Ayn Tizgha. "He was always a giver, never a taker," another neighbor said. Raddad's civility also contrasted with the temperament of his father and two paternal uncles. In his youth he witnessed great acrimony among the three of them: they fought for weeks over the

division of a small parcel of farmland they had inherited from Raddad's grandfather. Kitchen knives and a wooden club are believed to
have been employed in the negotiations. Raddad would have known
all about the fighting and probably seen some of it up close, because
his father, paternal uncles, aunts, and cousins live in a family compound of thin-walled houses where no one has much privacy.

"What would turn a boy like that into a wild animal?" Bari
asked aloud when we told him what we'd heard. "Ibrahim Dey was
also a peaceful man. How could they have fought at all? It doesn't
make sense."

Around age twelve, Raddad followed a custom of his village and
dropped out of school to help tend to the family farm. In his new
spare time, he learned to trap and shoot small game in the dusty for-
est beyond the farmland, and he found a favorite fishing spot, a few
miles from Ayn Tizgha, in the glistening Bay of Buzniqa. I visited the
place. Part of the shoreline is flanked by luxury housing, and the
people who live there, by local reputation among the fishermen, are
military generals who grew rich off the drug trade. This claim is a
recurring trope in Morocco; I have encountered it in several other
places up and down the kingdom's Atlantic coast. It may be true to
a limited extent, but more likely it is a poor man's way of explaining how some Moroccans grow rich. There are only so many generals in the country, after all. A semiliterate teen like Raddad would
be likely to believe such stories nonetheless. His ideas about the
army may even have been partly formed by them. He knew about
the value of hashish, in any case, because his father smokes it often
and Raddad acquired the habit himself in his early teens.

Why he decided to join the army is complicated to explain. In a
way, the reason stems from the family quarrel over land that
haunted Raddad's childhood. The breakup of farmland is so prevalent in Morocco that a farming expert I spoke with claimed that it
factors into the overall decline of Moroccan agriculture. As rural
populations grow and sons divvy up the plots of their fathers, he explained, more and more precious space is divided each year by
fences and chicken wire, and land use grows less efficient. The problem of efficiency may have been one reason why the Murtaziqs gave

up on farming wheat and corn a few years back and opened a green-house. Because most of the demand for the ornamental plants they now grew was in big cities like Casablanca and Rabat, they would have had to transport their yield, en masse, fifty miles at a time, and this crucial task required a van. They found the money to acquire one, and the business ran smoothly until the van began to break down repeatedly. Bari learned all about this family crisis from the Murtaziqs' competitors in the greenhouse business whom he met at the market. Several of them recalled how pleased they were when-ever the Murtaziqs' van broke down, and one of them hinted that the vehicle was not a lemon; rather, acts of sabotage lay behind the van's problems.

Whether or not the story of the van is an oversimplification of the family's financial woes, like stories about corrupt generals at the Bay of Buzniqa, we do not doubt the main point that around nine months ago, the family went bankrupt. Somebody had to step in and deliver some cash. True to form, Raddad volunteered. For poor rural youth in Morocco, the readiest means of earning a modest yet clean and reliable salary is to join the armed forces. Classmates say that as a boy, Raddad had already shown interest in becoming a sol-dier. The army is a prestigious institution in Morocco, despite the reputation for corruption among the officer corps; and among the children of Bin Sulayman, martial sentiments run especially high. Raddad has distant family in the armed forces, though none of his relatives in the Ayn Tizgha compound is a veteran. His mother ap-pealed to an uncle who is based in the training camp of Bu Arfa, a tough garrison town at the eastern tip of Morocco near the Algerian border, to help enlist Raddad. By the time of his conscription he had spent the past four years working in the thick, sweet air of the fam-ily greenhouse, where nobody wielded knives anymore, or fought, or even yelled. He knew that his life would change when he joined the army—but he had no idea, relatives said, that he would be de-ployed to Casablanca, where the air is polluted and life is fast-paced and noisy. At basic training in Bu Arfa, they broke him down and built him up again with a new fighting spirit. They moved him to another base in a region called Tadla for weapons training, from heavy artillery to knives and clubs. It was there that a recruiter for the nascent Rapid Intervention Forces decided he had the temperament to serve an urban policing role.

"The army must have changed him," Bari observed. "They made him more violent, taught him to get what he wants through violence. But they can't change a man's personality, can they? God only knows what they teach there."

No one in Ayn Tizgha or the surrounding villages knows much about what happened to the young man in the three months between his initial deployment to the big city and his arraignment for murder. All the family has to go on is what Raddad says when his mother visits him in jail once per week, and his stories contradict each other. During her first visit, Raddad told his mother that he had been drunk along the railroad tracks that night and climbed over the wall of the warehouse in search of a place to sleep, only to get in a fight with the man who guarded the place. Being in a drunken stupor, Raddad said, he had killed a man without intending to do so. On the mother's second visit, he told an entirely different story: someone in the army, he claimed, gave him milk to drink that was drugged. He fell into a psychologically weakened state, vulnerable to suggestion, and received instructions that he no longer remembers. Nor does he have any memory of his actions on that fateful night, he said. During her third visit, Raddad said he killed Ibrahim Dey for a reason, but he would reveal that reason only to the judge at his court-martial.

"So you see," Bari said in reaction to the latter two explanations, "there *is* a secret in this story. Maybe he was drugged by a commanding officer and given instructions to kill Ibrahim Dey, or maybe it's something completely different, but now we know for sure that there was a conspiracy to kill Ibrahim Dey, God have mercy on him."

No, we don't know for sure, I think. What we do know, however, is that whether one of Raddad's excuses to his mother is a lie or all of them are, they suggest, viewed together, that he is hiding something.

The three of us relax the following afternoon at the sidewalk café where our visit started. We have plenty of leftover cigarettes for Bari.

"I'm disappointed," Bari declares. "We still don't know the true story of what happened that night."

Well, I'm disappointed that Bari is disappointed. We just milked this town for two days straight. "Look, we made progress," I tell him. "We know enough about Raddad's character to rule out the police claim that he went in there to steal a little money, for one thing."

"I knew that all along," Bari says.

"Be patient," Muhammad of Ayn Sabaa says. "The truth is closer than you think." He clasps my forearm in a fatherly sort of way and maintains eye contact with Bari. "You have a good friend here," he tells him. "Ask him to go to the Jew who owns the warehouse and pump him for information. Because that man is a Jew, the police will tell him things that they never tell any of us. And he can tell his fellow Jew whatever he wants. They are beyond our system of power. I never understood why, but that's how it is." Then he bumps my shoulder with his fist, and in my ear he whispers that he has better schemes in mind now than to sue the Jew Toledano and would gladly let me in on the ground floor. For the right price, moreover, he is available to take part in any investigative project I might want to carry out in the future—"even in America," he says.

My mobile phone rings just as we are about to leave the café and look for a shuttle taxi back to Casablanca. It's a woman's voice.

"This is Fatima Dey," she says. The sister of Ibrahim Dey. "Our father has died. Our days of mourning begin tonight."

"Who was that?" Bari asks.

I tell him that the father of Ibrahim Dey is dead.

"We have to pay a visit to the mourning," he says. "A lot comes out when families mourn."

NINETEEN

The stars are out when I reach my apartment. I sit on the couch and spoon the remaining peanut butter out of the jar. Turning on my digital camera, I peer into the tiny LCD screen, rewinding past images of Bin Sulayman, Jadida, and Precinct 5, until I find the old passport photograph of Ibrahim Dey that we snapped in his mother's home. I zoom in on the murder victim's wide brown eyes. Under the half-light of the streetlamp outside, his eyes seem to telegraph a mixture of hurt and fear. I don't see the levity that Bari was drawn to, the power to bring good luck that kept him fed by strangers and friends. But I rewind one image more and there it is. Dey is all bliss in the smiling photo with his cousin and nephews in Jadida—a happier, easier, wilder time in his life, albeit a time that ended badly for reasons Bari and I do not fully understand. We know that he was dreaming about those days a few weeks before he died: his uncle, his cousin, the money he so easily doubled just by asking, "May I have a little more?" It was of course a wish that went unfulfilled; I switch back to the passport photo and notice the poverty in his gaunt, bearded face. Yet something made him dream of those days not long before his death. I turn off the camera and try to imagine the victim in the moonlit warehouse, pondering his dream. Then I try to picture him, moments before the end, looking into the eyes of a young soldier wielding a wooden stick.

Who are you, Ibrahim Dey?

I had been wondering whether it is harder to imagine an entire city you've never been to—like Baghdad, the city of my own dreams—than to understand a single human life you've never encountered—a life, like so many, that left barely more than the waning memories of family and friends behind? I think I have my answer: it's the shrouded individual life that defies the imagination. My hunger is growing to resurrect the memory of this soul I don't know—not because he represented something bigger than himself, not because he was possibly a jihadist or a victim of jihadism or a link to a globe-straddling drug cartel, but because he was the most confounding thing of all in any attempt to make sense of the world. He was an individual, shaped and pushed and pulled by the forces of his time—forces that ultimately brought him into one final bloody confrontation. My desire to understand Dey's life is only spiked, moreover, by the fact that the government, or some faction of the government, wants us not to.

But it is Bari for whom this pursuit matters most, and Bari whose life I am getting to know more easily. I am still placing a kind of hope in him—the hope that he can demonstrate that individuals like himself, in countries like Morocco, can press their demands on an authoritarian establishment and gain liberty and individual rights, one step at a time. I'm watching Bari with this in mind. He doesn't always seem to know what he's doing—though who does? He made a serious mistake in Bin Sulayman that jeopardized his quest—our quest. It took two friends, Muhammad of Ayn Sabaa and me, to redeem the investigation by applying our own skills that Bari did not have. Would he have had the courage, determination, and wherewithal to brave this journey on his own? For that matter, does his partnership with a foreigner like me make his quest less authentic, less replicable on a grand scale? I would like to think not. It was Bari who influenced *me* to join *him*, not the other way around. Bari persuaded me to drop everything I was doing and help him. Bari recruited Muhammad of Ayn Sabaa, against my wishes, to help in ways I couldn't have foreseen to be necessary. Bari built a team, and the team has been filling in his missing pieces. He even found himself a Jew to put on staff, with natural qualifications to figure out how to poke around a warehouse owned by a Jewish man.

Because of the importance I attach to his success, I am worried about what we are yet to uncover—about the possibility that whatever it is will overwhelm him, or underwhelm him, and make him wish he had never embarked on this journey to begin with, or worse still, cause him to quit. This concern unsettles me.

Something else is unsettling me, too, something I feel even more deeply but do not know how to put into words.

In any case, at Muhammad of Ayn Sabaa's suggestion, it's time I play that role for which I am uniquely qualified: seek out Marcel Toledano, the Jew who owns the crime scene, and pump him for information about the events of that brutal night.

Here's a paradox: the killer al-Raddad Murtaziq was once the kind of sweet boy who shared candy with all his brothers before taking a piece for himself, whereas his victim Ibrahim Dey dreamed of a lopsided scale, the heavy side with all the money on it belonging only to him. Murtaziq gave and Dey received, or dreamed of receiving.

Or maybe Dey was just dreaming about a lopsided scale.

There are many imbalances of power and wealth in an Arab capital—in any capital—but Dey appears to have taken a particular interest in one of them. Of all the warehouses in Casablanca, he chose to squat in one that belongs to a Jew. Only 3,000 Moroccan Jews remain in a country of 31 million people, down from an all-time high of 265,000 in 1947. Back then, there was nothing mysterious about their presence here. They had been around for centuries, and most Muslims in the country knew at least one or two of them. Today, the few who remain are an enigma to the general population, often cordoned off by tight security, high walls, and, in some cases, great power and wealth. A poor man has to go to some lengths to catch a glimpse of one.

Most of what Moroccans hear about Jews comes from Arabic satellite television, much of which emanates, in turn, from countries like Saudi Arabia and Qatar where there are no indigenous Jews at all. It isn't glowing coverage. Audiences learn about Israel's harsh treatment of the Palestinians and take in conspiracy theories about global Jewry's alleged aspiration to control the world. They learn to regard the Jewish people as enemies of the Arab and Muslim world. These messages naturally inspire hatred; but they also arouse curiosity.

I'll never know for sure what sort of curiosity Ibrahim Dey might have had about Jews, but I can make an inference based on the ruminations of some of his neighbors. When I first met Precinct 5 chief Sharqawi, for example, he wanted to know "why Jews love Morocco so much." Muhammad of Ayn Sabaa claimed that Jews enjoy a privileged status, far outside the country's legal norms. Coming from a man who games the legal system for a living, that's quite a statement. And the day I met Muhammad Bari, he marveled at the overwhelming police presence that surrounded and swarmed the Jewish-owned warehouse when a dead body was discovered on the premises. Not every dead body in Casablanca wins so much attention, after all.

The phenomena these three men observed are indicative of a special relationship that ties the Moroccan government to its Jewish community as well as Jews beyond its borders. The general population of Morocco knows relatively little about it, because their government tends to avoid revealing the details.

Life wasn't always rosy for the Jews of Morocco, and when opportunities arose to flee the country, many did. Over centuries they were pent up in ghettos and periodically subjected to mob violence as well as mistreatment by the ruling sultans—though the dark times were offset by periods of tolerance. In the twentieth century, the worst oppressors of Moroccan Jews were not Muslim. A wave of Jewish exiles fled discriminatory practices by the Vichy French government during the Second World War; Jews were banned from owning businesses in European neighborhoods, from procuring any form of credit, and in many cases from practicing the legal and medical professions. Then-Sultan Muhammad V boldly defied instructions from the pro-Nazi occupiers to make the country's Jews wear a yellow star and protected the Jewish community from greater persecution. He is remembered by Moroccan Jews as a hero. Only a few years later, however, the general population made Jews their object of rage following the 1948 Arab-Israeli war: Muslim-led riots broke out in two Moroccan cities, killing forty-four Jews. Eighteen thousand subsequently fled to Israel. Jewish emigration ebbed and flowed in the years hence—banned at times by King Muhammad V, slowed by periods of relative calm—and accelerated in the years surrounding the Arab-Israeli wars. By the mid-seventies, the Jewish population had fallen to twenty-five thousand, and it has been shrinking ever since.

A consequence of this mass emigration has been the establishment of Moroccan Jewish Diaspora communities. It has been estimated that 1 million Jews of Moroccan descent now live in Israel, for example, and though many are of modest means, some hold senior government positions, others are icons of popular culture, and no small number have grown wealthy. Moroccan Jews have also amassed economic power in North America and Europe. Successive Moroccan kings, sensing that these communities could serve as bridges to their adopted countries, have sought out and warmly engaged Moroccan Jewry everywhere—with the remnants of the country's indigenous Jewish community serving as bridges to their brethren abroad. "Morocco never loses a Jewish citizen," King Hasan II once said. "We gain an ambassador." In a poor economy reliant in large part on tourism, a significant chunk of tourist traffic into Morocco now stems from American, Canadian, French, and Israeli Jews, many of Moroccan origin. The cash-strapped kingdom has also been working, somewhat successfully, to persuade these communities to invest in Moroccan business. Most significantly, Jews have become a vital geopolitical asset—and a staunch ally in the Moroccan government's struggle against its enemies, both foreign and domestic.

Understanding the geopolitical side of this special relationship requires some background.

When Ibrahim Dey's confessed killer al-Raddad Murtaziq joined the army, much of what he learned about the army's mission would have concerned a long-standing conflict over a 103,000-square-mile portion of the Saharan desert. The region is sparsely populated, mainly desert flatland. For nearly one hundred years it was a Spanish protectorate, a vestige of Spain's imperial adventure in Africa. In the mid-seventies, when Spain began rapidly to divest from its colonial possessions, this chunk of the Sahara was left up for grabs. Morocco, citing its historic ties to the Sahara and tribal and ethnic links to the Saharan people, annexed most of the territory. It now amounts to half the kingdom's landmass. Algeria, a friend of the Soviet Union, and Morocco's bitter rival throughout the cold war, came to support a nascent Saharan fighting force opposed to Moroccan rule in the region, known as the Polisario. What ensued was a grueling war over the territory between the Polisario and Morocco that lasted more than fifteen years.

A U.N.-brokered cease-fire in 1991 put an end to the fighting, but not to the bitterness or the conflict. To this day, the Polisario controls a small portion of the Saharan territory and, from its base in southern Algeria, demands control over the rest to form its own desert republic—presumably in the mold of its chief state supporter, the Algerian military dictatorship.

Morocco has offered limited autonomy to the Saharans, but stands firm on its claim to sovereignty over all 103,000 square miles of Saharan territory. From the Moroccan government's perspective, the Polisario is essentially a puppet of Algeria, the kingdom's long-term rival, with which it is still in a state of cold war. Moroccans believe Algeria exploits and perpetuates the conflict just to sap Morocco's energies and military resources. Political developments surrounding the conflict are covered daily in the Moroccan media, and the kingdom clamps down hard on pro-Polisario activism within its borders. Meanwhile, tension in the south and along the Algerian border is a fact of life in Morocco, and the possibility of renewed hostilities is never far off.

Soldiers in Morocco by and large watch the same pan-Arab

satellite television everyone else does, and learn about their country's struggles from the national media and their commanders in the field. Ibrahim Dey's killer, al-Raddad Murtaziq, for example, would probably not have learned from these sources that for decades running, a key ally in Morocco's Saharan struggle has been the State of Israel, working in cooperation with American and Moroccan Jews.

The Moroccan kingdom's ties to the Mossad, Israel's secret service, date back to the 1960s, when the Israeli intelligence apparatus provided training and equipment to Morocco's security services in their struggle against domestic opponents, notably Nasserist and pro-Soviet elements. Assistance was a two-way street: Moroccan monarch Hasan II made numerous efforts to help broker a peace agreement between Israel and the Palestinians. During the Moroccan war in the Sahara, Israeli Defense Forces advisers made repeated visits to the war front. The Mossad assisted Morocco's army in the construction of the "berm," a vast wall that protects Moroccan Sahara from cross-border attacks by the Polisario. Senior Moroccan officials have credited the berm with saving Moroccan lives.

Since the 1970s, the Moroccan government has also turned to Israel and Diaspora Jews—including but not limited to Moroccan Jews—for political assistance. In 1979, for example, the monarch approached prominent American Jews for support in lobbying Congress to provide F-5 fighter jets to his kingdom for use in the ongoing war. Phillip Klutznick, president of the World Jewish Congress at the time, urged his constituents to support the king's request. "The Jewish community that lives in the country is facing severe challenges," he wrote. "We have to be especially attentive in order to maintain the safety of our brothers and sisters in Morocco. We should do everything we can to secure the safety of the state in which these Jews live." Jewish leaders in Washington responded to the call, making use of their political capital, and Morocco's request for fighter jets was authorized by Congress.

Thirty years later, with only a sliver of Moroccan Jewry remaining in the country, the present king continues to turn to his local Jews as emissaries to the broader Jewish world, especially for support on the Sahara issue. Casablanca-based Serge Berdugo, the appointed head of the Jewish community, has also been made special ambassador, with a mandate to lobby Israel and American Jews to advocate for the Moroccan government. In 2006, Berdugo is credited with having persuaded AIPAC, the influential pro-Israel lobby in Washington, to press Congress to endorse Morocco's new limited-autonomy plan for the Sahara. One hundred fifty-nine members of Congress were enlisted to write a letter to President Bush urging his support for the Moroccan position.

These successes, thanks to Moroccan, Israeli, and American Jews, make the welfare and protection of the remnants of Moroccan Jewry a high political priority for the kingdom. Though the country does not have formal diplomatic relations with Israel, families are permitted to travel freely to the Jewish state and send their children for summer courses in Jewish religion and the Hebrew language. Synagogues and Jewish community centers, obvious targets for jihadist groups, are secured by the police and the Rapid Intervention Forces. It is hardly surprising that the security services in Casablanca would move heaven and earth to catch the man who committed a violent crime on the premises of a Jewish man's warehouse—and to keep the matter out of the public eye. It might have been a hate crime, or a terrorist act, targeting the family that owned the warehouse. If the fact that a Muslim man had been murdered on Toledano's property came to be known to the general public, moreover, the result might be a further security risk for a prominent member of the Jewish community. Such extraordinary measures, viewed by the likes of Bari and Muhammad of Ayn Sabaa, fuel the perception that Jews enjoy preferential treatment. Meanwhile, the two men, like so many of their fellow citizens, are unaware of the extent to which the Jewish community contributes to the country's national security.

As for Ibrahim Dey, he would likely have perceived the warehouse as a place imbued with power and importance by the authorities, a kind of princely haven. Of course, if he believed he was especially safe there, he made a tragic miscalculation.

I ride a cab on Saturday morning to the King David synagogue in the swank Casablanca neighborhood known as California. Though thirty synagogues still functioned in the city, this thirty-first was built to serve the wealthy who had moved away from the older parts of town. Down a broad street with gated housing and a children's private school next door, the synagogue lies unmarked, behind a sumptuous wooden gateway. A detachment of uniformed police and soldiers from the Rapid Intervention Forces guards the entryway. I step inside the sanctuary to a crowd of eighty or so men in black-and-white prayer shawls, many huddled around the center rostrum, while a handful of women look over from their separate balcony seating. The rabbi opens the holy ark, which is set in silver and gold and adorns the far inner marble wall, and an honored congregant removes a Torah scroll from inside the glittering doors. He holds it high under a giant arched banner with the Hebrew words *I always place God before myself.*

I have only just walked in when a stout man with auburn hair and spectacles at the far end of the room snaps his fingers in my direction. Somebody instantly grips my arm and points me toward him. He is seated near the ark, in the section reserved for dignitaries and big donors to the synagogue—the coterie who get first dibs at the coveted commandment of welcoming a guest. The man motions me to take the seat next to him.

"I am Marcel Toledano," he says to me in French. *"Shabbat shalom."*

That was easy.

"Nice to meet you," I reply in Hebrew.

He locates this week's Torah portion in a copy of the Pentateuch and hands it to me. By cosmic coincidence, it's *Parashat Mishpatim,* the section that includes the penalties for murder, kidnapping, assault, and theft.

"You will be our guest for lunch this afternoon," Toledano whispers in slow-moving, guttural Hebrew.

"It would be an honor."

The rabbi chants the portion swiftly, running through the laws with authority in the somber Nihawand musical mode. "Although you are all now wealthy because of the booty you took in Egypt and at the Sea of Reeds," he recites, "there may nonetheless come a time when things will be different. Thus, if in the future one of you becomes so poor that he steals something and cannot pay back its value, the court may sell him for a period of service in order to pay back his debt."

"Where are you from?" Toledano asks.

"America."

"What are you doing in Morocco?"

"I'd love to talk to you about that over lunch. I've been looking for you."

A slim, dapper man nearby is leafing through his copy of the Pentateuch a little more intently.

"My brother Jacob," Toledano says.

I remember that Jacob is the man with legal trouble who was arrested at Kennedy Airport and extradited to Paris.

After the Torah and subsequent Haftarah portions have been chanted, the rabbi delivers an earful to the congregation in French about the impropriety of socializing during worship. No one in particular is singled out for reprimand. French, not Arabic, is the language of idle chatter and preaching alike for the worshippers at King David; like most of the country's remaining Jews, the congregation is firmly ensconced in the Francophone stream of Moroccan society, who still hold the reins of political and economic power. There is much for them to discuss on a Saturday morning.

Marcel Toledano and his family live diagonally across the street from their synagogue in a sprawling guarded compound with palm trees and a glistening pool in the backyard. It feels like Beverly Hills. We walk over in a group of four, including Marcel, Jacob, and Marcel's son, Ron, a handsome twentysomething with almond eyes and thick black hair. Near the front gates, three bearded men in tattered clothing about the quality of Bari's hold out their hands and beg passionately, yelling formulaic blessings at close range.

"God keep you and protect you!" one cries in Arabic.

"A thousand mercies to your parents and children!" yells another.

Jacob Toledano demonstrates that his pockets are empty. "Shabbat," he explains. "We are forbidden to carry money on our holy day. Sorry, brothers."

The beggars sullenly retreat, their heads lowered.

"So what do you do?" Marcel asks me.

I tell him I'm a writer who has been following the trail of the murder that took place in his warehouse, and he briefly freezes at the door to his home.

"You want to write about *that?*" he says.

I nod and my mind drifts to the murder scene, Ibrahim's head bashed in and gushing blood. *That.*

With a sigh and an air of reluctance, he motions me to head inside to a palatial sitting room and walks alone up a spiral staircase.

Colorful Berber tapestries adorn the walls alongside oil paintings of revered Moroccan Jewish holy men. I recognize the face of Rabbi Yisrael Abu Haseira, a leading rabbi and Kabbalist who was believed to work miracles through his prayers. There is crystal on the coffee table, chandeliers above each corner of the room.

Jacob Toledano takes a seat on an overstuffed couch and crosses his legs. Diagonally from him, a beautiful young woman with raven hair introduces herself to me in English as Ron Toledano's fiancée.

"My parents are Moroccan, but I'm from Paris," she says. "After we marry, I'll be coming here to live with Ron."

"What do you do in France?" I ask.

"I'm trained as a lawyer," she explains. "But I won't be able to practice here. The legal system is too corrupt."

I take a seat near Jacob and gently ask about his legal troubles. "I read about them in the Moroccan press," I tell him.

"What you read were lies," he says. "I'm taking them to court over it."

"But is it true that you were arrested at Kennedy Airport in New York and extradited to Paris on an international warrant?"

He flutters his right hand in slow motion, as if to diminish the importance of the question. "Okay, that is true," he concedes, "but the whole issue was exaggerated."

Tell me about it, bro, I say to myself.

Marcel Toledano returns from the second floor in a regal house robe and runs after his seven-year-old daughter to snatch a kiss. Fleeing her father with a major case of the giggles, she is overtaken beside one of the couches and raised briefly into the air like a pudgy ballerina. She makes a roller-coaster scream on the way down. Marcel's wife, Sophie, meanwhile, emerges from the kitchen and joins her husband on the couch.

"*Barukh haba,*" she says in Hebrew, an expression of welcome for a guest.

Marcel lowers his shoulders in my direction. "So, why do you want to know about that incident?" he asks.

"I've been working with the police at Precinct Five, and I got to know some friends and family of the victim."

"You interact with those types of people in Morocco?" he asks. "You talk to them in Arabic?"

I nod.

"No, you have to stay clear of them," Sophie chimes in. "We warn you as friends."

I thank her for the advice and pretend to give it careful consideration.

Marcel clears his throat and moves his head closer to me. "So, you want to know about that ugly incident. Well, that man, what's his name? He didn't belong on my property."

"Ibrahim Dey."

"Dey. He was a *fqih*. You know what is a *fqih*? Somebody who practices magic. He was using the damn bedroom in my warehouse at night to weave curses and spells for clients who came in to visit him. It was satanic magic, you know? I didn't find out about any of this until he had been killed. I didn't even know he existed. This kid, the soldier, was one of his clients. He had been coming in there for days or weeks at night. They were some kind of friends."

I can feel my heart racing. "How do you know all this?" I ask.

"The chief at Precinct Five. What's his name."

"Sharqawi?"

"Yeah. I was at his office and he told me. Anyway, that night Dey put the boy in a trance, and you don't mind if I use some language, do you? He tried to fuck him up the ass. I don't know how far he got. The soldier woke up, infuriated, and they struggled and the soldier overpowered him. Sharqawi told me there were scratch marks all over the boy's back. One of them was trained to fight, obviously, and the other wasn't."

"Sharqawi said they had never met before that night," I tell him. "He said the killing was over some pocket change."

Marcel Toledano chortles. "If you know about Morocco, you can understand why he would say that. Look, we have workers at the warehouse who watched the soldier confess to this, and my son Ron has become something of an expert on what happened. I can have Ron show you around tomorrow or the next day if you want."

A server in a suit emerges to announce that lunch is ready. We all enter the dining room. It's the most abundant and succulent feast I've seen in the kingdom, perhaps in my life. I'm not hungry, but I try in vain to eat away my worries.

TWENTY

You see, I *knew* something like this was going to happen.

Toledano's story, if true, would cast Ibrahim Dey in a swirl of social and religious taboos that would severely trouble Bari, the victim's family, and most any conservative Moroccan who regarded the victim as a friend. This is exactly why I warned Bari about digging into his friend's murder in the first place. I told him the day we met that he might find out something about his friend that would hurt him, or get him into trouble—or that maybe Ibrahim Dey was hiding something and he wasn't as good a friend as Bari thought.

Now Bari is going to regret he even started on this journey.

I take a taxi home, bloated from the meal and reeling from the table talk. I open the window in the living room, fall into the couch, rest my legs on the coffee table, and sigh. I marvel at Toledano's jam-packed little story. It won't just unsettle the people I have been spending time with here. It's worse than that. The details straddle the fault lines of a Muslim society in its conflict between modernity and tradition, and they have the potential to pit the state and its security services against powerful, dangerous social forces. The country sustained a similar shock only recently—and containing the damage proved costly and messy, with enduring consequences. No wonder the police would want to cover up the true story of Dey's murder. No wonder we were warned to back off.

I'd better explain the shocking events that rattled the kingdom a few weeks back. Some context first.

Magic, in Morocco, can be a good thing or a bad thing—but increasingly these days, it's a bad thing. The idea of magic harks back to ancient African shamanic practices that long preceded the advent of Islam. So widespread and cherished was magic to the polytheists and Jews of medieval Morocco that successive Islamic state builders thought better than to try to supplant it with a rigid faith. They chose instead, much like Catholic missionaries in Haiti, to allow elements of the tradition to be incorporated into Muslim religious practice while attempting to marginalize the rest as alien to Islam. The Qur'an, after all, acknowledges the existence of good and evil spirits known as *jinn*—"genies" to English speakers—as well as the magic of pharaonic Egypt. A distinction similar to that between Haiti's "white" and "black" magic was made, in Morocco, between the "divine" and the "satanic." From an anthropological standpoint, both these categories of ancient ritual flow from the same primordial source. But to modern Moroccans who embrace the traditions of magic, drawing a line between the two is serious business, and practitioners of the ancient art who fall on the "satanic" side of the spectrum deserve to be shunned—if not murdered. These convictions have taken on a new bite in recent decades, with the arrival of reactionary Islamist movements in Morocco that are influenced by Saudi Arabia's dogmatic, militant ideology of Wahhabism. Among their many aspirations, Wahhabis would like to stamp out "black" magic once and for all.

Homosexuality, meanwhile, remains the great taboo of the Muslim world. Punishable by death in some interpretations of Islamic law, it is a form of human intimacy that can be practiced only in secret. Across the Arab and Muslim world, suspected homosexuals have been rounded up and tortured, and in a few countries, notably Saudi Arabia and Iran, some have been executed. Yet for much of Islamic history, the permutations of sexuality in North Africa and the Middle East have been more complex than Islamic law could easily define, let alone suppress. Even today, there is a mind-set in Muslim countries, harking back to antiquity, that draws a distinction between the "receiver" in anal sex, who is the "true," "effeminate" homosexual, and the "giver," for whom the gender of his sex partner is barely relevant. More complex expressions of sexuality survive as well in some Muslim spiritual traditions. Witness the sensual dance rituals of Morocco's Gnawa mystical tradition—centuries old and widespread to this day—in which it is not uncommon for young men to dress up as women and dance effeminately to an enthralled traditional audience. Writers like Paul Bowles, based mainly in Morocco from the 1960s until his death, wrote admiringly of these performances—the likes of which used to be too risqué for a general audience in the United States.

One might expect that in the twenty-first century, with cultures coming together in a new global village, the rituals Bowles observed a few decades earlier would continue to flourish in Morocco as the rough edges of Islamic sexual taboo begin to taper off at last. But that is not the way globalization has been working in many Arab and Islamic societies. Instead, new conservative strains in the local culture, imported from Iran and wealthy Gulf states farther east, have grown dangerous, if not deadly, to some of these old traditions and the people who practice them.

This is what happened just a few weeks before the murder of Ibrahim Dey.

There was an incident in Al-Qasr al-Kabir, a small agricultural town in the kingdom's north with a rich history of pluralism and religious tolerance. A local event planner decided to organize a mystical Gnawa soiree in a hall for private parties. One hundred ninety guests showed up, including forty women and children, for the performance of a medieval folktale in which a young man is asked to dress in a woman's clothes and offer a gift to a female patron saint. One member of the audience captured the event on a camcorder and made the fateful decision to post it on YouTube.

Big mistake.

Within hours, the local branches of three Islamist movements

had come together to lodge a formal complaint and demand a police investigation into an alleged "perversion of public morals."
Two mosque preachers, in their Friday sermons, called on their
flocks to head off the "wrath of God" and take to the streets to
protect their city from the spread of sexual iniquity. Sympathetic
local media published front-page stories falsely alleging that a gay
wedding—dubbed a "perverts' marriage"—had taken place in Al-
Qasr al-Kabir. Thousands of people took to the streets chanting ho-
mophobic slogans. A mob threw rocks at the party hall in which the
performance had taken place and shattered the windows of a nearby
jewelry store that, they believed, belonged to the organizer of the
party. Nor were the homes of those involved in hosting the performance spared similar attacks. The man behind the show suffered
wounds to the head and fled to a nearby hospital, begging the police
to protect him.

The security services, under enormous popular pressure stoked
by Islamists, were compelled to act—and not on behalf of the embattled partygoers. Twelve members of the mob who had been arrested for acts of violence early on were released without charges
within three days. Meanwhile, police rounded up six participants in
the Gnawa soiree and charged them with "sexual perversion and
breach of public morals." The interrogations began immediately.

Within days, news of the incident had spread kingdomwide.
Spurious national headlines read Two Perverts Get Married in
Al-Qasr al-Kabir and Marriage of Perverts Is Attended by
an Official of the Public Prosecution, a University Professor, and a Retired Judge. The Islamist Justice and Development
Party's representatives in parliament castigated the interior minister
for failing to prevent the incident, calling on him to "take the necessary measures to prevent the repetition of this practice of corruption." Meanwhile, the Judiciary Police in Al-Qasr al-Kabir prepared
hasty transcripts of the interrogation of the arrested partiers, which
the latter were not even given a chance to read, and arraigned them
for trial. All six defendants denied that they were "perverts" or homosexual and pled not guilty to the charges. No substantive evidence was presented against them. They were denied due process,

promptly convicted, and sentenced to six to ten months each in prison. In a break with Moroccan media convention, their full names were also released to an angry public.

This is not to say that the Gnawa performers and the man who hired them were entirely alone in struggling, unsuccessfully, to defend themselves. The Moroccan Organization for Human Rights came on the scene to inquire about their well-being while in police custody, monitor and protest the violation of their legal rights, and provide a team of defense attorneys to represent them in appeals court. A handful of newspapers criticized their media peers for printing lies about the Gnawa performance. The minister of the interior, facing enormous political and popular pressure from the Islamist movement and its supporters, tried to articulate a middle ground—hailing Moroccans' zealous defense of public morals while noting that Gnawa traditions are a treasured part of the country's heritage. The Gnawa, it should be recalled, are viewed by senior Moroccan officials as a potential spiritual counterweight to hardline Islamist movements. Yet all these liberal voices could not stem the tide of popular rage, or manage to dispel the fiction that a time-honored Gnawa ritual was actually a gay wedding. The security services and the courts, caught in the middle between a thin liberal stream and a massive conservative base, played to the latter—and civil society in Morocco suffered a setback.

A few weeks ago I had read about the Islamist-led backlash against the mystical dance soiree with only passing interest. Now, my interest is piqued, since homosexuality, magical tradition, and prevalent attitudes toward both have taken center stage in our investigation of Ibrahim Dey's murder. I feel vested somehow in the fallout from this national drama.

Which brings me back to the lewd, dark story about Ibrahim Dey and his killer as recounted on the Sabbath by Marcel Toledano. Who knows what kind of magic, if any, the victim really practiced. Who knows what kind of sexual relationship, if any, brought the two men close together. Assuming my source faithfully narrated something he heard from Chief Sharqawi, the details may have stemmed from the kind of witnesses who also believed a "perverts' marriage" had taken place the month before in Al-Qasr al-Kabir. The mystical and the sexual inhabit a kaleidoscope of confusion in a country torn between its complex roots and the modern world. I would only know from Toledano's account that the police, in digging into the mystery of Dey's murder, appear to have struck something they deemed threatening to the "social fabric" that they presume to guard. To this delicate situation they may have factored in the risk of further shaming the Rapid Intervention Forces, their allies in the struggle against terror and vice—and, of course, compromising the security of a prominent Jewish businessman—and calculated that the true story of a man's untimely death did not merit the chaos its release would cause. If police had leveled with me about the situation at the outset, I might have commended the chief and his deputies for keeping the matter under wraps. I might have felt compelled to leave the story alone myself.

But that was then. My priorities are different now.

What kind of rituals Ibrahim Dey may have practiced and what sort of relations he may have had with a young soldier go to the heart of who he was and what his tragic death meant. Have we been struggling for weeks now to redeem the life of a rapist? As a Westerner, I am not fazed by his alleged homosexuality or proclivities toward magic. But for Bari, all three possibilities will put his cherished friendship with Dey into conflict with his conservative Muslim worldview—and force him to confront the likelihood that some of the secrets he has been seeking are secrets Ibrahim Dey kept from him. He had many theories when our quest began, but all of them cast his murdered friend as a righteous victim.

How do you confront a man with information that will pain him and threaten the romantic memories of a past friendship that sustained him for so long? I ask myself how I would want to be confronted with a secret about my loss of Ali that would devastate me. For years now I would have told myself that I'd prefer not to know at all. They say that what you don't know can't hurt you. Maybe I still feel that way. But here we are in a country in which the burial of hard truths by the state has tortured thousands, and here is a man who said he would fight to have his truth at any cost. I am going to hold him to his word.

What you don't know can kill you.

The stakes are very high—bigger than Bari and me—because how he copes with the release of a painful story is either a vindication of authoritarian practices or a sign that this population can handle its own autonomy. I would like nothing more than to prove somehow that Ibrahim Dey was not a rapist, and to persuade Bari to come to terms with the murder victim's alternative lifestyle. To accept him in death for what Bari might never have accepted him for in life. Yet spilling the beans may set off a chain reaction, if Bari informs too many people about what he learned, that could spur another blood-soaked scandal in Morocco akin to the incident in Al-Qasr al-Kabir. A Jewish businessman could be pitted against Islamists for hosting abominable behavior on his premises. Do I want to be the reason for a mess like that, or should I deny Bari the story he wants to know and make myself complicit in a police cover-up?

In my heart, this dilemma is less important that my prime directive: uncover Ibrahim Dey's true story. We haven't even gotten to the bottom of it yet.

How would *I* want to be confronted with a hard truth? Doling out the news slowly with a spoonful of sugar would only prolong the agony for me. I would prefer to have it all at once.

So I'm going to hit Bari over the head with it—and to hell with the bloody consequences.

TWENTY-ONE

On the third and final night of mourning for Ibrahim Dey's father, friends and neighbors of the bereaved organize a traditional Muslim feast to ease the family's burden of hospitality. A large tent of colorful striped cloth has been pitched outside the Dey home in the neighborhood of Timseet. Underneath it, sixty or so male guests have taken seats around wooden tables, and a local cleric leads a handful of his followers in Qur'an recitation and a series of slow-paced dirges. "If we live a thousand years and two thousand more," he sings in Arabic, "we will still one day end up in the grave." A large sheet of white plastic is laid out to cover each table. Bowls of ground almonds, argan oil, and honey come out first with sweet loaves of bread. Next, whole roasted chickens are set directly on the plastic for communal hand picking. Mounds of stewed vegetable couscous are served on giant platters. A dessert of sugar-sweet noodles caps the meal.

I listen in on the table talk.

"Mark my words: Moroccan slang is a mere dialect of Arabic, not a language," a young man insists.

"I tell you it is becoming a language all its own," his friend replies.

God only knows the truth, they agree, but whatever it is, the fact that there's a dispute between two Moroccans is probably the fault of the French.

There is sports talk, discussion of the Israeli-Palestinian conflict, and gossip unrelated to the Dey family or its second recent loss. There is talk in Shilha that I don't understand. Here and there, I pick up a muffled buzz in Arabic among the crowd. It is striking, people say, that the father of Ibrahim Dey passed away precisely one month after the murder of his son. This is a family that has been touched by the cold hand of fate, they whisper, and when tragedy strikes twice, there must be a reason.

The women are all inside, taking in a similar feast. Khadija Barrada Dey, the widow, will not leave the house for four months and ten days, in keeping with a Muslim tradition that many Arabs in Morocco have abandoned but to which Berbers hold fast. Her daughter Fatima will oblige her with the groceries and all her household needs. It's house arrest without the ankle bracelet.

After the meal is through, men will be welcome again to pay their respects inside. I bide my time with food in my mouth, waiting for Bari to show up as planned.

He eventually saunters over to my table from outside the tent, an eager smile on his face.

"I was here earlier today," he says. "A man pulled up in a big fancy car with a driver to pay his respects."

"Did you find out who he was?"

"His name is Abdullah Barrada. It turns out that he is a senior official from the Directorate of National Security in Rabat—and Ibrahim Dey's first cousin."

"So what do you make of that?"

"What I knew all along—that somebody very high up must have been paying close attention to the case. He is such a close relative, after all."

For reasons he doesn't know yet, I muse, Bari's theory rings true. Abdullah Barrada would be yet another member of the security services with a vested interest in squelching the true story of Ibrahim Dey's murder—both to avert a violent scandal like that of Al-Qasr al-Kabir, and to protect his own family from the shame of homosexuality and satanic magic.

"Just you wait," he replies. "There will be other high officials mixed up in this, too."

Bari's eyes dance as if he's just made a crucial deduction in the case. He finds a chicken drumstick on the table and picks off the juicy flesh. There's an innocence to the conspiracist, a kind of magical wishfulness that governs his logic. But how will he react when he can no longer evade the truth with selective reasoning? I'll soon find out—but not here amid the mourning.

"I met Toledano."

"Oh?"

"I'll tell you about it later."

The crowd quiets down as the cleric clears his throat to sing another dirge. This one focuses on the enduring light of the prophet Muhammad through time and space, a light that will last forever. Between each slow-moving couplet of rhyming verse, the crowd sings a chorus of "There is no God but Allah and Muhammad is his prophet." Most of the crowd drops off after the meal, but a small number of family and friends make their way inside to the Dey family sitting room. Khadija Barrada Dey wears a gown of snow white and a white headscarf. She is flanked by her older daughter, Fatima, and a younger woman with thick eyebrows and a stern, pale face.

"I am Jamila," she tells me, "the younger sister." She puts her hand on the shoulder of the small man beside her, who sports a warm, nonstop smile. "This is my husband, Jami."

Men line up to greet the nuclear family with formulaic expressions of comfort.

"We all belong to God and to Him we return."

"Your mourning and our mourning are one."

"Only God lives forever."

They take seats on the cushions that hug the sitting room walls and mostly keep to themselves.

"We know that you have taken a special interest in our brother, God have mercy on him," Jamila says. "We miss Ibrahim especially tonight, because it would have fallen on him to take the place of his father as the head of our family now."

"Your mourning and our mourning are one," Bari replies.

"After the night crowd has left," she whispers, "maybe we can talk some more."

By 10:30 or so the rest of the guests have departed and only Bari and I remain to talk to the family. Fatima and her mother head off to the kitchen to prepare another round of mint tea, leaving Jamila and her husband to spend some time alone with us.

"So you have been looking into the death of my brother," Jamila says. "But tell me, is it just one of several cases you are following?"

"Yes, of course," I tell her, "I've been looking at other cases, too."

She lowers her gaze and briefly takes her husband's hand, then restores it to his lap.

"I am younger than Ibrahim and Fatima by several years, and my life has been very different because of it," she says. "I had the opportunity to finish high school because by the time I was old enough to study, my father had stopped forcing the family to move every year between Casablanca and the mountains. It was terrible what he did to Ibrahim and Fatima. How can anybody get an education when half the time they are in a place where all there is to study is Qur'an at the mosque?" She chuckles. "As you can see, I am the rebel in the family."

"An education is vital in this world," Bari says. "I grew up in the mountains, but I wish I had had the opportunity to study."

"Anyway, my father was very cruel to Ibrahim, that is what I remember," she goes on. "I was just thirteen when he came back from Jadida, but I remember that he returned from there a broken man, destroyed by something, and all my father could say was, 'Why don't you get up and work, Ibrahim?' 'What are you doing at home, Ibrahim?' No one gave him the attention he needed. And what he really needed was to be treated for his curse."

"I'm sorry?"

Jamila smiles a teacher's smile. "My husband," she says, putting her hand on his lap this time, "he is a practitioner of divine magical healing. He has over one hundred clients. He should explain."

Jami clears his throat. "I didn't know Ibrahim well because he rarely came to see me," he says gently, "but I know enough to say that what he suffered from was a magical curse."

He speaks Arabic with a thick rural accent, perhaps a recent arrival to Casablanca.

"This is something that can affect every aspect of your life," he goes on. "You can take medicine and it has no effect, go to the doctor and it doesn't help. Try to earn a living, and everything you put your hands to will fail. The root of this magic is Satan himself. Medical doctors don't usually believe in these things, but the truth says otherwise."

"Ever since we were children our family has been the target of satanic magic," Jamila adds. "We would open the door of this house and find that someone had poured dirt or filthy water on our property—a puddle of filthy water, filthy with cursed substances, to try to harm us. This magic is powerful, and if you should doubt it, you need only look at the Jews in Washington. As we know from Morocco, they are very strong in magic, and you can see their profound influence on power and politics all over the world as a result."

Jamila's observation about global Jewry strikes me as another idea about Jewish power that her big brother might have shared— another reason for Ibrahim Dey, allegedly a practitioner of magic, to want to live in a Jewish installation.

"Ibrahim could have come to see me," Jami says. "I perform *ruqya* on my clients, meaning that I read the Qur'an over water and wash their faces in it. But from what I understand, he went to see others, people of ill repute. And this, too, can be part of the curse— that a man looks in the wrong places for help in removing it."

I have an informed question for the couple that I am going to have to put delicately. Bari will soon have it all, but I'm not sure about the family yet.

"Do you think that maybe," I ask, "in the course of meeting so many others for magical healing, Ibrahim may have been learning to become a practitioner of magic himself?"

Jamila laughs. "Ibrahim? A *fqih*?" She laughs again. "My husband took years to get his certification in magical healing from the preeminent institution for these studies in Agadir. This is not something you pick up casually. No, I don't believe it."

"But isn't it a little easier to learn, say, the other kind of magic?"

"*I take refuge in God from the accursed Satan,*" Jamila says fiercely. "No one in our family would veer in that direction, ever."

Fatima and her mother return from the kitchen with tea and cookies, settling down by Jamila's side.

"Do you hear what these men are saying?" Jamila asks them. "They think Ibrahim was a *fqih*."

She chortles again. Her older sister laughs politely. Their mother, who is of course mourning a husband, does not laugh at all.

It isn't easy to keep Bari's curiosity at bay. Having insinuated to Jamila and her husband that Dey might have practiced some form of magic, I have his antennae up, and he wants to know what I learned from Toledano. I have in mind to share the news with him as soon as possible, but only when we are more or less alone and he is sitting down comfortably. It's a ten-minute walk to his home, which will be crowded with children, and his favorite café along the way is closed for the night.

"Why don't we stop at that chicken rotisserie for a snack," I suggest.

"We just ate a feast," he says.

"Maybe they have hot drinks."

He accedes to my request with a shrug.

The sight of whole chickens turning slowly in a greasy glass tank is enough to turn my stomach after all I just ate—and maybe Bari's, too. I volunteer to take a seat facing the poultry so that Bari, sitting opposite me, will have a more serene view of the windy Ayn Sabaa roundabout by night and the neon pharmacy light flashing above us like a slow-ticking clock. The waiter approaches. He wants to know whether we would like a quarter or a half chicken each, with or without "chips."

"Do you have anything like tea?" I ask.

"Fruit cocktail. *Laban.*"

Bari opts for the liquid yogurt and the waiter walks away.

I scan my friend's scruffy face. He blinks, caressing the childhood cut marks on his temples, and combs his beard with the fingers of his right hand. I remember that a couple of weeks ago on our train ride to Jadida he said it might have been the hand of God that brought us together. I wonder, alas, whether our friendship will survive the night.

"Muhammad, I learned some things from Toledano about what the police might actually know, aside from what they told the public."

His eyes widen and his nostrils flutter.

"I know the Dey family believes in magic, but do you believe in it, too?" I ask.

"Of course," he replies. "This country is drowning in it."

"Both kinds of magic, right? The divine and the satanic."

"*He who eats a watermelon must swallow black seeds,*" he says.

"Well, Toledano told me Ibrahim Dey was a *fqih*, and he practiced satanic magic in the warehouse at night."

The fluttering stops. Bari's eyes freeze for a moment. He taps a finger nervously on the table and takes a series of short breaths.

"No, it can't be."

"I don't know, but he offered to let me look at the magical effects Dey left behind in the warehouse. We might have concrete evidence."

"Every day in the café I saw him with his prayer beads and Qur'an," he protests. "We went to the mosque together at the crack of dawn. He was a simple man of God. Toledano is wrong."

"I'm just not sure he would have a reason to make up a story like this."

"It can't be," he pleads softly. "Ibrahim was a man of God."

"Muhammad, it's not only about the magic."

The waiter delivers a tall glass of yogurt to Bari, who promptly slides it over to my side of the table.

"You told me in all the years you knew him, you never saw him with a woman."

"Never. He was too poor to take a wife, and where would he take a girl?"

"The poorest of men can fall in love and have children. Is it possible you never saw him with a woman because by the time you got to know him, he preferred men?"

"*I take refuge in God from the accursed Satan!*" he exclaims. "This is my friend you are talking about, and you are saying he was a pervert. Fear God!" He points an index finger at me. "Who are you, anyway, to tell me these things! You come from far away and dig into our secrets and disgraces. And you go see your Jew friend Toledano and he tells you a pack of lies about us. Why don't you go home and look for your own disgraces! *I take refuge in God!*"

My heart rate picks up. It isn't just the comment about my "Jew friend" Toledano that bugs me. I'm angry—infuriated, actually. I've donated my time to help this man, and look what gratitude it gets me. How dare he talk to me like that.

"You know something?" I go on. "Let me tell you about this guy your friend. According to my 'Jew friend Toledano,' police say he tried to rape the soldier in his sleep. Your friend of ten years—a rapist. How do you like that, brother Muhammad. Shows what you know about picking friends."

He turns red. I've hurt him now.

"You know, it sounds to me like you're taking some pleasure in telling me these things. The way you're talking sounds calculated to hurt me."

"Oh, don't go blaming me for hitting you with this. It's what you wanted all along. I've been putting up with your obsession and you should be a grown-up and deal with what we found."

"Why are you so angry?" he asks softly.

"Stop changing the subject."

"What's going on with you?" he says.

"This isn't about me," I tell him. "It's about *you.*"

Bari begins to regain his composure. "You know, I've had children, nine of them. Two are grown up, one's your age, and the other is a couple of years older."

"So what."

"So I know something about growing up."

He takes my hand. I snatch it back.

Bari smiles and slowly gets up, pulling his tattered coat straight with an air of dignity while balancing carefully on his two feet.

TWENTY-TWO

All right, maybe it's time for me to check in again with Julia, my psychology grad student friend, because we have new information about Ibrahim Dey and his nocturnal activities. You have to go through a dream many times in order to properly make sense of it, and now that we have more information about the waking hours surrounding the man's dream, it behooves me to run it by an expert.

I wait again until it's evening in Providence, Rhode Island, and make myself some chamomile tea before sitting down on the couch to call her. My breath is short—obviously, because the Dey case is wearing on me.

"So you've learned more about this dead dreamer," she says. "How do you feel about it?"

I brief her on the alleged black magic, the alleged homosexual tryst, the possibility of a rape. I recount the details of Ibrahim Dey's dream, though this time I remember to fill in the image of the scales.

"You didn't mention the scales last time," she notes.

"It slipped my mind," I reply.

"You sleeping all right?"

"Not bad. You know, some of this is exhausting."

Julia says she is skeptical of the classical Freudian interpretation of sexual drive determinants in dreams. Nonetheless, she points out that on the face of it, the dream now appears to have as its centerpiece a passive homosexual image. Dey is given a portion of "money" and he would like to have more, so he asks for it without demanding it. Thankfully, he gets what he wants. "What's strange," she says, "is that this does not appear to be the wish fulfillment of a rapist. Your rape allegations might be suspect."

"Could the soldier have been the rapist?"

"Obviously that's not a question for me," she replies, "unless of course you have a dream from the killer. Bear in mind that in traditional societies, the question of who gave and who received is extremely important. The recipient of a homosexual act is thought to be purely homosexual, whereas for the giver, it's almost just another act of masculinity. You have to factor this into whatever you're looking at."

"Maybe there was no rape at all," I suggest. "Maybe they had a friendship that developed into sex."

"Yes," she replies. "It might have been a first for the young man. The murder could even be explained in terms of a 'homosexual panic.' Of course, that might put the murder victim in the place of the giver, not the recipient, which would make the dream all the more perplexing."

"Homosexual panic" is a term coined back in 1920, describing an acute, brief reactive psychosis that the target of an unwanted homosexual advance experiences. It can lead to violence. In American trials of some violent assaults following gay sex, the "gay panic defense" has been used to exonerate the defendant.

"And the scales?" I ask. "Any thoughts about the scales?"

"By the way, Joseph, is everything well?"

I swallow some air. "I'm keeping busy," I tell her, "making some new friends here."

Pause.

"Well, it's good that you're asking questions."

The following morning, I decide I'll leave Bari alone a little while and give him a chance to reflect. Hopefully he'll forgive my outburst. Half of what I said, he needed to hear anyway. Maybe he will come around to the view that we should press on together, if only to try to disprove the story told by Toledano. Maybe he will even open his mind to the possibility that Toledano's story is true, and Bari did not know Ibrahim Dey half as well as he'd thought. Then again, maybe he won't. I do not regret having confronted him head-on, though I wish I had done so more sensitively. It pains me to sit alone and think about writing an epitaph for our friendship—and to admit that I made it worse by hitting him harder than was necessary.

With free time on my hands, I ride a train an hour north to the manicured capital of the kingdom, Rabat. The Moroccan Organization for Human Rights has scheduled a press conference there to present findings on the violent incidents in the northern town of Al-Qasr al-Kabir.

My cab spins off a main road of imperial palm trees in parallel rows, onto a quiet cul-de-sac filled with parked cars. I get out and open a steel door to a white-walled conference room furnished like a classroom. Three speakers, seated behind a platform and backed up by portraits of the present king and his late father, face an audience of twelve or so reporters from TV, radio, and print media. The woman at the center, Organization president Amina Buayash, is gesticulating passionately. Journalists are flipping through copies of a staple-bound, typewritten document in Arabic. I snag one. It is a blow-by-blow account of the Al-Qasr al-Kabir affair and its fallout—critical of the press, Islamist groups, the security services, and the courts.

"I come from the north," Buayash says, "from a town not far from Al-Qasr al-Kabir. We were tolerant, we were peaceful. We had Jews in the town when I was growing up. We had Spanish people living among us. We always welcomed the stranger and the guest. It was shocking to me that an incident like this would erupt in a place so close to where I grew up. . . . And since we are holding a *press* conference, let me emphasize that especially disappointing was the manner in which some of the local and national press stoked the fire with spurious reports of a 'gay wedding.' Our inquiry has confirmed that there was no wedding, and no homosexuality."

"How can you fault the newspapers for exercising their freedom of the press?" a man calls out from behind a TV camera. "And the Islamist groups were only exercising freedom of assembly!"

Buayash cringes, then summons a gentle smile. "In Morocco we have an unusual phenomenon," she replies. "Some groups are using freedom of the press and freedom of assembly to *undermine* personal freedoms rather than uphold them. That is not the purpose of the freedoms we have only recently been granted and are struggling to build on."

A young man with a beard raises his hand and stands up. He introduces himself as a reporter from *Al-Tajdid,* one of the country's Islamist newspapers and a leading purveyor of the "gay wedding" story. "Even if there wasn't a gay wedding," he asks, "wouldn't you agree that there was a ceremony of black magic and corruption, inimical to Moroccan values?"

Buayash sighs. "The question is, whose Moroccan values? The Gnawa is a part of our cultural heritage. And even if there were something new and innovative about the ceremony, what of it? Our society is in a state of flux, and new values should be able to enter the mix within a democratic framework. When we encounter a group of people whose value system is different from our own, how are we going to deal with it? We can print spurious rumors and throw rocks at them, or we can reach into our rich tradition of tolerance and agree to live alongside others, even if we differ with them."

"Even homosexuals?" a woman asks.

Buayash turns to the elderly man to her right, who taps his finger on the microphone in front of him and hunches in toward it. "At the Moroccan Organization for Human Rights," he says softly, "we do our work on the basis of the human rights of every human being, regardless of the choices they make in life. Our defense of the human rights of others does not stop if we suspect they are homo-sexual."

The little crowd buzzes, and the print reporters in the front row scribble furiously.

"Let me add that we do not fault the press and the Islamist groups alone," Buayash interjects. "The society and the state were equally culpable here. Look at the behavior of the police and the courts. In the worst days of the 'Years of Lead,' the most bitter ene-mies of King Hasan, God have mercy on him, were given a chance at legal representation before they entered the courtroom. Yet these young men, based on rumors of homosexuality, were denied legal counsel. If we are really going to move toward democracy and the rule of law, the state should not be treating its citizens this way."

A woman in a headscarf unplugs the microphone from her tape deck, wraps the cord around the microphone, and walks out the door.

I watch Buayash and her colleagues field more tough questions as the journalists peter out. Buayash is unflappable. The more stri-dent the question, the more articulate and insightful her response. I marvel at the hostility she attracts for her defense of liberal values—from members of the fourth estate at that. Unfortunately, she ap-pears to be outnumbered.

In numerous Arab countries, similar scenes are playing out be-tween traditional societies and their own proponents of novel, progressive ideals. Arab liberals are not foreign, Western-backed implants, as their opponents sometimes claim. They are authentic native sons and daughters, struggling to compete in a local market-place of ideas heavily weighted toward Islamists. They have not re-ceived sufficient backing from the United States in its intended war against extremist groups. Some of them might not have accepted it, for that matter, even if American funding and training were of-fered to them. Meanwhile, many of their hard-line opponents have been bolstered by foreign funding themselves—from the petro-endowments of Islamism in Saudi Arabia and Iran. It would be helpful to Arab liberals if they could find a reliable ally in their local governments, which are themselves on the defensive from Islamist opposition groups. But these governments tend to reject aspects of liberalism for reasons of their own—namely, the liberal expectation that the state will further relax its grip on civil society, the political system, and official government narratives. Morocco, with all its flaws, stands several steps ahead of its Arab neighbors in progress toward civil society and the rule of law. Yet the showdown between Islamists and their opponents over the incident at Al-Qasr al-Kabir demonstrates that freedom is embattled—not only on account of the government—and in danger of regressing.

Just after sunset, Ron Toledano, Marcel's son, picks me up from my apartment in a shiny black Mercury Mountaineer. I didn't sleep too well last night, and it's starting to catch up with me, but never mind. Gangsta rap is playing softly from the car's crisp stereo speakers. The driver, an employee of the family's, flashes a grin of stained teeth under a fierce black mustache and introduces himself as Omar.

"So you want to see what happened that night," Ron says to me in French-accented English. "I tell you, if I were the soldier and that man tried to do that to *me,* I would have done the exact same thing myself."

"We are going to show you *everything!*" Omar cries in Arabic.

We speed along a familiar eastward route, past the white concrete apartment buildings of Ma'arif and the hotels and restaurants of Anfa, into the mixed assemblage of historic architecture that weighs down the sprawling center of town. The long shadow of the coffee-colored stone clock tower glides over us like a phantom as we drive past the keyhole-shaped Marrakesh gate, toward the tall white buildings of Casablanca's prime commercial district. Then the storefronts grow wearier and the housing less desirable as we pass into the city's eastern half. A mile beyond the modest headquarters of Precinct 5, we are in Ayn Sabaa again, turning past the round-about onto the "passageway of the villas." We park in front of the spiked red metal gate of warehouse number 18, and Omar runs out and bangs on the door.

The same curly-haired Berber guard whom I met with Lieutenant Jabri earlier opens up. At the sight of Ron, he promptly stamps out his cigarette—a courtesy he did not show Jabri, as I recall.

"The police said I would have made a good cop," Ron boasts. "I helped them try to piece together what happened on the first morning of the investigation."

We enter the gnarly warehouse of derelict freight carcasses, still with a tractor and some trucks parked under a giant canopy full of holes. Spurts of blood have faded to the slightest shadow stains up the stairwell to the guard's room, and the thick mess of fallen leaves in the distance appears untouched.

Omar the driver puts his arm around the guard's shoulder. "This man was here when the murderer confessed. They brought the soldier back to the scene of the crime and he was limping, because they beat him hard to make him talk. They brought him here more than once, in fact—the second time with men in army uniforms to go over the whole story again. They brought video cameras to film the whole thing."

This is the first I've heard that army personnel also visited the warehouse, apparently to independently investigate or document the crime.

"Tell him what you heard the man say, brother," Omar says to the curly-haired guard.

The guard puts his head down, silent.

"Well, tell him, tell him!"

The guard only whispers, "That story about the incense. Come on, you tell it better than me."

"This *fqih* Ibrahim," Omar says, "he used this whole facility to perform magic on his clients, his victims. Every place in the warehouse, practically. The bedroom, the second floor of the building, the bathroom. That's why the blood was everywhere that night. Not all the blood came from their big fight, you know. Some of it was part of his magical practice. Anyway, this *fqih* summoned *jinn* by reading the Qur'an backward and pissing on it. And then he burned the special incense to make the boy fall asleep. You know who I mean—that soldier, who had been coming to see him every night for days. And when he fell asleep, Ibrahim tried to fuck him."

I turn to the curly-haired guard. "Is that actually what you heard?"

He lowers his head again and sighs.

"Ron," I ask, "were you there when the killer confessed?"

"I missed that part," he replies. "I was here at the beginning, when they were combing the crime scene for clues and interrogating our old guard, Hasan."

"The cops told me the killer climbed over the wall to get in here," I tell Omar. "That he came here to steal and immediately got in a fight with Ibrahim Dey, who was a total stranger to him."

"Brother, that's not true," he replies. "He walked right in through the front door and only escaped up the wall. Just look at the spurts of blood. They only lead in one direction."

"He's right about that," Ron adds.

"And when they found his dead body," Omar says, "his pants were down and there was semen around his penis. What more do you need to know?"

Ron motions for us to enter the bedroom where Dey slept. I walk in first and he turns on the light behind me. I recognize the same acrid smells, the same unmade bed, the same yellowing sheaf of printed Arabic on the coffee table—even the teacups on a round tin tray, still untouched.

Omar clutches the Arabic sheaf. "You see? He probably pissed on this." He restores it to the table.

"Nothing has been moved," I tell Ron.

"The new guard doesn't want to sleep here or even clean the place up. He sleeps on a cot near the gate. He's afraid of evil spirits, and he's angry we didn't tell him there was a murder here before we hired him."

The curly-haired man only reluctantly steps into the room to join us.

"It's almost the same as before," Omar adds. "I remember there used to be a big mirror in this room, but it's been gone a long time. Otherwise, the same."

By now I have my own insights into the secrets of the room. I recognize the honeydew color of the blanket as identical to the cushions in the living room of Dey's parents' house where he used to sleep. I can faintly make out the smell of wormwood, boiled green leaves, that was wafting out of the kitchen of his cousins' home in Jadida. The worn-out carpet with an embroidered image of Jerusalem's Al-Aqsa mosque, a holy symbol and a reminder of the Israeli-Palestinian conflict, brings to mind Dey's flirtation with an Islamist preacher. Perhaps in ways that I know and ways that I don't, the bedroom is a shrine to the lives Ibrahim Dey used to live.

Omar opens one of the drawers under the high table, which is actually a writing desk, and produces a plastic grocery bag. "These are his magical effects," he says.

"May I keep those?" I ask.

Omar gets the nod from Ron and hands the bag over eagerly.

"Take it all," Ron says. "The police didn't want to have anything to do with these things."

I stuff the yellowing sheaf of Arabic print into the plastic bag, which does not smell good, and carry it under my shoulder.

"I want to show you something upstairs," Ron says.

We ascend the spiral staircase in the dark. On the second floor, Ron switches on another overhead light, exposing a cot, pillow, and blanket tucked in a corner of the landing.

"You see what I mean? He was running a real show in this place, that guy. Guests staying overnight up here, magic and sex down there. Who knows what else? He was a real businessman."

A real businessman.

Ibrahim Dey, who used to be admired for his entrepreneurial spirit, would probably have taken that as a compliment. But between Jamila Dey's dismissive talk about her late brother ever becoming a *fqih* and Omar's thirdhand testimony about the dead man's lewd and lascivious behavior at the warehouse, there is plenty of confusion about what sort of business Dey was transacting.

It's getting dark.

Ron Toledano gives me a ride back to my apartment. He doesn't say much along the way. I tighten my grip around the bag of Ibrahim Dey's personal effects.

Dropped off in front of the building, I ride the elevator upstairs. I reach the front door of my apartment. The lights in the corridor aren't working, so it is pitch dark.

I hear a splashing sound under my feet.

I bend down and run my index finger along the ground. It's a puddle of muddy water. I squeeze my knees further and drop my head down toward the puddle. It doesn't smell like ordinary mud. There's some rotten substance mixed into it.

What was it that Jamila Dey said about puddles of filthy water left in front of their home?

Who knows where I live?

My heart rate speeds up again.

I stand up and take the key out of my pocket. I fumble with it until it fits into the keyhole, then turn on the lights inside my flat. I take off my shoes. I make for the couch and try to forget about the puddle outside.

Bari must be lying in his bed, wide awake, pondering the news I laid on him yesterday. I really ripped into him. I shouldn't have done that.

My mobile phone rings. The caller ID registers "Unknown."

"Hello?"

There's no sound on the other end. Cold silence.

"Hello?"

Someone is breathing now. A husky male voice, I think.

"Hello?"

Whoever it was hangs up. Now my heart is beating faster and my mouth is drying out.

I go back to the door and double-lock it.

I'm glad I have a project to work on tonight, to keep my mind occupied: go through Ibrahim Dey's personal effects to figure out what they betray about his relationship with magic; what they might reveal about him.

I sit down and take a few deep breaths. Take longer, deeper

breaths and eventually your heart rate slows down. Usually. The bag of Dey's personal effects is there right in front of me. The puddle of water and mud lies waiting for me outside. I take a few more breaths.

Should I call the police?

All right, on to the analysis.

I am going to start off by dismissing the dead man's younger sister's claim that Dey could only have become a practitioner of magic after years of study at the likes of the prestigious institution from which her husband graduated. That is just the modern bias of professional certification talking. Traditional Arabic sources on the subject note that private teachers abound in Morocco who can train the earnest seeker in the "secret sciences," and even a determined autodidact can make significant headway on his own. For a student to become a professional healer of the "divine magic" variety, he is encouraged to seclude himself and pursue his learning in secret. A warehouse by night would do admirably for the purpose. He should stop shaving his face and eat a limited diet of mainly dates, milk, and bread; witness Ibrahim Dey's black beard and gaunt frame. Several times a day he should burn a mixture of salt, African rue, and the skin of a snake—and the rest of the time it's cram, cram, cram. After his hundredth day of studying, the student should peer by night into a mirror by the light of a candle. If he finds instead of his own reflection an image of the saintly *jinn* who will serve him in his ritual practices, then he has all the certification he is going to need. The rest he can learn on the job.

The "satanic" side of the spectrum allows for a similar learning track, though the details are slightly more exacting. It is preferable for the seeker to withdraw to one of the valleys on the outskirts of the city, though for Casablanca, which is not surrounded by valleys, the seclusion of a warehouse in the heart of town might pass. He should plan on changing clothes every hour or so, because the learning process is messy. The diet involves a particular type of bread prepared without salt and very little yeast, together with dried dates and raisins. Some of the day-old flatbread Bari used to donate might have done the trick. On graduation day, the trainee must use a mirror with a frame of ebony wood. The *jinn* that appears in the mirror will make a brief announcement: "You have disturbed the entire lower house." Then the sultan of all *jinn* will ride by on a chariot followed by his seven armies—a parade of scorpions, vipers, and various animals. A pillar of smoke will rise, transforming into a wooden stick, then a snake, and finally a handsome young man. He is the newly minted sorcerer's *khadim,* bound to serve his every need.

Maybe Dey fancied he had found his handsome young *khadim* in the soldier who eventually killed him.

Which of these two tracks Ibrahim Dey would have pursued may possibly be deduced from an examination of his personal effects. I open the bag and find two books, for starters, and one of them is a hardcover Qur'an. Whether Dey read from it backward to summon evil spirits, as Omar claimed, I cannot tell, but his incendiary charge that the dead man debased the holy book appears untrue. I flip through the pages and find it to be well taken care of—unstained by urine, blood, or any other fluid.

The other book is a softcover volume published in Egypt called *People's Defense from Jinn and Satan.* "Since the beginning of humankind," reads the promotional blurb on the back cover, "Satan and his helpers have been in hot pursuit of humans, setting traps for them and deceiving them in every way possible in order to make them stray from God Almighty. This book tells the story of that conflict . . . and explains how to protect family and the home from Satan and his *Jinn.*" It is a familiar book to me because it is immensely popular in the Arab world; I've seen it in bookstores all over Morocco and in Egypt, Jordan, and Lebanon. The cleric who wrote it, Abu Bakr Jabir al-Jaza'iri, is a university lecturer in Saudi Arabia, dubbed a sworn enemy of "satanic" magic, who believes that whatever strays from the "divine" variety should be stamped out forever.

So these two books, at least, bespeak a man who held fast to the tenets of his faith and shunned the magic of Satan—as Bari so vehemently insisted. It might even be said that there is a straight line to be drawn from the hard-line Islamist cassette tape Dey used to listen to in Jadida and the straight-and-narrow variety of divine magic espoused in the softcover book.

But the bag also contains a few other items. One of them is a small pouch of fur, sewn shut. I cut it open with a knife and find a dried white substance in a tiny blue plastic bag. It is in all likelihood a small chunk of a dead animal. Animal parts are common in the field of North African magic: the bones of a snake, the skin of a lion, the testicle of a wolf, the blood of a bat. The shoulder bones of a sheep slaughtered during the Eid festival, for example, are believed to hold the power to reveal the future until the following Eid. These talismans of the dead are typically not the "divine" variety of magic.

What remains in the bag are a couple of small sacks of sand—scooped, perhaps, from the tombs of Moroccan holy men or sorcerers—and a can of rotten tomato paste. Foul-smelling substances are used in "satanic" magic to support the weaving of spells that target other people's prized assets. One might aim, for example, to effect the dissolution of a marriage, the failure of a business, or ill health.

It is a mixed bag of magic, defying a binary classification as "divine" or "satanic." A visitor to Ibrahim Dey's place of "business" by night would have found, evidently, that he had a little something for everybody. Or maybe each item represented a facet of Dey himself—the dark as well as the light.

As for the yellowing sheaf, which was lying on Dey's coffee table the night of his death, I vaguely recognize the Arabic prose from my studies.

There's the mobile phone again. I restore the sheaf to the coffee table.

"Hello, who is this?"

A clicking sound. Some static. More breathing.

My heart isn't beating so fast this time, but I feel cold and my teeth are chattering.

I shut the windows and lock them.

The phone rings again. I don't want to answer it. It keeps ringing and ringing.

"Hello what do you want!"

"It's Muhammad Bari. Something happened. My head—I fell on my head outside. It was crowded. I tripped, or somebody—"

The living room shrinks to half its size and my head starts spinning.

"Who, somebody?"

"I don't know."

I throw on a sweatshirt and run to the nearest busy street.

TWENTY-THREE

Just when you need it most, it's hard to find a cab in this town.

After ten minutes' waiting in the chilly wind tunnel down Gandhi Street, I see a beat-up *petit taxi* sputtering down the road and flail my arms as if there were competition for a ride.

"Up to the roundabout of Ayn Sabaa," I tell him.

"Iraqi, my brother?"

He recognizes the accent I learned from my old friend.

"Land of manhood!" he cries.

I've been through this in a Moroccan taxi before. *Here we go again,* I think. The speech turns out a little different this time—though only slightly.

"All the forces of evil have conspired against you, brother. The Zionists, the Americans, the crusaders. But you were never destroyed. Long live Iraq! I say this as a Moroccan citizen, only one of millions who pray for your victory every day, five times a day."

"Thank you, brother."

"The Jews will never destroy you. They are weak and you are strong! They are few and you are many! Never surrender! Never relent! Resist oppression and darkness!"

"God keep you, brother."

"As for the Americans, God destroy their homes. They were not even suckling infants when you were a great civilization."

"God lengthen your days."

Hey, I'll take a little encouragement wherever I can get it.

Muhammad Bari appears to have narrowly averted a concussion. There is a gash and a severe bruise mark on his forehead. When I arrive at his flat I find him lying on the cushions in the living room, a bootleg New York Yankees baseball cap holding together the bandages on top of the stitches in his head.

"I am so sorry," I tell him.

"Sit down," he grumbles.

Bari tells me the story without looking at me once.

It was getting dark, he recalls. He had picked up some groceries for the family and begun walking home along his usual route. He passed a cracked stretch of concrete sidewalk that overlooks an old, dilapidated Muslim shrine, known, ironically, as the tomb of Muhammad of Ayn Sabaa. Long ago it ceased to be used as a Sufi place of worship and was taken over by practitioners of magic, mostly women, who sacrifice small animals, tell fortunes, and solve clients' problems through incantations. Locals say much of the magic is not the "divine" variety. This evening Bari could smell burnt chicken wafting up in smoke as he passed by.

Out of nowhere, men walked up from behind him at top speed. Bari tripped on somebody's leg and hit the ground, hard. The men around him were not good Samaritans. They just kept walking.

Bari noticed blood coming down fast in front of his eyes and put a finger on his forehead. Without panicking, he rushed home, which fortunately was not far away. He did not go to the hospital because he doesn't have the money. His wife, an expert seamstress, managed to stitch up the gash herself.

"I'm so sorry," I tell him again.

He looks sullen and emotionally wounded. I don't know how to express my sympathy for him. I feel guilty for my meanness the other night, partly responsible for his injury today. The guilt disorients me, and I'm afraid to open my mouth.

"You know I have been sick ever since we last spoke," he grumbles. "Absolutely sick."

Besides the head wound, his nose is running and the whites of his eyes are watery and pink.

"Do you understand the implications of what you said for *me*?" he goes on. "The closest person in the world to me after my own family, the man I spent hours with every day, like a brother, would be lying to me about everything. If what you told me is true, I never even knew him! He never really trusted me. He was never honest with me."

"I'm sorry," I reply. "It must have hurt you terribly."

He looks away and waves his right hand wearily. Facing the wall, his jaws move slightly up and down at a quickening pace, but no sound comes out of his mouth. He looks into my eyes, then looks away—twice.

"You did not behave respectfully toward me the other night," he says. "You disrespected *yourself*."

"I'm sorry about that, too. I don't know what came over me."

Bari gets up and sits next to me. "You don't know. Are you sure?"

"I really don't know."

"Tell me, my friend, do you have problems back home in America? Is something wrong there?"

Of course not, I think. "Everything's fine in America."

"Why are you spending all this time *here,* chasing the secrets of a man you've never met? You don't have any reason to do this that I can understand."

Bari, as has already been established, is a man of the street. To explain the complex policy questions that underlie this case—the future of authoritarian states, the tension between individual lives and the government's agenda to control their personal narratives— would be irrelevant.

"I like you and I want to help you," I tell him. "I'm a student of this region. I'm trying to find a relationship between our quest and some of the big political questions people are asking about Arab countries—in Washington, London, Paris, you know."

He grins. "That's all you're after," he says. "You have no personal motive of your own, aside from helping me and Washington and London and Paris."

I think about my relationship with the memory of Ibrahim Dey. That, too, is complicated to explain.

"Of course not," I tell him.

"My friend," he says, "when the time is right, I only hope that you will open up to me in ways that I have opened up to you. Maybe you need to open up to yourself first. I don't know. But remember that I am your friend."

This time my heart rate doesn't quicken. It's just one beat that thuds, harder than the rest, and I feel my hair standing on end.

After what I put him through and what he's been through, he still wants to be my friend.

One of his little boys is passing through the sitting room en route to the kitchen. Bari snaps his fingers and whispers something into the boy's ear. The boy nods and continues on his way.

"I have decided to introduce you to someone," Bari says.

A compact woman in a loose-tied veil, with a round face and a warm glow in her eyes, shyly enters the living room and sits beside her husband.

"This is a first for my wife," Bari says. "She wanted very much to meet you, and I decided to grant her permission."

Avoiding eye contact, she says, "Welcome. A thousand times, welcome. My name is Mahjuba."

Here at last is the long-unseen woman who cooks up a storm, raises Bari's nine children, and supports the family by working full-time so her husband can prowl around Morocco with me. For all the energy and strength she must expend throughout the day, to a foreign guest she exudes the timidity of a docile homemaker.

"My wife told me I shouldn't give up on what you and I have been doing together," Bari says. "That I should follow through until the end."

Mahjuba simply nods.

A threat from the Interior Ministry and now a wound to her husband's head, and this shy young woman is pressing her husband to press on.

"I worried that I had lost him," I tell her.

"You have given my husband a new source of vitality and strength," she replies. "I want him to keep it and build on it, despite what happened to him tonight. We are strong, and my husband is brave. He doesn't always reveal it, but he is brave."

Bari takes her hand in his lap and envelops it between the two of his. Their eyes meet. She tips her head in the direction of the kitchen. Bari gets up, as if instructed to do so, leaving the two of us briefly alone.

"Where do you work?" I ask her.

"I sew jeans in a big factory down the street, near the soccer stadium. It's a Moroccan company called Samir. We have European bosses and they serve American clients. I sew buttons onto the jeans, two hundred jeans an hour."

Bari returns with three glasses of *laban* and a plate of cookies.

"There's a guard at the door of the company and he won't let anybody in who doesn't work there," he says. "What they make her do at the factory is terrible. She gets paid less than a dollar an hour, and she works thirteen or fourteen hours a day, seven days a week. Three times a month she has to work twenty-four hours straight. One of the girls she worked with tried to complain to the boss and she got fired immediately."

I notice that Mahjuba has dark circles under her eyes. She continues nodding while her husband speaks, adding only the formulaic expression, "God is noble. God is noble."

"Tell him something about the company," Bari says.

She smacks her lips and grins. "Minimum wage in Morocco is supposed to be about a dollar fifty an hour," she explains, "but my company bribes the Ministry of Labor so they don't have to pay it. A strike is impossible because the workers are too poor and they have to get paid. Look at us. We are a big family and we need to eat."

"Someday," Bari says, "we hope that she can save enough money to buy herself a sewing machine, start a little business on her own. She could earn more that way. But saving money is hard when we barely have enough to eat at the end of the month."

"God grant you sustenance," I tell them.

They acknowledge the kind words with their eyes and bless me in return.

I feel, however, that I should be able to do more than ask God to help them out.

Over lamb cooked in a clay *tajin,* I update Bari on what I learned from the outing with Ron Toledano. I'm gentle this time. His eyes stay half closed and he nods, as if he were inebriated, at all the tawdry details, one at a time, as they come out. When I tell him the killer may have walked right in through the front gate of the warehouse, contrary to police claims, he cringes and shakes his head. "We all walked right in," he laments. "Ibrahim Dey never turned down a visitor, unless there were other visitors inside already. That night I knocked on the gate and he turned me away. He said, 'I have guests.' It was the killer in there, God curse him. Who knows who else?"

"Remember, we can't be sure of any of this yet," I caution him. "It's just a bunch of Toledano employees talking about what they say they overheard the killer say, and Toledano's memory of something Chief Sharqawi said. Maybe some of them are imagining things, or mixing stuff up. All we can be sure of is the physical evidence from Dey's room."

I walk him through the short list of magical effects retrieved from the warehouse, moving delicately, this time, from the divine to the satanic. I have brought along the talisman containing what I believe to be a chunk of a dead animal. I hand it to Bari.

"What do you think this is?" I ask.

After a fleeting glance at the tiny object, he tosses it back into my hands with a look of fear. "Do you know what this is?" he demands.

"I thought it was some animal part."

"It's a hyena's brain! He was keeping a hyena's brain in the warehouse, God protect us!"

I have a vague recollection of the meaning of a hyena's brain in North African folklore, and Bari helps me fill in the rest. It is a staple of Moroccan magic—and not the divine variety. According to the country's traditions, the hyena has unique powers of influence over humankind. Its brain is the tool of the weak against the strong. Whoever possesses a piece of it can control other people according to his whims. So coveted and feared is the magic of the hyena, in life and in death, that the animal has been hunted down to endangered species status in Morocco. Some kill the animal to harvest its body parts for magical purposes, while others mean to rid the world of its dangers. It has recently become necessary for Moroccans to import hyenas' brains from the Central African Republic, where the animal is still plentiful, and the cost of the substance has skyrocketed. How a poor man like Ibrahim Dey could afford to acquire this talisman is unclear, but his desire to influence the minds of others must have been particularly strong.

I restore the item to my briefcase.

"Be careful, my brother. Never bring it back here. I have a wife and children. And keep it far away from where you eat and sleep. Keep it far away from the bathroom. It's best not to keep it in your apartment at all."

Bari cleans off his fingers vigorously by rinsing them in a bowl of water, then freshens up his face with his wet hands.

"By the way, another thing I learned at the warehouse is that the killer was brought back there several times, once or twice by the army. They videotaped the warehouse and him. Apparently they videotaped the soldier explaining what he did."

Bari places an index finger at the space on his beard that covers his chin. "In my opinion, that confirms that there was sexual perversion," he says. "They wanted their own version of the killing that would clear their soldier of being a pervert. Maybe they told him to lie for the camera."

A rooster crows over our heads somewhere. I reach for the bowl of water and rinse my hands in it as well.

We take stock of the new information and agree that every party with a connection to the killer or the victim would have its own interest in keeping sex out of the story. The army would like to avoid a sex scandal that implicates one of its boys. The police, as "guardians of the social fabric," want to avoid any public controversy with potentially seismic effects to match those of the incident at Al-Qasr al-Kabir. The killer's family would sooner their son confess to theft and murder and spend years in prison than admit to being sexually assaulted. Even Ibrahim Dey's family, if they knew the truth, would not want anyone else to know. Though Dey's mother and sisters are probably unaware of what we have learned, Dey's first cousin Abdullah Barrada at the Directorate of National Security in Rabat has access to the police files—and the power to weigh in on police investigations at Precinct 5.

Another point emerges from our discussion that echoes an observation by my psychology grad student friend: anyone who was affected by this sordid affair might easily want to know who was the "giver" and who the "receiver" in the sex act that preceded the murder, since the greater shame rests with the receiver.

"Doctors must have examined the killer's body for signs of penetration," Bari says. "They surely did the same for Ibrahim Dey at his autopsy."

As he utters Dey's name, Bari frowns.

"Now *you're* angry," I tell him.

"I'm deeply troubled," he says. "I hope everything you learned from Toledano was a lie, and I would like to be able to prove it so that I can still think of Ibrahim Dey as a friend."

"And if the story proves true?"

His eyes open wide. "Be friends with a pervert? Impossible!" He sizes me up as if we have just met. "You probably have different ideas about perverts than we do, being an American. *I* do not accept them. I could never accept them. If all this is true, then Ibrahim Dey was never my friend to begin with."

I notice that Bari has dropped the formulaic "God have mercy upon him" that he used to throw out at every mention of his friend's name. "Maybe he really did consider you his closest friend," I suggest, "but he knew the only way he could maintain that friendship was to keep certain parts of his life a secret. Wouldn't you feel sorry for him that he had no choice but to pretend all these years?"

"I am so hurt, you cannot even imagine, that he did not trust me with his secrets—even though I hate the secret that he kept from me—because I shared so much of my life with him. He was a pretender. He never trusted me. And pretenders are themselves never to be trusted. On principle, one should never be friends with a man who hides something important about himself, even if he is not a pervert."

"Oh, really," I reply, thinking of the aspects of my background that I routinely conceal during my travels in this region. I pick one with which to challenge Bari. "In some countries I've visited—Iran, for example—I decided to pretend I wasn't Jewish, for reasons I think you can understand. Does that mean you can't trust me? I mean, I may be immature and annoying, but have I given you a reason not to trust me?"

He smiles charitably. "Of course not. But you are a follower of one of the monotheistic faiths, an authoritative faith. There are powerful extremists in Iran. I understand why you had to do what you did there. There is no comparison between your being Jewish and Dey being a pervert."

"Well, if you're so disgusted," I ask him, "then why do you and your wife want so much to continue fighting for the truth about his death?"

"We just have to know the truth," he says, "whatever it is. We can't live without it. And I think the truth is more complicated even than what you learned from Toledano. I can't bring myself to stop. That's all."

"Do you think there is something you could discover about what happened to Ibrahim Dey that could change the way you feel about him?"

He stops to consider the question. "First of all, I just know in my heart that Ibrahim Dey was not a rapist. It's important to me that you believe me on this point. Even if he lied to me, I know my friend was a gentle man."

"I believe you."

"Well, I would like to prove that somehow. Second, well, there is something else. Yes, there is something out there that could change the way I feel about Ibrahim right now. I don't know what it is, but I'll know when we find it."

"All right. So what do we do next?"

The last time I asked Bari to build an investigative plan in his living room, he stammered and hesitated and finally resorted to parroting old TV cop shows and Al Jazeera. Now, wearier and physically wounded, he stares off into the wall, breathing deeply, and contemplates the question for a minute or so.

"You have to confront the police," he pronounces at last.

My heart skips a beat.

"Why?" I ask him.

I would like to talk him out of this.

"They know what happened. They must have documents they never showed you—medical examinations that could prove or disprove the stories of Toledano. The police need to know that you are onto them and they need to be talked to plainly, so that they open up to you and let you see the rest of the file. Only you can do this. My head is wounded, and you are an American. You may infuriate them, and they may blame me for putting you up to it, but it's the only way."

Bari is right—but he has no idea how averse I am to angering another bunch of cops. My hands are shaking.

"It is the least you can do," he says.

TWENTY-FOUR

S o all tracks lead back to the security services—and hopes that a Westerner will confront them. Bari's demand reflects a broader sentiment. In numerous Arab countries, people tend to fault the United States for backing the hard regimes that rule them and wish that Washington would act to soften or change them. They feel that their hopes have fallen on deaf ears.

Only a few years ago, former American secretary of state Condoleezza Rice visited the American University in Cairo and told her audience that American foreign policy was undergoing a radical shift. "For sixty years," she said, "the United States pursued stability at the expense of democracy in the Middle East, and we achieved neither. Now we are taking a different course. We are supporting the democratic aspirations of all people."

But the United States is reeling from the toll democratization experiments in Iraq and Afghanistan have taken on its soldiers and resources, and many of its decision makers have been stunned at the democratic gains registered by Hamas and other Islamist groups thanks to democratization efforts in Palestine, Iraq, and elsewhere. Washington has resisted intervention in countries whose people cry out for American help. In Arab states like Jordan whose rulers have long served America's interests, the U.S. government still accepts se-curity at the expense of justice, stability at the cost of freedom. The Baris of the Muslim world and beyond are expected to confront po-lice on their own, if at all.

Some Westerners still speak of the need to spread democracy, freedom, and individual rights to the autocracies of the world. We marvel at the bravery of dissidents in countries like Syria, whose government we hold at arm's length, and Egypt, whose government we support. We are astounded by the capacity of ordinary people in Tunisia to come together in overthrowing their ruler. But it remains unclear what form of governance, what style of politics, will sup-plant the authoritarian model. There are liberals in every Arab and Muslim country, like Amina Buayash of the Moroccan Organiza-tion for Human Rights, who are struggling to advance the same val-ues we cherish. Occasionally they achieve remarkable things—but when they achieve too much, they run up against the cold iron hand of the state and its gun-toting enforcers. As I noted earlier, one form of hope is that these societies will gradually pressure the autocracies that rule them to grant greater freedoms and individual rights. But the regimes wield so much raw power through their security ma-chinery that their ability to arrest liberal initiatives has largely gone unchallenged. And why would Western governments want to inter-fere now, when instability brings chaos and the potential for Is-lamist rule? The prophet Muhammad himself said, "Forty years of tyranny is better than one hour of civil strife."

As for my little quest with Muhammad Bari, never mind that I am shell-shocked about getting into a confrontation with police anywhere after my experiences in the United States. Never mind that it seems foolish to me to expect that they would willingly cede the kind of information Bari believes they are withholding. It would be so utterly ungrateful of me to insult them that I hesitate to do it for that reason alone. These are the police who protect the syna-gogues in which I've worshipped, block the Islamists who hate me from achieving power democratically, and foil al-Qaeda-affiliated terrorists who would kill me, week in and week out. These working-class fighters have welcomed me into their midst, allowed me to watch them work, and treated me like an honored guest in their homes. They caught the man who killed Ibrahim Dey, and they appear to have buried the truth about his death in order to spare Morocco another bloody scandal like the one at Al-Qasr al-Kabir. What the hell do we want from them?

The problem is, we still want the truth.

Could I possibly retrieve the information police are apparently concealing without angering them—amicably, dare I say diplomatically? It would save me a lot of anxiety, for one thing. So it occurs to me to try to have a talk with the most genteel cop I know in Casablanca, the man in the charcoal gray blazer who cracked the case of Dey's murder. Maybe we can work this whole thing out as friends.

Lieutenant Rashid Jabri lives with his wife and three sons in the humble district of Sidi Barnusi, northeast of Ayn Sabaa, in a large housing complex zoned exclusively for officers of the security services and their families. I take him up on his open invitation to visit for a meal, and the door opens to an elegant apartment of embroidered chairs, colorful handmade carpets, and a coffee table topped with fine silver and fresh fruit. His wife, Samira, in glasses and a cloak of black, waves from the kitchen, and Jabri and one of his boys sit in the living room glued to the TV. The lieutenant is wearing a soccer jersey, the uniform of his beloved home team, Raja—an annoyance to his youngest son, who roots for the opposing Casablanca team, Widad. The two local franchises are squaring off this afternoon, and family tensions are heating up in living rooms across the city. I join them on the couch and watch them hang on every play.

"The police and the Rapid Intervention Forces are stationed in full force around the stadium right now," Jabri notes. "Fights break out all over the place after Raja and Widad go at it."

At length the voice of his wife calls out from the kitchen, "Young men, time to pray!" Jabri's son puts the volume on the TV down, and the two of them make for the largest carpet in the living room.

They position themselves facing east toward Mecca and commence their ritual prostrations. I sit quietly on my own and watch the silenced game.

God hears those who praise him, they whisper in unison. *God hears those who praise him.*

Meanwhile, Samira emerges from the kitchen with bottles of Coca-Cola and lemon Fanta and places them symmetrically at opposite ends of a table set for four. There is an empty space in the middle of the table for something very large. She returns to the kitchen and comes back again with a giant decorated platter of *couscous tfaya,* the stunning queen of Moroccan cuisine. Over a sculpted yellow mound of couscous, large chunks of lamb lie immersed in a stew of apricots and squash infused with cinnamon, saffron, and the meaty, aromatic Moroccan spice blend known as *ras al-hanout.* The stew is topped with caramelized onions, plump raisins, and fried blanched almonds with ginger zest. I watch the steam rise slowly from the center of the plate and sniff the heady air. Thank God the afternoon prayer in Islam is over in less than five minutes.

Jabri's son returns to the soccer game while his father signals me to join him at the table alone. "My wife has been working at this for hours," he says.

"Long live her hands," I reply.

Jabri laughs. "Always Iraqi idioms with you."

Eating slowly and savoring his wife's special feast, Jabri asks me to tell him about my family. I walk him through a few cursory details: an Iraqi Jewish mother, an Ashkenazi Jewish father, a younger brother whom I'm close to, rabbis on both sides of the family.

"My story is a little different," he says.

Jabri tells me the story of his career all over again, as if I have forgotten. His parents died when he and his four brothers were very young. He had always wanted to be a doctor, but suddenly he bore responsibility to help support a struggling family. He became a cop because the pay was adequate, the training took less time than medicine, and he viewed it as another type of opportunity besides medicine to serve the public good. Twenty-three years later, he regrets the choice. "I work long hours every day and I'm called away from my family at all hours of the night. My children will never work in this field—I won't allow it. My oldest wants to be a doctor, and I pray we will help him get there."

The lamb flakes off as tenderly as a piece of fish and is thoroughly infused with the flavor of the stew. I scoop another helping onto my plate.

"When you started your work as a cop," I observe, "Morocco used to be called a police state. Now people aren't sure what to call it."

Jabri puts down his fork and lifts an index finger into the air. "I don't like the term 'police state' for any Arab country. All right, the Iraqis made mistakes under Saddam. But for the rest of the Arab world, governments do what they have to do to maintain order. It is the circumstances that determine how police secure the country, not the other way around. And if you want to talk about brutality, look at the French occupation of Algeria. They killed a million and a half people and still have not even apologized for it."

As Jabri speaks, his wife emerges from the kitchen again, a look of keen curiosity in her eyes. Without seeking permission from her husband, she takes a seat at the table.

"Have you ever read about the police work of the caliph Abu Bakr?" she asks me, referring to the esteemed successor to the prophet Muhammad for political and religious leadership of the Muslim polity, known as the Umma.

"He was the great sleuth of early Islam," I reply. "He would dress up as an ordinary man and listen in on conversations to get to the bottom of a mystery. And he handled his cases very gently."

"If only our police today would emulate the ways of the early caliphs," she says brightly, "then we would have perfect justice throughout the Muslim Umma."

Jabri looks away for a moment, then returns his gaze to his wife with a lips-shut smile.

"Rashid," she says to her husband, "isn't it so?"

"Of course, God willing," he replies.

The table is silent for a moment. Samira lowers her head and gets up again, returning to the kitchen.

Jabri looks at my plate. "You haven't eaten anything," he says, though I have eaten quite a bit.

"I still haven't quit talking to people about Ibrahim Dey, you know," I tell him.

"Ibrahim Dey, *every* day!" he says in English. Back to Arabic: "So, have you turned up something new?"

His grin is wide open and full of teeth this time. There is an Arabic poem from the fifteenth century that reads, *"If you see the fangs of the leopard protruding, do not assume that the leopard is smiling."*

"I don't know what to make of it all," I tell him. "But the men who work for Toledano say the dead body was found with its pants down. Is that true, or are they making it up?"

There is a pregnant pause.

"It is true," Jabri says. "We found him that way, and we immediately suspected that sexual perversion was at the heart of the case. But when we eventually found the perpetrator and he confessed to us, we figured out what really happened. The body had been dragged from elsewhere in the warehouse where Dey was killed. He was dragged by the bottom of his pants. So his pants had naturally come down."

"And his zipper undone."

Whoops.

"Look," Jabri goes on, "we still didn't know what to think. So we submitted the body of the dead man as well as the living body of the perpetrator to a thorough medical examination at the city morgue. Dr. Farida Bushta determined conclusively that there had been no sexual contact between the killer and the victim. So we have the scientific evidence that proves our position."

"Any chance I could read the autopsy report?"

He bites off another chunk of lamb.

"Perhaps," he replies. "But it is beyond my authority to give it to you to read. You would have to get authorization from Chief Shar-qawi."

Samira returns from the kitchen again, ostensibly to check on our progress with the couscous.

"You like it?" she asks.

"Long live your hands!"

She takes a seat beside her husband.

"So you are talking about one of my husband's cases," she says. "He is a very thorough man."

"Indeed," I offer.

"What else have you heard?" Jabri asks.

I inspect the loose black cloak and tight-fitting headscarf covering Samira, which would satisfy the official dress code of the Islamic Republic of Iran.

"Magic," I tell him. "I heard something about Ibrahim Dey practicing magic."

"Magic?" he replies, wrinkling his lips as if it were a dirty word.

"*We take refuge in God from the accursed Satan,*" his wife says. "Our holy book teaches that a man who practices the wrong kind of magic will definitely come to a bad end. Definitely. And he was murdered? *God makes his determination and what He wills, He does.*"

"That said," Jabri interjects, "almost nobody deserves to die."

Jabri looks distraught after Raja loses the soccer match to Widad. His son turns off the TV and goes off to his room to celebrate quietly out of respect for his father, who briefly leaves my company as well to change out of his soccer jersey. The lieutenant comes back and ushers me into the living room to join him for a fruit dessert. Samira, having cleared the table and washed our dishes, takes a seat next to him.

"How do you like being a writer?" he asks me.

I take a deep breath.

"Money is tight, but I love the work. Sometimes you get to meet a lot of people, and other times you get to sit around by yourself and think."

"Working in an Arab security service today," he says as if I had just asked him, "it's like being a cleaning woman. The pay is bad. The master of the house can't make up his mind what he wants you to do. The children and the wife have instructions of their own. And you are always bending down to clean up after others."

"Rashid is a sensitive man," his wife cuts in. "He is a good husband, a loving father, too. In a few years he will retire and our life will change for the better."

"What are you planning for your retirement?" I ask.

Jabri smiles and puts his arm around his wife. "Samira and I have the same tribal affiliation. We are both from the clan of Mdhakra, on the outskirts of Bin Sulayman. You know Bin Sulayman, I think. You told me you visited there. I have some property there, a few hectares of farmland that my brother is tending to right now. We will retire to the farm. I'll take care of it, and the family will live there with me. There will be no one to disturb our peace of mind over there."

"So you and the Murtaziqs will be neighbors."

"Yes, we will," Jabri replies, chuckling a bit. "A nice, quiet place to retire."

I thank Jabri and his wife for their hospitality and leave. They are a lovely couple, and I don't doubt that Jabri is a good husband and a loving father. And he is no less loyal to the hierarchy he serves at Precinct 5, so there is no way around confronting the leadership there head-on.

On my way home in a taxi, my mobile phone rings.

"It's Hasna," a girl's voice says.

I do not recognize the name.

"My brother is Safwan bin Suda, the boy you saw in the interrogation room with a soldier from the Rapid Intervention Forces."

Now I remember. Each suspect had accused the other of assault, only the soldier was trained to kill and big enough to end the boy's life just by sitting on him. Safwan's family had been standing outside—a grandmother, a mother, and a sister, by the looks of them.

"You said you'd call, Hasna. I remember."

"My brother is home from jail," she says. "Twenty-four days. He was cleared of the charges. We want you to come over and talk to him."

It is early enough in the evening. I hand the cabdriver my mobile phone and ask him to follow the girl's directions. We drive back into Ayn Sabaa, to the drab neighborhood of Al-Hay al-Sikakiya, past a train caboose melded into the concrete by the sidewalk, ornamenting a large community center for urban youth. A little way down the road, every balcony in the corner apartment complex harbors a long clothesline, and each roof is a typical jungle of rusty satellite dishes. Hasna is a good-looking, voluptuous girl with Berber blue eyes and Arab jet-black hair. Waiting out front, she asks me to follow her up the stairs.

"We want you to understand how much you helped my brother at a terrible moment in his life," she says. "He wants to say thank you."

"But I didn't do anything."

She opens the door to her home.

Safwan bin Suda sits humbly on a living-room couch, his right arm in the hands of his mother. There is a guitar next to him.

"Ever since he got home," Hasna says, "we've been trying to get him back to playing it, but he is too hurt to return to his music. He is too scared to go back to school."

Safwan does not say a word.

"What happened?" I ask. "I don't understand."

Mrs. Bin Suda points to a silver *siniya* of tea and cookies on the table and asks me to sit down.

"As soon as they picked my son up in the van they started beating him," she says. "They beat him on the way to the precinct headquarters. When they got upstairs, even the soldier who accused him of assault joined the police in beating him some more. Then you walked in, and for twenty golden minutes they treated him with respect."

The story makes me feel ill.

"Who beat him? Does he know?"

My digital camera contains photographs of the various cops I have come to meet. I show him my collection, and he points to a picture of Abd al-Qadir Marzuq, and another man in a winter cap whose name I don't know.

"There were four of them," he says quietly, looking over his shoulder. "They blindfolded me first, but I could see a little through the bottom. One of them stamped his boot over my sneaker so I wouldn't move, and the others kicked me and punched me. Then the soldier himself joined in—the same soldier who was denying that he beat me before. Would you believe it?"

I believe it all right. I remember Bari's description of the beating of Hasan al-Attar. It's virtually identical.

"Here, look," Safwan says.

He rolls up his right pants leg to reveal a long horizontal scar.

"This is what's left, after twenty-four days in jail."

"Are you a human rights worker?" Hasna asks me.

"No."

"Well, we want to thank you for standing by our son, even for twenty minutes. For a short while you gave him the strength to defend himself in words. But what are you doing with police if not human rights?"

I tell them briefly about the story of Ibrahim Dey.

"But you are not Moroccan, you're not a human rights worker. Why are you doing this? Isn't your mother worried?"

Again I face this question of why. "I'm doing this to help out a friend," I tell her.

"This friend must be very close to you," she says. "You must have been friends for a long time."

"Not exactly," I tell her.

She looks perplexed.

"Well, it is kind of you to do this, anyway," she says. "And you are an outsider. You can press for things in Morocco that we cannot."

The stinking puddle awaits by my door when I get home. I skip over it on the way inside. The windows are all shut and the apartment smells like the musty belongings of Ibrahim Dey, still laid out on the coffee table in the living room. Bari warned me to keep the hyena's brain far away from where I eat, wash, and sleep, but the apartment is small, so nothing lies far away from anything else.

Among the murder victim's personal effects, only the yellowing sheaf in Arabic that was sitting on his coffee table the night he died remains for me to examine. It's a forty-page section of a longer book that appears, from its fragility, to date back half a century or more. I sit on the couch, carefully take hold of the pages, and begin to read:

> If in a dream one forgives someone a sin, or a mistake, or an error, it means that God Almighty will forgive him his sins. It also means that he will live a long life, earn fame for his piety, live in God's protection, have a good heart and a forgiving nature.*

The language is familiar. I turn a few pages, trying to remember.

> A book peddler in a dream represents someone who has vast knowledge or someone who gathers amazing stories. Seeing a book peddler in a dream also could mean overcoming one's trouble, solving one's problems, marriage, or the repentance of a sinner.

The style is distinctive. Dream interpreters in early Islam were rare. *That's it*—I know exactly what this is. Suddenly the pages rattle in my hands.

---

*These translations by Muhammad M. Al-Akili, *Ibn Seerin's Dictionary of Dreams: According to Islamic Inner Traditions* (Philadelphia: Pearl Publishing House, 2006).

If one sees a valley filled with blood in a dream, it means that he
may be killed in that locality. If one sees blood emanating out of
his body without cupping or cuts in a dream, it means giving
money to someone. If he is a poor person, then it means receiving money from someone.

This is Ibn Sirin's classic treatise on the interpretation of
dreams. I know why I remember it now. I know why my hands are
shaking. A tear falls and wets the yellowing page in my lap, bruis-
ing a cluster of Arabic words. This is one of the manuscripts a portion of which Ali and I worked through in our first seminar
together at Yale, so many years ago, where we first met. Remembering those days, I forget how fragile the pages are and clutch
them tight. I can see Ali showing up late in the musty little reading
room at Yale's Sterling Memorial Library where the seminar was
held. I see us walking across the campus green and drinking coffee
at Machine City. I remember more now: frequenting the same coffee shop for years, sharing our own dreams and memories with
each other—and finally, out of nowhere, the calamitous circumstances, some of the details clear and obvious to me and others
mysterious, that tore our friendship apart. Here in Casablanca, in
the story of Ibrahim Dey and Bari, I have stumbled upon a situation that resonates with so much of my own distant past. But in
Bari's brave quest to uncover the true story of his loss, the symme-
try is gone: I am watching a man do something I have not had the
courage to do.

Baghdad is a city I got to know in dreams—but Casablanca is
real, and so are the people and problems I know here. It's time for
me to wake up.

I let loose my clutch on the fragile pages that belonged to
Ibrahim Dey and breathe in the air of his few earthly possessions.

Muhammad Ibn Sirin, the book's author, was a revered Muslim
scholar of the eighth century who lived in Basra, now the largest city
in southern Iraq. Dreams were a specialty he cultivated on the side-
lines of his expertise in recounting the sayings and doings of the
prophet Muhammad. Like Ibrahim Dey's, his life is cloaked in mys-

tery, and he, too, is remembered as having two sides to his personality: "I used to hear him weeping during the night," a contemporary wrote, "though he was a most cheerful host during the day." Though he dealt in symbols and visions from the perspective of an eighth-century man—each image in a dream was believed to have one or several fixed interpretations—irony and duality of meaning come through in some of his writings as well. Consider his take on the police, which I also locate in Dey's worn-out pages:

> A policeman in a dream represents security and peace, prayers, a secret friendship, a hidden love. . . . A policeman in a dream also represents the angel of death, a fright, or distress. If a policeman brings his helpers with him in a dream, it means a scare, sorrows, sufferings, punishment, or danger.

So a policeman, to Ibn Sirin, might as easily represent the angel of death as security and peace. The author leaves it up to the dreamer to find his own meaning in a constellation spanning dark and light.

I picture Ibrahim Dey poring over the dream book the night he died—out of the same desire for understanding that caused him to share his dream with Bari, the same yearning to know, to understand, that drives Bari on his quest. He was probably not an Islamist after all; he may have listened to the preaching of a radical cleric out of the same restless curiosity that led him to obsess over his dream, to learn the practice of magic, to have sex in a secretly rented apartment in Jadida, and to experience homosexuality clandestinely in a warehouse in Casablanca. Ibrahim Dey, a poor man with a fifth-grade education, was a student of life and a student of the dream world until the day he died.

I continue turning pages and notice a series of pen marks that encase a particular paragraph:

> Seeing the scale of the Day of Judgment in a dream means the vulnerability of people's secrets, exposing one's actions in public, recognition of the ultimate truth, joy, happiness, victory, and justice.

This would be Ibn Sirin's advice to Ibrahim Dey about the dream of the money and the scales that he related to Bari a few weeks before he died. Of all the dreams Dey might have had, only the vision of the scales perturbed or fascinated him enough for him to mark up its interpretation in the book. I picture the dual interpretation Ibn Sirin offers as having reassured and frightened Ibrahim Dey at the same time. "Exposing one's actions in public" would have been a terrifying prospect for Dey, assuming it is true that he was hiding a stigmatized sexual preference and a proclivity for magic shunned by Morocco's stern traditional society. On the other hand, the promise of "joy," "happiness," and "justice" would have encouraged him to believe in a brighter future. It stands to reason that he could have only one or the other; as in the dream, the scale would be lopsided. He must have wondered which version of the dream would come true.

Ibn Sirin's book conforms to a particular set of ideas about dreams dating back to the ancient world that were reaffirmed by the prophet Muhammad himself. The prophet once told his followers, "A dream sits on the wing of a flying bird and will not take effect unless it is related to someone." In other words, a dream is waiting to come true in one way or another, but it won't until you recount it to another person. Elsewhere in the prophetic tradition, Muslims are advised to share their dreams only with their most trusted and pious friends, lest the fulfillment of the dream turn tragic. If Ibrahim Dey believed in these principles, then his choice to share a perplexing dream with Bari is a sign that he had the deepest trust in his friend. We had taken this for granted, until we learned about the secrets Dey seems to have kept from Bari—and now Bari is reeling from the belief that Dey never trusted him at all. It occurs to me to tell Bari that Dey had been reading Ibn Sirin. The likelihood that, in sharing a perplexing dream with Bari, Dey thought he was putting its fulfillment in his hands may give some comfort to my troubled friend. It could help make up for my arrogant behavior toward him, too.

Perhaps, each in his own way, both Bari and Dey were brave men, unafraid to pursue the questions that haunted them. The psychoanalytical interpretation of the dream by my grad student friend Julia held that Dey was passive, waiting for the magical fulfillment of his fondest wishes. There may well be something to this, Ibn Sirin's more traditional interpretation notwithstanding. But when Dey needed to find out something about himself, he was not so passive after all. He turned to a book and a friend to help him understand, even at the risk of divining news of his own imminent tragedy. He had courage—which is what I need right now as I prepare to confront the police about the Dey case. I'm a foreigner and a Westerner, as Bari and the Bin Suda family have pointed out, so I should have little to fear. All I have to do is overcome the fears that haunt me from far away.

TWENTY-FIVE

The next day I put on my best pair of slacks and a dress shirt and avoid my morning coffee because I am jittery enough already. Though spring is on its way, it is a cold, rainy Casablanca morning. The traffic down Grand Army Avenue sputters through a black asphalt lake, the headlights reflecting off the dank, sopping streets. The cabdriver takes me well past precinct headquarters to the Ayn Sabaa roundabout, and I tell him to let me off at the Tizi Ousli Café. Inside, I find Bari at his post, smoking his usual Cleopatra, and take my seat.

"I've been meaning to ask you something," I tell him. "How much would it cost to get your oven back, get your business started again?"

He smiles graciously, landing the chair back on its front legs, and puts the palm of his hand on my shoulder. "Thank you for asking, my friend. But it is very expensive. It's not just the oven, which costs a great deal. It's also the lease of the property where I would install the oven. And the cars to deliver the bread. And the men to drive the cars. It is hard to start from scratch. I don't know if I would have the strength to do it anymore—no matter what my wife thinks."

I would have liked to help Bari onto his feet again.

"What about your wife? The sewing machine?"

He pats me gently on the back. "Ibrahim once said he prayed that one day, God willing, the day would come that she would find the money to buy one."

"By the way, in the past, whenever you mentioned Ibrahim, you used to always say, 'God have mercy on him,' as Muslims should. Now you've stopped saying that."

Bari's smile fades. "I've rested and I've had the time to think about it," he says. "I don't know whether God *should* have mercy on Ibrahim Dey, because of the abominations he might have practiced. I won't know until I really know."

Precinct 5 is buzzing this morning. Another haul of stolen carpets, home appliances, and mattresses clutters the first-floor landing, while two men drag in more heavy items from a truck outside. Three women sit on the linoleum bench crying into their dresses over a family member who has been taken away in handcuffs. Just outside, a crew of officers on motorcycles are converging with Rapid Intervention Forces for a foray into the Al-Hay al-Muhammadi district to put down the beginnings of a street protest. One of the detectives explains to me that several dozen locals have been up in arms about plans by the local telecommunications company Wana to install a base station atop a building surrounded by dense housing. The protesters believe the presence of a base station is a health hazard to everyone who lives nearby. They do not have a permit to stage a proper demonstration, however, so the police have a free hand to break them up—after a series of warnings, that is, as per a new law.

I look for Chief Sharqawi in his office. An aide sits at his desk.

"He's upstairs, with Abd al-Jabbar," the aide says.

My heart pounding, I walk up to the second floor.

Sharqawi stands over his beefy deputy in the sun-drenched corner office. Abd al-Jabbar is working through his breakfast of four doughnuts strung on a long, thin twig.

"Have a seat," Sharqawi says, and takes a call on his mobile phone.

"I heard about the protest at al-Hay al-Muhammadi," I tell Abd al-Jabbar.

"It's barely a protest," he replies, his voice muffled by a dough-nut, "really more of a scuffle. They are silly, these people. They are reacting to rumors of a health hazard, but I think that is all just pro-paganda. Their grievance would have to be proven through a scien-tific study. Meanwhile they are interfering with the freedom of the owner of the building to enter into a contract with Wana to install the antenna. It's the affair of the owner of the company, I say, and these rabble have no business entering into it."

Chief Sharqawi hits the red button on his mobile phone and takes a seat opposite mine. "You want to talk to us about your mur-der case, I am guessing."

I nod.

"We have been waiting for this," he says.

I take a deep breath.

"Chief Sharqawi, are you sure al-Raddad Murtaziq said he never knew Ibrahim Dey before that night, and he only came into the warehouse to steal?"

The chief looks at me sullenly. "Why do you care so much about this question? What does it matter to you, this nobody who died that night?"

"He isn't a nobody to me anymore. I know his family, I know his friends, and I've been trying to piece together his life story. He has become a part of my life."

"But there are hundreds like him every year who die," the chief persists. "He wasn't a celebrity, he never had any power on this earth. Why have you gone to all this trouble?"

I hesitate for a moment. "Like I said, he's a part of my life now. And I think you guys are hiding something."

Sharqawi looks at Abd al-Jabbar and they share a quick smirk. My heart is pounding.

"What Murtaziq confessed to is what we put in the police file," the chief says. "It's as simple as that."

"I'm not sure it is so simple anymore," I reply. "People are telling me the two of them had a relationship and I want to know what it was."

Sharqawi slams his hand against the table. "People will say all sorts of things! What *we* say is what actually happened. This is what we do, and we do it every day under extraordinary pressure. So what do you want from us?"

"Okay," I tell him, extending my hand. "But didn't you say something other than what's in the report when you talked to Toledano about the case?"

The chief's scowl ebbs. He probes my eyes cautiously. "You've been talking to Toledano?"

"Just a little bit."

Pause.

"Why would you talk to him?"

"I figured maybe he knew something. I assume you are aware, by the way, that his family has had some legal troubles in France."

Abd al-Jabbar grins. "The troubles a man has in other countries don't concern us, as long as they behave themselves here. Surely you can appreciate the wisdom of *that*, Mr. Braude."

That was slick. He put me right in my place.

"Were you in touch with Ibrahim Dey's cousin Abdullah Barrada," I persist, "in the national security directorate headquarters in Rabat?"

A vein pops up on Sharqawi's forehead. "You are insinuating that Abdullah Barrada edited our file on the murder, aren't you? Well, I'll have you know I didn't talk to Abdullah Barrada *once* during the whole investigation. Look, what is it you're trying to get out of this case?"

"I just want to know what happened."

"Don't you know enough? You know what our findings are, what the newspapers have printed. We have gathered the evidence and we have our proof."

"Did the two of them have a relationship, a sexual relationship?"

At this, Abd al-Jabbar cuts in. "Please, this is an Islamic country.

Sex between men is a secret no one would ever admit to. Besides the two people concerned, an outsider would have no way of knowing. It could never be proven."

"Besides," Sharqawi says, "we have scientific evidence that proves they didn't have sex! We have an autopsy report and a body exam, and the doctors at Muhammad V Emergency Ward performed tests on the dead body and the killer and determined conclusively that there was no sexual contact. Science doesn't lie, brother."

"May I see these reports? Can I visit the doctors at the emergency ward?"

Sharqawi raises an index finger and points it at my heart. "You know what your problem is? Your problem is the Moroccan people. They will lie to you, they will make up stories, they will say anything to you just to be close to you, because you are a foreigner—an American, at that. And you believe what they say as if they were accountable to somebody. You must know what I mean by now. Haven't they pulled on your heartstrings? Are you close to giving them money, or gifts? They fill your head with stories, and you come back to us demanding information that is totally insignificant and nobody's business."

Sharqawi's rant hits a nerve. In Arab countries of great poverty I've spent time with lots of people who fit the chief's description. And it may be true that I'm at the point of buying Bari's wife a sewing machine.

But I refuse to believe that our friendship isn't genuine.

"If the case is so insignificant," I practically whisper, "why not let me see the documents and clear me to talk to the doctors at the hospital? It means a lot to me and the victim's friend."

Sharqawi looks me over, sizing me up as if we have never met.

"These documents," he says. "What would you do with them if I gave them to you? Would you share them with the media?"

He fears another breach of the "social fabric," like the one provoked by the alleged "perverts' wedding" in Al-Qasr al-Kabir.

"Of course I wouldn't do that."

"Because you know," he goes on, "to do that would be against the law."

I'm frozen by the ice in his eyes. I say nothing.

"Fine!" he cries, and bangs on the table again. "You can have the bloody documents and talk to any doctor you want! Jabri!"

Lieutenant Jabri walks over from his office across the hall and stands casually over the chief.

"Get him the rest of the file on Ibrahim Dey. Get him an appointment to visit the hospital. Just get him out of our hair!"

I follow the lieutenant back to his office. Without saying a word, he retrieves a manila file folder from the cabinet by his desk and goes through its contents page by page, handing me certain pages and holding on to others. What he chooses to share includes a staple-bound file in French with a gruesome photograph of Ibrahim Dey's bloodied head on the top. It is the autopsy report, together with another report about the living body of the soldier al-Raddad Murtaziq.

"The boys downstairs can make you a copy."

I walk downstairs clutching the key to answering Bari's burning questions. At first, all I care about is that I've left the chief's company. Then I begin to wonder, in much the same way I wondered why he handed over the police file on Dey in the first place, why the chief has now surrendered this additional sensitive material to me without putting up more of a fight.

TWENTY-SIX

There are five doctors in all of Morocco with a four-year university diploma in autopsy medicine—and Farida Bushta, who examined Ibrahim Dey's corpse and the living body of al-Raddad Murtaziq, isn't one of them. She is the resident doctor at the Casablanca city morgue, a facility on the outskirts of town, near the vast Burial Grounds of Mercy where Dey is buried. The morgue is controlled by the Interior Ministry. With the assistance of a second doctor on weekends, she performs roughly two thousand autopsies per year. In the 1980s she participated in a one-day-a-month seminar in the field that was offered by visiting doctors from France. This light training puts her ahead of most physicians in the kingdom who perform autopsies in local hospitals at the request of police; their background typically does not extend beyond the field of general medicine.

I procure Dr. Bushta's mobile number and ask whether we can meet to discuss the Dey autopsy and her examination of Murtaziq. She declines my request. I visit the morgue anyway, just to get a feel for the place. The entry hall is decorated with numerous photographs of Dr. Bushta flanked by long rows of men in uniform. I look at the photos more closely: these are Moroccan army officers.

I form the impression that Dr. Bushta is particularly close to the military Murtaziq serves.

Occasionally, in cases of extreme importance to the security services, Dr. Bushta's work is submitted for reexamination, in the form of a second autopsy, to Dr. Hisham Bin Ya'ish, a properly licensed autopsy physician, at Ibn Rushd hospital in Casablanca. I make an appointment with Bin Ya'ish, bringing along the documents police provided, and ask him to help me make sense of Bushta's findings. His office lies in a pristine campus of two-story medical facilities behind a long gated wall. Bin Ya'ish is a gentle man in his forties, wiry and slight.

He notes first off that the file includes Bushta's original handwritten notes together with the printed version of both reports. "This is unusual," he observes. "Ordinarily she would be allowed to keep the handwritten notes for her own records."

The report on al-Raddad Murtaziq indicates that Dr. Bushta had been asked to examine the young man's body for signs of sexual penetration. Along the way, she observes that thin scratches were found on Murtaziq's shoulders, back, and stomach—"though she doesn't say whether they are new or old," Bin Ya'ish notes. This detail, as I recall, confirms Toledano's claim that Chief Sharqawi told him the killer's back was scratched up. Bushta finds a stitched wound on Murtaziq's left wrist as well—apparently the one he suffered while scaling the glass-topped wall, the stitching presumably thanks to the emergency medical care he received at Muhammad V Emergency Ward that night.

As for Murtaziq's outer sexual organs, Bushta reports that no bruises or abrasions were found in those areas. There was, however, "a reddening of the anus caused by friction."

"What does that mean?" I ask.

"She leaves it vague," Bin Ya'ish replies. "It could be the result of sexual activity. It could have been some ailment. She does not attempt to explain the specific source of the friction. From my perspective, however, this suggests a strong possibility of sexual activity."

Dr. Bushta took samples from Murtaziq's mouth, groin, and

anus for evidence of semen and submitted them to the "Scientific and Technical Police" for scrutiny.

"These samples wouldn't do them any good," Bin Ya'ish observes. "I see from the date of the report that they were taken from Murtaziq's body six days after the night of the murder. It is virtually impossible that sexual microbes would remain on a living person's body for that long, so there was no story for these samples to tell."

Ibrahim Dey's autopsy report is of course a more gory and extensive document. Each blow to the head and neck is thoroughly parsed, together with the drops of blood on his legs and feet—the result, Bushta concludes, of the victim's having been dragged a significant distance. In his stomach, she finds squash, peppers, and turmeric—in all likelihood, she writes, a hearty bowl of the Moroccan peasant's soup known as *harira*. Bushta takes an interest in Dey's sexual organs as well. She observes, for example, that his pubic hair was neatly trimmed. She notes that his anus was "closed"—"not a significant point," according to Dr. Bin Ya'ish, "because the anus of a dead body opens easily and closes easily. What matters, in terms of a sexual attack, is whether there are wounds in the area, and on this issue she is oddly silent."

Bin Ya'ish observes that no effort was made to examine the victim's groin for traces of seminal discharge—"an obvious place to look," he says, "if there is a possibility he may have penetrated the accused."

What it all adds up to, he says, is "inconclusive reporting that nevertheless suggests Murtaziq was penetrated sexually."

"Why would police claim it proves the opposite?" I ask.

Bin Ya'ish sighs. "In Morocco the police have a special reverence for science," he explains. "They believe our findings are always definitive—that we can 'prove' or 'disprove' their theories about a case. But a scientific finding is not the same as a legal finding, and in this country we have a way to go before some of our police appreciate the difference."

"So what will they make of an inconclusive report like this one?" I ask.

"What will they make of it? Pretty much whatever they want."

The following morning I return to Precinct 5, hoping Chief Sharqawi will clear me for a visit to the Muhammad V Emergency Ward, as he has pledged to do. I find him in his office—blowing his nose into a Kleenex, shivering, and sipping a hot cup of tea.

"Work is crazy," he says. "My back hurts and I need a day off. What do you want now?"

I remind him.

"All right. You will have to be escorted to the hospital, and I barely have a free man today. Let me see."

Presently a thirtysomething officer walks in with a document for Sharqawi to sign. A tight leather jacket hugs his frame and an old, thick scar drapes diagonally over his right eye.

"Aziz," the chief says, "this young man could use your help."

We ride in the backseat of a red Peugeot *petit taxi,* past the colorful shantytown markets of Al-Hay al-Muhammadi toward the drab housing projects of Dar Laman. The band Nas al-Ghiwan is blaring from speakers behind us—a song in which a farmer prays to the sky to water his thirsty land. Policemen in Morocco are generally careful not to talk about their work in taxicabs, but the driver has opened his window wide and the breeze is blowing in his ears.

"So, what have you been working on?" Aziz asks me.

"The murder of Ibrahim Dey."

"I was on that case, you know."

My head swivels involuntarily toward him.

"It was a very strange few days."

Aziz explains that he works as a liaison officer between the Judiciary Police and the Scientific and Technical Police, who maintain their headquarters elsewhere. Though he is based in Precinct 5, he does not report to Chief Sharqawi and is often not even aware of the chief's directives to his men. It occurs to me that if an instruction went out to suppress details of the Dey case from the public, Aziz might never have gotten it.

"What happened that night?" I ask him.

"Sex," he replies.

Bingo.

"You mean between Ibrahim Dey and the man who killed him?"

"Between the killer and somebody, that's for sure. That's what the doctor told us."

I am shocked and refreshed by a policeman's candor.

"The doctor said the boy had been sexually penetrated," he goes on. "I think Dey and the boy were lovers. They were together in his warehouse every night for months, anyway. That's what he told us when he confessed."

"Who else heard him say these things?"

"Jabri, Abd al-Jabbar—the usual guys. But the boy was vague about why he killed Ibrahim Dey. He said they were doing something in his room, I never fully understood what, and they got into a fight. It escalated, and Murtaziq beat him to death."

"Did he say anything about black magic?"

"Yes, I remember hearing something about magic."

The driver pulls in past the gates of the familiar split-level hexagonal building with a Moroccan flag out front—the Muhammad V Emergency Ward. I remember visiting the place by night with Officer Abd al-Qadir Marzuq and his prisoner, the banged-up sheep slasher.

Aziz and I walk in together. As we wait in line to speak to the front office receptionist, I tap the young officer on the shoulder.

"Aziz, there's something I need to ask you. Jabri, Sharqawi, Abd al-Jabbar—all those guys insist that Murtaziq told them he had never even met Ibrahim Dey before that night. They keep insisting, no matter what I tell them I have learned from others. Why would they do that?"

Aziz smiles. "They are from an older generation of police," he says. "They don't feel they owe you the truth, and they hold on to their version of what happened because they think it is safer—better for the country, even. Probably they are covering up for the army, to protect its reputation. Maybe they are covering up for the owner of the warehouse because he has money or because he's a Jew. These things happen all the time. They happen everywhere—even in America. In Morocco it is a culture that has to change, and it *is* changing, but slowly."

He presents his badge to the receptionist and moves on, with her nod, to an office in the corner of the main hall. A doctor in white sits behind a desk piled with ledgers and looks up from his reading.

"We are from the Judiciary Police," Aziz says. "We need to see the doctor who was in charge the night of December eleventh."

With a dour expression, the physician consults a worn-out book on the corner of the desk.

"Gharshi," he pronounces. "And he happens to be in charge right now."

We proceed to a larger office down the hall. An affable-looking man in his sixties sets a paperweight statue of the Al-Aqsa mosque gently atop a pile of documents. Stray curls from a full head of gray hair drop casually down his forehead.

"Dr. Gharshi," Aziz says, "this is an American researcher attached to our precinct. He has some questions about a patient you admitted on the night of December eleventh. The one who signed his name 'X the son of X' and turned out to be a soldier."

The doctor raises his eyebrows and peers curiously at me. "From America," he says. "And are you researching terrorism?"

"Not exactly," I reply.

"Most American researchers who come here care only about terrorism."

"Can you help him?" Aziz asks.

Gharshi moves a book and a few papers aside from the center of his desk, as if clearing the area where he rests his arms would help him concentrate.

"I do remember the boy," he says. "We treated him here for a few days, and he was whisked away to the military hospital in Rabat after that."

"What happened to him?" I ask.

"What we understood at the time was that he had been raped—by a commanding officer."

Blood rushes to my head as if I were standing upside down.

TWENTY-SEVEN

At last we had begun to fill in some details. We had cut through layers of deception. We could almost begin to piece together the secrets of Ibrahim Dey's life that led to his tragic death. The police had given in and granted me the keys to the kingdom— or so I thought. I squeezed what I could out of those autopsy documents like a good little researcher and pushed to see the doctor at the emergency ward. Now, from out of nowhere, comes the tantalizing possibility that Murtaziq had been raped by one of his superiors in the army, and our investigation demands a whole new line of inquiry that would lead us straight into a brick wall. We will never be able to snoop around a military barracks in Morocco. All we can do is speculate. Maybe there was a cover-up before the cover-up, for example: maybe police tried at first to protect a predatory military officer by blaming Dey for the rape of Murtaziq. Then—at the behest of Dey's powerful first cousin, or simply in light of the scandal that was likely to ensue—they decided they'd be better off taking sex out of the picture entirely. And if it's true that someone from behind the barracks walls raped Murtaziq, then what led the young man to kill Dey? Bari and I were of course fuzzy on that question to begin with, and now the answer is fuzzier. My friend Julia's theory that Murtaziq experienced a "homosexual panic" may explain his violent motive, but it would not explain his choice of a target.

I had wondered why Chief Sharqawi gave up the autopsy documents so easily. I had thought he was succumbing to the same sort of sloppiness, perhaps hubris, that caused him to hand over the police file on Dey in the first place. I know from hubris. But now I think I foolishly underestimated him all along. Now it seems more likely that the chief got to be the chief, and my host, for a reason. He and Lieutenant Jabri have known for years, and through dozens if not hundreds of homicide investigations, what I had only begun to learn over the past few months: that the more you delve into the mysteries of an obscure life, the complexities of an obscure murder, the more the questions, the fewer the answers—the more elusive the story, the more inscrutable the man. Maybe the chief sized me up as someone for whom evidence matters, and simply knew that the true story of a poor man's life and death is typically so convoluted as to be confounding.

I'll be flying home soon, yet the situation now is as unresolved and frustrating for me as it is bound to be for Bari. We shared the hope of snatching back the truth from the state machinery that is designed to conceal it. What we have captured instead is a handful of shards. To assemble them into a coherent story would leave too much to the imagination to yield a credible truth.

I was inspired to help Bari investigate Dey's murder in part because I wanted to know what happens when an ordinary person like Bari presses his unelected rulers for something that may threaten the status quo. Will they yield to his demands? Will they learn to do the same for others? Now I'm struggling to decide whether they have yielded much at all. Meanwhile, I had also acquired a new ambition along the way: to redeem a lost life from the abyss of obscurity. So I'm struggling, as well, to figure out how much of Ibrahim Dey remains obscure, and whether what we have uncovered qualifies in some way as a redemption of his memory. But the most important question—ultimately, what drove us on this quest—has been Bari's burning desire to know what really happened to his friend in order to achieve some sort of closure. Whether the retrieval of an incom-

plete story can provide him anywhere near the peace of mind he
craves is beyond me. But incomplete stories may well be the best
people can hope for in thousands of situations like this one, across
the Arab world and beyond—and so Bari's reaction to our incomplete investigation is important for me to understand.

The morning's gray fades into a warm, dry spring afternoon of
sunshine in Casablanca. Outside my apartment, a heavy wind
shakes the palm trees towering over the noisy traffic. I put on some
clothes and have coffee and a croissant at the swank café near
where I live, then return to my flat and pick up a piece of machinery
that I procured secondhand the other day from a sprawling elec-
tronics market in the east of town. It's a sturdy old Singer sewing
machine. I lug it downstairs and hail a cab in the direction of Ayn
Sabaa. I am going to miss this ride across the stark chain of con-
trasts that stratify the city.

My taxi brakes hard in front of the stubby three-story precinct
headquarters, and I walk up the nine concrete steps one last time. I
ask the Auxiliary Forces private behind the linoleum counter to hold
on to my sewing machine a little while, and he gladly obliges. The
cushioned door to Sharqawi's office is wide open. The chief waves
me inside, a tissue to his nose, and rings an aide down the hall.

"Round them up," he says.

A few minutes later, the precinct's principals are assembling in a
semicircle. I hear the squeaky rubber boots of Marzuq and wave to
him as he walks in the door. Four officers I don't know well who
work upstairs, handling car theft among other crimes, walk in together. The last man in is Jabri, in his trademark jeans and charcoal
gray blazer. Beaming regally, he takes the seat nearest the chief and
his deputy, Abd al-Jabbar.

"We are going to miss you," Sharqawi declares.

The team nod in unison.

"Have you found Casablanca to be a safe and peaceful place?"
asks Abd al-Jabbar. "Do we handle our responsibilities with devotion and efficiency?"

"Absolutely," I reply. "It has been an honor to know you all, and I'm grateful for the opportunity to watch you in action. I think Morocco has the best police force in the Arab world, and you should be proud of yourselves."

Sharqawi silences his cell phone. He looks down at the cigar ashtray centered on the little table in front of his desk and takes a sip of sweet mint tea. "The next time you come here, brother," he says, "we are going to prepare a special welcome. A *really* special welcome."

Perhaps he didn't mean for this to sound as sinister as it came across.

"Thank you."

"And now," he goes on, "Lieutenant Jabri, the hero of your story, would like to add something."

Jabri stands up and clears his throat. What comes out is soft, nearly a whisper, marked occasionally by a slight crack in his voice. "On behalf of my division, I would like to thank you for taking an interest in our work," he says. "And we would like to apologize that, for reasons of national security, it was not possible for us to respond thoroughly to all of your inquiries."

I look into his eyes and ponder the layers of command and control standing over him, the years of acculturation to opaque police work. In his voice there is weariness and a trace of humility.

"Lieutenant," I tell him, "I know that you have done all you can."

Now I'm walking down the alleyway that leads to Bari's squalid home.

He comes to the door in his pearly white gown, probably just back from midday prayers. He notices the sewing machine and stretches out his arms for a hug. He shouts his wife's name in the direction of the kitchen. "This has always been her dream," he says, tapping an index finger on the metal. "It will change our lives."

Mahjuba emerges from the kitchen, and I am thrilled to watch her jaw drop at the sight of my modest gift.

"But we wouldn't be able to afford this," she says.

"You owe me nothing."

She lifts a finger into the air and spins around, back toward the kitchen. It smells like couscous in there.

"Have a seat," Bari says.

We sit close to each other on cushions along the far wall.

Bari stares down at the cracked linoleum. "My sister in Paris, she is sick," he says. "Cancer of the stomach."

I remember his own bout with cancer.

"The doctors there, she's not happy with what they say. She asked me to send her three owls. She wants to try the same treatment that cured me. Today I am going back to the Jmi'ah market to buy them. You can come with me if you like."

Mahjuba returns to the sitting room with a platter of couscous topped by seven stewed vegetables and a plump chicken. She is breathing heavily. Her dark eyes glisten, perhaps having welled up in the kitchen.

"May God reward you," she says. "I don't know how to express my gratitude."

"Your husband's friendship has been a much greater gift to me," I tell her.

At Bari's nod, she leaves us again and lets the couscous speak for her.

I move my hand in the direction of the chicken, but Bari grabs hold of it and pushes it back, peering into my eyes intently. "So tell me what you learned," he says. "I need to know."

"Of course. I'll tell you everything I know."

The Jmi'ah market, at ground level, resembles open-air bazaars across the Arab world. Tall mounds of spices sit on display in long rows of burlap sacks. Olives swim in large white buckets; dried fruit, nuts, and salted seeds fill plastic tubs. Live chickens run around in cages, and veiled women beside the market stalls sit with their hands stretched out to every visitor. Ascend a flight of outdoor steps to the upper level of the market, however, and the stalls carry a different variety of product. Hanging from each canvas roof is a row of dried whole animals: snakes and lizards, gazelles and deer, hawks and doves, wolves and sheep. Mounds of leafy dried herbs fill the sacks out front, and inside each stall are bottles of bright-colored powders and potions. There are live animals, too: turtles in tanks piled from the ground; woodpeckers at eye level in round hanging cages. The herbs and powders, when boiled in water, are meant to cure various ailments. Some of the dried animals are for ornamental purposes, others to ward off the evil eye. So say the vendors, anyway. Ask and you will learn about the curative powers of traditional medicine, the decorative beauty of animal skins, and the merits of keeping a woodpecker as a household pet. But one important word you will hardly hear whispered is "magic"—the great hushed secret of the market.

I follow Bari down the lane of vendors. He is breathing more heavily than usual, walking unevenly. The old cut marks on his temples glisten in the sunshine. I remember the black wound on his stomach. How long does he have to live? There is no doubt in my mind that dead owls don't cure cancer. His chain-smoking can only hasten the inevitable.

Correction: there is *almost* no doubt in my mind that dead owls don't cure cancer.

Bari now knows what I know. His only reaction when I told him about the autopsy documents and the rumor about Murtaziq's rape by a commanding officer was to listen and gravely nod. I have no idea what he is thinking or feeling. "Let's go to the market now" was all he said to me, and we took a taxi here in silence.

He finds the vendor he was looking for—a short, mustached man—and begins to haggle. The back-and-forth doesn't last long. The vendor walks into his stall, rummages through some boxes, and returns with three clumps of something wrapped in newspapers.

"Let me see," Bari says.

The vendor unwraps a full-color sports section to reveal a small dead brown-and-white-feathered owl. He applies a little pressure on its cheeks to show off the beak, then gently pulls away a lower corner of the wrapping to stretch out its right wing.

Bari nods and produces 150 dirhams from his pocket.

"God help my sister," he says.

"God keep her and protect her," the vendor replies.

We walk together slowly along the row of market stalls, an ocean breeze at our backs. Bari peers thoughtfully at the animal skins and produces a cigarette from his coat pocket. A vendor is on hand to light it for him.

"I rarely come here," he says. "I never came here with Ibrahim Dey, God have mercy on him. But now we know that he probably came here by himself."

The Arabic language brims with formulaic blessings, gallant tropes from a bygone age, that embellish even casual conversations with literary beauty. Some speakers of the language throw these expressions around without thinking about them much. Bari, I have learned, thinks long and hard. When I first met Bari, I thought he was a simple, humble man. I was right about his humility, but there is no such thing as a simple man.

"You said 'God have mercy on him.' I thought you never would again."

"God only knows whether I should," he replies. "But Ibrahim Dey was my friend, and those are the words we must say for those we love whom we have lost."

We walk down the stairs, back to the fruits and vegetables and meats and spices. The steps are made of stone, fairly clean. Bari sits on one and I join him.

"Tell me," he says, "did you lose a friend, too?"

The question jolts me. I hesitate.

"Yes, a very dear friend."

"Do you know why it happened?"

"No, I really don't."

"Well, how can you live without at least trying to find out?"

A woman just ahead of us begs for food or a few coins. Bari quiets her with a blessing or two. I watch him do so with grace and a show of sympathy for the lady, such that she understands he would give her some money if he had it.

Before my months in Casablanca, over the course of fifteen years of travel in Arab countries, I had acquired the habit of walling off the life I live back in the States from the relationships I form in this region among Muslims. But here in Casablanca, the walls have begun to crumble. Bari feels like a friend from back home.

"You know, what happened is confusing," I tell him, "and it's not so easy in America to get to the bottom of something like that."

Bari chuckles. "Harder than in Casablanca?"

I squint in the sunshine. "Not harder, but sometimes maybe about the same."

"Well, do you have a theory, a working theory of what might have happened?" he asks.

Sure I do.

"It doesn't make a lot of sense, Muhammad."

He laughs at me again and pats my shoulder. "You might as well start somewhere, my brother."

So I ignore all my instincts, open my mouth, and begin to tell.

EPILOGUE

It isn't easy to communicate with Muhammad Bari by phone. When I call him from the United States, his words drift in and out amid the sound of static and occasional clicks. Sometimes when I ask about the months we spent together back in 2008, I hear hesitation in his voice, as if he fears that someone is listening in, even now. In October 2010 I had occasion to visit Morocco, after a trip to neighboring Algeria on an unrelated matter. Bari and I had a tearful reunion. He told me he had quit smoking, and I confirmed it by smelling his breath. That was the good news. I asked where his wife's use of the sewing machine had led them financially and learned, to my disappointment, that she had never managed to start her own business with it. She needed additional equipment and raw materials, he explained, and they would cost more than the sewing machine itself—more than they could afford, more than I could afford. So she still works miserably at the sweatshop. I visited their apartment and found the sewing machine veiled by a musty cloth in a corner of the living room. Bari is still unemployed, of course. And I had dreamed that my foreign aid would change their lives.

There is another way to reach Bari from my home, albeit indirectly. Among his eight children, his son Sulayman, now twenty-two years old, is on Facebook. I didn't know the boy well when I lived in Casablanca, but not long after I departed the country, Sulayman reached out and we began to correspond by email. He shared stories about his life, and updates about his family and conditions in Ayn Sabaa. Two years ago he wrote that he had tried to join the civil service in Morocco but learned that he needed to know somebody just to be considered for a government job. A bribe would have helped, he said. Next he applied to college. That door turned out to be closed to him as well. He claimed a bribe would have been necessary to win admission, though I didn't know whether to believe him. I didn't believe the state of affairs in Morocco was quite that bad. More likely, I figured, his grades were not high enough. I have other friends across North Africa and the Middle East who send me emails, too. Nearly all of them relay these sorts of grievances, at once minor and life altering. Over time, one grows numb to such stories.

The Arab revolutions that began in January 2011 hit me like a sock in the jaw. I had never imagined that Bin Ali's iron rule in Tunisia would collapse at the hands of largely peaceful demonstrators organized into a movement by a cascade of Tweets. For centuries the region had known regime changes only through foreign invasions, bloody uprisings, and military coups. This somber history must have weighed down my imagination. A thousand years of medieval manuscripts, mostly penned by court historians, told no story like that of the street vendor in Tunisia who set himself on fire to protest the confiscation of his wares by the government. Yet his kind of story—his degradation by the state, the theft of his individual rights and dignity, the fear that he would live and die without his grievance being heard—is perhaps the one constant of life in North Africa and the Middle East dating back to the ancient world. Thanks to the new, democratic medium of the Internet, the street vendor's tale was not buried. It ripped across borders and ignited millions of young people who felt they shared in his plight. Even after the Bin Ali regime had fallen, several renowned Mid-East experts promptly wrote that what had happened in Tunisia would stay in Tunisia, precluding the possibility of a domino effect. I have to admit that I agreed with them. But within a couple of weeks, the most populous country in the Arab world, Egypt, saw its dictator of thirty years relinquish power. Protests broke out in Algeria, Bahrain, Djibouti, Jordan, Sudan, and Yemen. In Libya, the dictator responded to demonstrations against his rule by waging all-out war on the population. At this writing, the people of Libya are fighting back. God help them.

The dust will eventually settle, and where rulers have been deposed, new politicians will struggle to build an alternative. I feel humble about predicting what these alternatives will look like. For the past few years I had pinned my hopes on some of the region's liberal activists, like Morocco's Amina Buayash, who aspired to work within authoritarian systems to bring incremental change. Now all eyes are on Arab youth—Sulayman Bari's contemporaries. They are the generation of the greatest baby boom in the history of the world. In numbers they dwarf their parents' and grandparents' generations combined. As anyone who reads the news now knows, many of them are techno-savvy. Through satellite television and the Internet, they have been exposed to free societies. Many of them want to build liberal democracies, while others subscribe to militant, reactionary ideologies that are also part of the global village.

The wave of demonstrations reached Morocco, too, last week. Reports indicated that the protests were comparatively small, less ambitious than their counterparts in Tunisia, Egypt, and Libya. A twenty-five-year-old Moroccan mother of two set herself on fire and some protestors called for the ouster of the king, but most demonstrators confined their activism to demands for more aggressive economic and political reforms. For now the king appears to be persuading demonstrators that he will address their grievances.

Muhammad Bari is on a bus to the northern city of Tangier when I reach his son on his mobile phone.

"What does your father think about what's going on?" I ask the young man.

The ocean breeze of Ayn Sabaa is blowing into Sulayman's phone. I picture him cupping it with his hand as the ambient noise dies down.

He says that Bari was seated at his post in the café when the Bin Ali regime began to teeter, and it was like no soccer match he had ever seen on TV. Pent-up rage swelled in his stomach, and his heart rate was up for hours. Then Bin Ali fled the country. Perhaps for the first time in Bari's life, Al Jazeera made him cry. By the time Egyptian president Mubarak squared off on screen with a crowd of several hundred thousand in Tahrir Square, the coffeehouse was crowded beyond capacity, and people inside relayed news the old-fashioned way to people outside. Men were banging on tables. Ashtrays were rattling. Uniformed Casablanca police, seated among the regulars, appeared to be off-duty all day. "We think the cops had instructions to lay off everybody," Sulayman reports. "My friend was driving 140 where the speeding limit is 80, and they let him go with a slap on the wrist."

"But what's going on with these demonstrations? Are you guys going to bring down the king?"

Sulayman says absolutely not: "We don't suffer the same oppression here. People aren't starving. We have no emergency laws. There is political opposition in parliament. The king is a good man; only the government is corrupt."

I remember the band Nas al-Ghiwan's ambiguous song about the nature of a monarchy: "The king is a doctor and his subjects are wounded, but there is not a single government official to tell him of their plight." Such fables, widely believed by the population, can hold a system together for a very long time.

"How can I reach your father?" I ask. "What's he doing in Tangier, anyway?"

Sulayman says I can't talk to Bari today because he left his own mobile phone at home with his wife. He is going to Tangier because he has reason to believe the equipment and raw materials his wife requires are cheaper there, and over the past few weeks the couple decided to make a go of acquiring them in installments.

"Does he still talk about Ibrahim Dey?" I ask.

"Nobody does," he replies. "Not my father, not my mother, nobody. Even the family of Ibrahim Dey has forgotten him."

ACKNOWLEDGMENTS

Before the events of this book took place, the project was nothing more than a gut feeling and an offer of access to a unit of the Moroccan police. That was sufficient for Spiegel & Grau executive editor Chris Jackson to embrace the concept and press for its acceptance. When I came back from Morocco, he provided guidance on how to make a manuscript out of my reporting and travails, and vastly improved successive drafts. I wonder whether the book would exist in any form without him. Both Chris and I, in turn, relied on my agent, Lydia Wills, for strategic, practical, and literary advice. In my case, she also provided unwavering support and boundless patience.

Meanwhile in Morocco, Sharqi Darees, the director of National Security, granted me the access that made the reporting possible and provided crucial assistance whenever it was called for. The openness of his directorate to the sustained prodding and critical gaze of a foreign journalist speaks to the kingdom's strength. Among Darees's deputies in Rabat, Fadel Atallah provided a tutorial on the machinery of Moroccan security. Mustafa Mawzuni, the chief of police in Casablanca, chose the precinct in which I was to be embedded and fostered my relationship with its leadership. Though no conditions were placed on my reporting, I have chosen to respect the shared wish of all lieutenants and officers at Precinct 5 that their real names not be used.

I owe a particular debt of gratitude to the family of Ibrahim Dey, God rest his soul, especially his mother, Khadija, and sister Fatima. They shared intimate family details and made introductions to many relatives at a time of pain and bereavement. The man whom I refer to as Muhammad Bari drove the independent investigation into Dey's tragic death, which is the core of this book. Along the way, he became a close friend. Umar Sayyid, the band Nas al-Ghiwan's lead singer and elder statesman, spoke to the country's heart and soul in ways that only a seminal artist can.

Professor Najib Akesbi at Rabat's Institut Agronomique et Vétérinaire Hassan II provided insights and data about Moroccan agriculture and aspects of the country's human and physical infrastructure. Professor Mohamed Cherkaoui at the Centre National de la Recherche Scientifique provided the benefit of his formidable scholarship in Moroccan sociology. Zaynab Mumin, a graduate student, donated the use of her dissertation on masculinity and sexuality in Morocco. Munir Muntasir Billah, a former judge, gave an insider's view on the workings of the country's judiciary. André Azulay, Serge Berdugo, Masud Waknin, and Jacob Perez offered their perspectives on Moroccan Jewry past and present. Dr. Hicham Benyaich at Ibn Rushd hospital in Casablanca helped me make sense of a most unusual autopsy report. Numerous Moroccan journalists imparted tricks of the trade. I am particularly grateful to Lubna Bernichi at *Maroc Hebdo* and Tawfiq Buashrin at *Al-Masa*. Another media man, Ahmed Charai, opened his Rolodex and his heart, and contributed invaluable advice and wisdom.

Family, old friends, and new friends enabled me to reach the stage of writing another book after difficult times, and rallied to help me reach the finish line. I will always be grateful to Marty Peretz. When I faced Federal prosecution, he stood by my family and me. After I emerged from the courtroom convicted of a crime, he gave me the opportunity to write a weekly column for *The New Republic*—the beginning of a new career. My mother, Rita, father, Joel, brother, Yoni, and uncle Ben Braude, continuous sources of love and encouragement, made numerous helpful suggestions as I produced the manuscript. Yoni and his partner, Emily Sadigh, also reviewed the manuscript, offering insightful comments. My former wife, Nitzan Pelman, showed kindness and support at critical stages of the project. I learned a great deal about writing from my editors Richard Just, Robert Love, and Timothy Mohr, whom I count as friends. Finally, I am grateful to my girlfriend, Ruth Franklin, who offered a fresh perspective on the manuscript that led to considerable improvements.

ABOUT THE AUTHOR

Born to an Iraqi-Jewish family, Joseph Braude studied Near Eastern languages at Yale and Arabic and Islamic history at Princeton. He is fluent in Arabic, Persian, and Hebrew, and has lived, studied, and worked in most Middle Eastern capitals. As a journalist, his work has appeared in *Best Life, Playboy,* and *The New Republic,* among other publications. He lives in New York.